Brian Power was born in Tientsin in 1918 and lived there until 1936, when he came to England to study history at London University. During the war he served with the Irish Fusiliers in North Africa and Sicily, where he was seriously wounded in action. Later he was seconded to War Crimes Investigation, based in Austria and Italy.

In 1951 Mr Power was called to the Bar. After practising for six years he became a teacher in the art of speaking in public. In 1964 he married Prunella Stack.

In 1973, during the Cultural Revolution, Brian Power returned to China. He travelled across the country and spent a short while in a commune. He has given many lectures on China, past and present, with specific references to the prevailing influence of her ancient ways and customs, in the United States and Canada as well as Great Britain. His book about his own early life in China, *The Ford of Heaven*, was widely acclaimed when it was first published in 1984, and it was among the Book of the Year selections in *The Observer* and *Financial Times*.

Also by Brian Power

THE FORD OF HEAVEN

and published by Corgi Books

Brian Power

THE PUPPET EMPEROR

The Life of Pu Yi, Last Emperor of China

CORGI BOOKS

THE PUPPET EMPEROR
A CORGI BOOK   0 552   99293 3

Originally published in Great Britain by Peter Owen Publishers

PRINTING HISTORY
Peter Owen edition published 1986
Corgi edition published 1987
Corgi edition reprinted 1988

This book is set in 11/12 Baskerville

Corgi Books are published by Transworld Publishers Ltd., 61-63 Uxbridge Road, Ealing, London W5 5SA, in Australia by Transworld Publishers (Australia) Pty. Ltd., 15-23 Helles Avenue, Moorebank, NSW 2170, and in New Zealand by Transworld Publishers (N.Z.) Ltd., Cnr. Moselle and Waipareira Avenues, Henderson, Auckland.

Made and printed in Great Britain by
The Guernsey Press Co. Ltd., Guernsey, Channel Islands.

To
the wandering story-tellers of China

CONTENTS

ILLUSTRATIONS

回

PLATES

LINE DRAWINGS

ACKNOWLEDGEMENTS

I am grateful to the following women, both of them poets, for so generously telling me about their personal memories of characters who appear in this book: Ling Su Hua, who attended the wedding reception for Pu Yi and his Empress Beautiful Countenance in the Forbidden City, and who later met the imperial couple on several occasions; and Innes Herdan who, from 1934 to 1935, attended the lectures given by Sir Reginald Johnston (one-time imperial tutor) when he was head of the Chinese Department at the School of Oriental Studies in London.

The picture of Prince Chun (plate 1), and those of Pu Yi and the Empress Beautiful Countenance (plates 5, 6, and 7), were presented to Nona Ransom by the Empress herself. They are reproduced for the first time in this book by kind permission of Harry Ransom Rose, to whom I am especially indebted.

B.P.

The Romanization of Chinese Characters

The beautiful and ancient (over 3,000 years old) Chinese script with its elegant and vivid strokes is based not on any alphabet, but on pictographs – that is to say, drawings reduced to essentials, which in time became stylized. Thus the character for *male* shows a plough and a field, clearly implying 'that which uses its strength in the fields'. Since the seventeenth century there have been many attempts to transliterate Chinese characters into the Roman alphabet for the sake of foreigners. None of those attempts has been satisfactory. Apart from being aesthetically dead, the various systems of romanization give but a crude approximation of the sound and nothing of the sense of the characters they represent.

In this book I have used a simplified version of the Wade-Giles system of romanization. It was widely used in foreign settlements in China during Pu Yi's lifetime, and is still used in the case of well-known personal and place-names. Where possible, however, I have translated Chinese names directly into English. It seemed to me that readers would rather know that the name of the last Empress of China meant Beautiful Countenance than be told merely that her name was pronounced Wan Jung. It should be noted that, in Chinese, the surname precedes the given name.

'The essence of history does not reside in recorded facts but in the thoughts, emotions, ideas and aspirations of the human beings who have made it. Facts are only the outer shell. . . . '

Amaury de Riencourt, *The Soul of China*

'L'exactitude n'est pas la vérité.'
Braque

INTRODUCTION

When I was a child I often listened to the wandering story-tellers who performed in the market-place in Tientsin, a river port of northern China. They spoke of emperors, peasants, warriors, mandarins, monks, courtesans and heroic outlaws who defended the oppressed. As if unfolding a Chinese screen, they presented their tales of chivalry, blending fact and imagination, in dramatic and unforgettable scenes.

I was born in Tientsin in 1918 and spent the first eighteen years of my life there. I must have been about three when our Chinese amah began to take my elder brother Pat and me to the market. So it was from an early age that I came under the spell of the story-tellers. Part of their lure was in the atmosphere of distant and exotic places that they brought with them. It was hazardous to travel in northern China in the 1920s and 1930s. There were hardly any roads, trains were frequently commandeered by the soldiers of rival war-lords, and few ships reached Tientsin on the Grand Canal without being boarded by pirates.

Travelling northwards by river and canal, the intrepid story-tellers would break their journey to give their recitals at the main landing-stages, such as Nanking. In the spring they would reach Tientsin. In midsummer they went on to Peking, eighty miles inland. By November, when the waterways began to freeze, they would be on their way south again.

The small Tientsin market was always full of mule-drawn carts, coolies and pedlars. Sometimes a camel train, bearing dust-covered packs, would arrive from the desert lands of the Interior, and the harsh cries of the camel drivers could be heard above the calls of the pedlars and stallholders, and the

11

din of the crowd. Against all this noise and bustle, the story-tellers had to work hard to hold their audiences. Few people would bother to listen, let alone throw any coppers at the feet of a story-teller who mumbled on with his nose buried in a book.

The story-tellers recited tales from ancient history that had been passed down from father to son for many generations, but the best of them also improvised a good deal. They did not try to resurrect history so much as relive it in their imaginations. (The great classic Chinese novels owe much of the richness of their plots to the inventive genius of the story-tellers.) Brilliant actors, they could move their audiences to tears and then to laughter with only a few gestures; and they would rouse their passions with lurid descriptions of cruel rape or with poetic touches on the delights of love-play.

Not even peasants and coolies can live by hard labour alone, and those who crowded round the story-tellers, must have found spiritual refreshment in the heroes and heroines they were given to admire, as well as some nourishment for their hopes.

One of the story-tellers also put on puppet plays from behind a wood and canvas stage which he set up in a corner of the market. He used only two figures, and he would rapidly change their costumes from a box hidden behind the stage. Once, after his performance, I stole behind the stage. One of the figures, in the bright pink robe of a concubine, lay on the ground. The other stood inside the open box, among the scattered clothes of an emperor that had just been stripped from it. About a foot high, its wooden arms were stretched out, making it look like the frame of a scarecrow. It had an iron mask for a face; its eyes, which could be opened and closed like a doll's, were two slits. Now that the play was over, this sinister figure with its iron mask gave me the uncanny feeling that it had a twilight life of its own.

Many years later, when I was writing the story of Pu Yi, the last Emperor of China, whom I had seen several times in Tientsin, that scarecrow figure with the iron mask kept returning to me, as if insisting that it was the real emperor.

Other things I had learned in the market-place came back

like the tones of a language, long lost but once well known and loved. Without meaning to, I found myself reliving parts of Pu Yi's story and arranging it in scenes as if I had witnessed them myself. It seemed to me only natural that history should be presented in this way. The story of a person's life should be true. But truth does not mean, simply, a respect for recorded facts. Beyond the fabric of facts, there lies the truth of the imagination. If I have been a truthful witness at some imagined scenes of Pu Yi's lifetime, I have to thank the wandering story-tellers of China.

PROLOGUE

THE GATE OF HEAVENLY PEACE

In Peking, the pleasure gardens of Kublai Khan's celestial city contain a fortified sanctuary, the dark red of whose high walls resembles the colour of dried blood. This is the Forbidden City, where for 500 years successive emperors of the Ming and Ching dynasties played out their remote, decadent and often fearful lives. Today its labyrinth of palaces is uninhabited, save for some ghosts from China's imperial past. Most of those dark red walls have been pulled down in recent years, but the watch-tower and battlements of the Gate of Heavenly Peace, Tien An Men, still command the southern approaches to the Forbidden City. Outside this massive gate, the no man's land of Tien An Men Square separates the bustling Chinese City to the south, from Kublai Khan's city (the so-called Tartar City) which encloses the imperial palaces to the north.

One day in the autumn of 1960 a group of twelve middle-aged men got off a bus in Tien An Men Square. They were dressed in drab grey uniforms, soft peaked caps and cotton shoes. The official in charge of them wore the armband of the ministry of state security. Two or three of the group had put on face-masks. A westerly wind was blowing and the darkening sky was a deep yellow, ominous signs that a dust storm was on its way from the Gobi Desert.

There were few people about as the men in grey shuffled along in the swirling dust towards the Forbidden City. A black government staff car, the curtains on its windows discreetly drawn, cruised past. Every now and then they would hear the tinkling of a bell, and a bicycle would appear out of the gloom and weave by them. They crossed the ceremonial stone bridge over the imperial moat and came to a modern, concrete reviewing stand, bedecked with red flags. Here, on 1 October 1949, Mao Tse-tung had proclaimed the People's Republic of China. A portrait of him was hanging over the stand. There was an earnest expression in the eyes, but the hint of a smile about the corners of the mouth.

Ahead loomed the watch-tower, crowning the fifty-foot-high buttressed wall in which the arched Gate of Heavenly Peace is set. Armed sentries were on guard at the gate. The men in grey were expected, and an official, the palace curator, was at hand to receive them. The Forbidden City was not yet open to the public. In a year or so it would be renamed the Palace Museum and on state holidays truckloads of peasants would be brought here from the provinces to gaze with bewilderment at this other world. For the time being some of the dilapidated buildings were being repaired, and only special parties of visitors were admitted. The men in grey were such a party.

Each of them was a war criminal and a traitor, having been in the pay of the enemy during the Japanese invasion and occupation of China, which lasted from 1937 to 1945. Three of the group were generals; most of the others were senior civil servants. After serving ten years in prison, where they had been 'politically educated and remoulded through labour', they had received special pardons from the People's Supreme Court. As part of their rehabilitation, the Peking municipal authority had arranged a series of visits for them to places of interest: a peasant commune in the country surrounding Peking, some newly built factories and housing estates, and the historic site of the Forbidden City.

At the Gate of Heavenly Peace the men in grey had their passes inspected. Then, accompanied by the curator, they walked through the gate's massive archway into the first of several forecourts on the long and daunting approach to the imperial palaces. A quarter of a mile on stood the Wu Men, the Meridian Gate, last bastion of defence of the inner palaces. The curator, the official from the ministry of state security, and the three former generals marched towards the gate at a brisk pace. At the rear of the group, out of step with the others, came a man in a mask. He walked with a jerking movement of the arms and legs, as if he were a mechanical toy that had been wound up and set in motion. His cap was much too big for him, and he had to tilt his head back in order to peer about him through large tinted spectacles. Although he cut a comic figure, the rest of the party treated him with deference. When he lagged too far behind, they would wait patiently for him to catch up.

They passed through the main arch of the Meridian Gate. Spread out before them was the Da Nei or Great Within, a sequence of six magnificent audience halls, each facing south and linked by bridges and long flights of steps with marble balustrades. On either side of this range of halls, clusters of palaces, temples and pavilions stood in the ancient gardens whose unearthly charm pervaded the atmosphere.

After a while the curator produced his notebook and began to recite: 'The Forbidden City was built by Yung Lo, the third emperor of the Ming dynasty, between 1398 and 1420. It measures 960 metres from south to north, and 750 metres from west to east....' These bare statistics, uttered in the official's matter-of-fact voice, seemed, if anything, to accentuate the silence of the empty halls and temples. The curved roofs of yellow tiles, which cover the buildings of this imperial sanctuary as if with a single canopy, merged with the ochre sky. It was time to enter the Great Within. The official from the ministry of state security took the man in the mask by the arm, led him to the front of the group, and said with a smile, 'You must be our guide now.' The others all clapped their hands and nodded in agreement.

Their shy companion began to fumble awkwardly with his mask. After what seemed a long time, he succeeded in removing it. He was Pu Yi, Son of Heaven, and the last Emperor of China.

17

CHINA DURING THE CHING DYNASTY

1644-1912

Chita

Trans Siberian Railway

Amur River

MANCHURIA

Harbin

Changchun
(Hsinking)

Vladivostok

INNER MONGOLIA

Talitzu

JEHOL

LONG WHITE MT.

Mukden

SEA OF JAPAN

Taho River

Yingkow

Tunghua

Jehol City

Kalgan

Peking

Shanhaikwan

JAPAN

Tokyo

N

A

Tientsin

Taku

Port Arthur

KOREA

Yokohama

CHIHLI

Sea River

Weihaiwei

Paoan

SHANSI

Ise

Yenan

SHANTUNG

Hiroshima

SHENSI

Yellow River

YELLOW
SEA

Sian

Grand Canal

HONAN

Nanking

Hankow

Shanghai

FORMOSA
(TAIWAN)

Canton

KWANTUNG

Hong Kong

SOUTH CHINA SEA

0   miles   500

PART ONE

THE FORBIDDEN CITY

CHAPTER ONE

THE SPIDER'S WEB

Early in the morning of 13 November 1908, the Manchu Prince Chun and his household were awakened by loud knocking at the iron gate of their house, the Northern Mansion, in the Tartar City of Peking. Nervously, the prince put on his bedrobe and slippers. It must be the outlaws, he thought. Twice this month a band of outlaw raiders from the hills had been seen in the neighbourhood. He was making for his usual refuge, the study, when he heard someone call out in a stern voice, 'In the name of Her Imperial Highness, the Empress Dowager . . . ' The prince turned and ran into the courtyard, shouting to the stupefied gatekeeper, 'Hurry! Open the gate. Can't you hear?'

While the gatekeeper was trying to draw the heavy bolts, the prince looked through the gate hatch, gasped, and then reeled back into the courtyard, beating his breast and moaning, 'What have we done? What have we done?'

Beyond the gate a small army was drawn up. At its head was the palace herald. Behind him was an escort of Tartar cavalry from the imperial guard. In the frosty air steam was rising from their shaggy Mongolian ponies as they wheeled and pawed the ground. Four sedan-chairs, surrounded by uniformed bearers, had been set down on the ground behind the cavalry. In the first chair sat a grand councillor, dressed in his state robes. The second and third were occupied by eunuchs of the imperial presence, wearing brilliant scarlet helmets and jackets. The fourth chair, which was covered with yellow silk, was empty. At the rear, lounged a company of soldiers in ill-fitting foreign uniforms. They were men of General Yuan Shih-kai's Northern Army. A small crowd, mostly servants from nearby houses, and some hawkers, had already gathered and were chattering excitedly.

As soon as the gates were opened, the sedan-chairs were carried at the trot into the courtyard. To the prince's relief, the soldiers remained outside. After he had exchanged bows with his distinguished visitors the prince led them to the reception-room, which was also a theatre, decorated partly in the style of Louis-Quinze and partly in traditional Chinese. Servants rushed about in confusion among the jumble of furniture while the prince's children, Pu Yi and his baby brother Pu Chieh, cried loudly in their nurses' arms. The prince's mother, attended by two maids, kept calling out, 'What is happening?'

'No! Not that chair, this one,' shrieked the prince, getting in everyone's way.

Eventually, the grand councillor was seated in the place of honour, a *chaise-longue* in front of the stage, which was draped with curtains.

One member of the household remained calm, surveying the scene with a cold eye. The Princess Chun, looking immaculate, ordered tea to be brought. Then, in a few words, she told her husband to leave the room and dress himself. Here was a woman of mettle, thought the grand councillor as he watched the handsome woman who was the daughter of the late Jung Lu, the great Manchu general and viceroy of Tientsin. He remembered the Empress Dowager saying once in audience, 'The Princess Chun fears nothing, not even me!' The Empress Dowager had given her in marriage to Prince Chun in 1901 as a reward for his mission to Germany. The prince had gone there to present an apology to the Kaiser for the assassination of the German minister, Baron von Ketteler, by Boxer rebels. Coming as he did from an upstart family the prince was fortunate to have been given so distinguished a

26

wife. It was common knowledge that his mother was a concubine of low degree and that his father, an officer in the secret police, had been created the first Prince Chun for assisting the Empress Dowager in one of her murderous intrigues . . .

At that disloyal thought, the grand councillor checked himself and gazed about him at the scrolls of characters that hung on the walls. They were mostly well-known maxims, attributed to Confucius, in praise of family life and paternal authority. But one scroll, which hung near the stage, was in the hand of the first Prince Chun. The grand councillor viewed it with distaste:

> Wealth and Fortune breed more Fortune,
> Royal Favours bring more Favours.

As they sipped their tea, the two eunuchs peered slyly over their bowls at the lithe figure of the princess. Every detail of her personal life was known to them through their spies: how she liked to disguise herself as a man and visit the theatres in the Chinese City, how often she went to the bawdy-house, the Golden Ship, in the company of young actors, how much she spent of the prince's annual pension of 50,000 taels of silver on her admirers. It was a pity she did not live at court.

The prince reappeared, bowing and mumbling his apologies. When he had settled down, the grand councillor rose and took from his sleeve a document, attached by strings to red wax seals, which he flourished for all to see. Entitled the valedictory decree of the Kuang Hsu Emperor, it had in fact been composed by the Empress Dowager with the connivance of the grand council.

A hush fell on his audience as he began to read in a solemn voice. The Kuang Hsu Emperor would soon ascend on high, borne by the dragon chariot, ran the decree. Therefore, His Imperial Majesty was pleased to appoint as his successor, Pu Yi, the infant son of Prince Chun . . .

The prince's mother gave a shriek and collapsed in a faint. Her two maids, who were unable to lift her up, called for help. The children began to cry again, and his nurse tried to quieten Pu Yi by breast-feeding him. The prince staggered to his feet,

27

muttering, 'Pu Yi, Emperor? How can this be? Prince Ching's son, Pu Lun, is next in line to the throne, surely. And General Yuan Shih-kai is his friend. What will the soldiers out there do when they hear about this? Suppose they open fire?'

The princess called for silence, and the grand councillor read on: Prince Chun was commanded to bring the child Pu Yi to the palace that day, to be shown to the Emperor and to the Empress Dowager.

When the grand councillor had come to an end, he and the eunuchs took their leave of the princess while the struggling Pu Yi was carried out to the imperial sedan-chair by his father. Just before the procession moved off, one of the ponies bent its head close to Pu Yi's window, bared its large yellow teeth, and snorted. Terrified at this monster, Pu Yi buried his face in his father's lap and wept.

On the mile-long journey to the Forbidden City, the procession passed close to the palace of Prince Ching, head of the senior Manchu clan of the Nurhachi, whose son, Pu Lun, was the rightful heir to the imperial throne. The very sight of the Ching palace alarmed Prince Chun. Fearful of a plot, he half expected to see Prince Ching's bodyguard rush out, join forces with the escort, and take him and Pu Yi prisoner. Only when the procession had passed through the Gate of Spiritual Valour at the northern entrance to the Forbidden City, did Prince Chun feel safe.

Pu Yi was two years and nine months old when he was taken away to the Imperial Palace that day. He was not to see his mother again for another eight years. To him, she would always remain a shadowy figure sitting alone in a theatre, waiting for the play to begin.

That night Prince Chun and his son were lodged in a pavilion near the Palace of Tranquil Old Age, the residence of the Empress Dowager. It stood in a maze of courtyards and palaces at the heart of the Forbidden City. 'Clear the city! Lock the gates! Light the lanterns!' Listening to the cries of the eunuchs on night-watch, the prince felt trapped. He longed to be back in his own home far from this city of ghosts. The strangely inanimate figure of the infant Pu Yi, soon to be Son of Heaven, made him uneasy. The name Pu Yi, or

Universal Rite, had been chosen by the princess. He had always thought it strangely formal, more fitting for the high priest of a temple. Now he was beginning to see how prophetic she had been. Long after the eunuchs' cries had died away, he remained awake, dreading the coming of dawn when he would have to present Pu Yi to the dying Kuang Hsu Emperor and to the old Dowager. 'Her Sacred Majesty' the eunuchs of the presence called her. Sacred Majesty! The prince trembled at the thought of the fearsome woman who had ruled over China for close on fifty years and was now venerated as a goddess.

The daughter of an obscure provincial inspector, the Empress had first come to the Forbidden City in 1852 to serve the Hsien Feng Emperor as a concubine of low rank. She was called Yehonala after her father's Manchu clan name. At court she was treated with disdain by the members of the imperial family who were all of the rival Nurhachi clan. Once mighty warriors and fine horsemen, the princes of that clan had been corrupted by the decadent life of the Forbidden City several generations ago, but they still possessed many hereditary privileges. Sensual and ambitious, Yehonala quickly saw that the way to find favour with the Emperor was by ingratiating herself with the chief eunuch.

There had been eunuchs at court ever since the tyrant Chin founded the first imperial dynasty in 221 BC. Self-styled the Son of Heaven, the Chin Emperor and his sycophantic prime minister, Li Ssu, established a central bureaucratic government to take the place of the old independent states. They did this by force of arms and by introducing draconian laws: 120,000 families of aristocrats were transported from their former lands and forced to live near the imperial capital, where they could be kept under watch; a civil service of viceroys, governors, magistrates and inspectors was appointed to administer the provinces into which China was now divided. Afraid that these new officials might try to make their offices hereditary, the Chin Emperor surrounded himself with a staff of eunuchs who, with their network of spies, provided a counterbalance to the civil servants. Being

29

unable to found feudal families, the eunuchs were unlikely to prove disloyal to the Emperor.

In time the eunuchs became all-powerful at court, and few dared to oppose these high priests of a dark world where sexual orgies and a medley of religious rites were intertwined in a grotesque cult. Towards the end of the Ming dynasty, the chief eunuch, Wei, was worshipped as a deity in his lifetime, and a shrine to his honour was erected in the Forbidden City. This was too much for a senior official, the censor, who had the courage to denounce the chief eunuch for sacrilege and for leading the Emperor into paths of depravity even while his enemies, the Manchus, were massing beyond the Great Wall to invade China. For his audacity, the censor was condemned to the slow death by a thousand cuts. His family came to fetch his body, for which they were charged a huge sum of money. They found it so horribly mutilated that they were unable to recognise him.

When the young concubine, Yehonala, arrived at court, there were 3,000 eunuchs on the staff. They were governed by a hierarchy of eunuchs of the presence, at the head of whom was the chief eunuch, An Te-hai. Apart from their many domestic duties, the higher ranking eunuchs were responsible for the Emperor's entertainment. They hired troupes of professional actors from the Chinese City, produced plays and masques, attended the imperial bedchamber, and in liaison with the fifty or so concubines, catered for the Emperor's sexual appetites. To that end, they made use of books on erotic love which had been compiled over the centuries. They contained detailed illustrations of a variety of sexual positions and caresses with commentaries by experienced eunuchs and concubines.

From the first night that he wrapped the naked body of Yehonala in a blanket, carried her to the imperial bedchamber, and laid her at the foot of the dragon couch, the chief eunuch knew that here was a goddess of love. Watching her play her part in the classical themes of love-play, *Approaching the Fragrant Bamboo* and *The Jade Girl Plays the Flute*, he was struck by the relish and versatility that she brought to her art. Other concubines might be skilled in love-making;

what distinguished Yehonala was her seductive voice. And the chief eunuch himself was roused as he listened to her whispering her erotic fantasies to the bewitched Emperor.

Yehonala rose high in the Emperor's favour. She was promoted to the first rank of concubines and, after she had borne the Emperor a son and heir, she attained the status of consort. Despite her rapid advance at court, she remained inseparable from the chief eunuch. It was possible, although rare, for visiting actors who were not castrati to be smuggled into the ranks of the eunuchs, and watching Yehonala's flagrant behaviour – she would stroll in the grounds arm in arm with the chief eunuch and exchange passionate kisses with him – her rivals among the Manchu nobility and the concubines were convinced that the father of Yehonala's child was not the Emperor but the chief eunuch. There were others at court who believed that the father was Jung Lu, an officer of the imperial guard. Forceful and decisive, Yehonala possessed just those qualities which, added to feminine charm, prove irresistible to military commanders. With the army and the eunuchs on her side, she was able to survive the attacks of her many enemies, including the wrath of the Hsien Feng Emperor himself.

In 1861 the sickly Hsien Feng Emperor died in his palace at Jehol, beyond the Great Wall. He had fled there with his court to escape the foreign devils' armies that had captured Tientsin and were marching on the Forbidden City. Fearing that she had designs on his life, he refused to see Yehonala. In one of his last edicts, he ordered her to be banished to the Cold Palace where concubines who had fallen from favour were imprisoned. But Yehonala with the aid of Li, a eunuch of the bedchamber, snatched the imperial seal from the dying Emperor. Without his seal, the edict had no effect.

Yehonala's son, then aged six, succeeded to the throne; he was given the reign title Tung Chih. Yehonala, now Empress Dowager, took the name Tzu Hsi, Motherly and Auspicious. In a brilliantly timed military coup, she had her three principal enemies arrested. They were the grand secretary and two imperial princes, one of whom was the Regent-elect. After a summary trial they were sentenced to death by beheading. The Empress Dowager gave orders for their heads to be displayed in Tien An Men Square. It was the first act of her long regency.

Women did not appear at imperial audiences, and it was the custom for an empress dowager, if she were Regent, to sit behind a curtain of yellow silk which hung beside the throne. When the Tung Chih Emperor sat on the dragon throne, the assembled courtiers, ministers and other officials who had been kneeling in their appointed places on the cold stone floor since before dawn prostrated themselves. But it was not the child Emperor whom they feared; rather it was the sinister figure of the Empress Dowager, hidden behind the yellow curtain. Like a voracious spider lurking beside the intricate web on which her victims danced, the Empress Dowager took up her position in the shadows of the Forbidden City. And as a spider, attached to its web a silken thread, can detect the faintest tremor on any part of it, so the Empress Dowager was sensitive to any hostile movement at court. With an unerring sense of timing, she would race to strike at her fluttering prey or, if needs be, she would lie in wait, watching its struggles become more feeble, before sidling in for the kill. In slow and horrible ways – none could equal her as a poisoner – she destroyed her co-Regent, Tzu An, the Empress Motherly and Restful, her own son, the disease-ridden Tung Chih Emperor, whom she encouraged to lead a dissolute life, and his wife, the young Empress, who was pregnant at the time of her murder. All three had shown signs of wishing to be independent of the Empress Dowager.

The Tung Chih Emperor died in agony in December 1874, and the next victim to be enmeshed in the spider's web was the five-year-old Kuang Hsu Emperor, the brother of Prince Chun. Kuang Hsu means Brilliant Succession, and the choice of title looks suspiciously like one of the Empress Dowager's devilish jests, for she had the wretched boy placed on the throne in defiance of all the dynastic laws of succession and the opposition of the Nurhachi clan. Once again the Emperor was a minor and a member of the Yehonala clan, and the Empress Dowager Motherly and Auspicious ruled as sole Regent. Brilliant Succession might be the boy Emperor's title, but he was to become known as 'the loneliest monarch in the world'. His every move was watched, and when he showed signs of wanting to be more than the Empress Dowager's puppet, he was condemned to spend the remaining years of his life in solitary confinement.

All had been well at first. At nineteen he had married the Empress Dowager's niece. The young Empress was given the title Lung Yu, Honorific Abundance. The old Dowager had then retired to the Summer Palace, seven miles west of the Forbidden City.

Under the influence of an imperial tutor, the young Kuang Hsu Emperor became involved in the Reform Movement, whose leaders advocated an interest in European learning and an end to many of the hereditary privileges of the Manchu courtiers. Throughout the nineteenth century peasant revolts and foreign invasions had led to the break-up of China. Defeated by Britain and France in the 'Opium Wars' of 1839-42 and 1856-60, and plagued by the Taiping, Great Peace, rebels who were active in central China, the enfeebled Manchu reigning house was forced to cede more and more territory, including the finest ports of China, to no fewer than nine foreign nations: 'the vultures' as Peter Fleming, the foreign correspondent, called them.

Many of the concessions yielded by China were sanctioned by the unequal treaties, so named because China had no choice but to give in. The final humiliation came when, in 1895, the small island empire of Japan, which the Chinese had always despised, annexed the island of Formosa (now Taiwan). The military might of Japan had grown as a result of her adopting foreign methods and equipment, and the leaders of the Reform Movement argued that China must do likewise in order to resist foreign aggression. In future, they urged, imperial generals should be selected on merit and trained in foreign methods.

These progressive ideas were anathema to that arch-reactionary, the Empress Dowager, who had a profound contempt for 'foreign devils', be they soldiers, traders or missionaries. With the help of her lover, General Jung Lu, Prince Chun's father-in-law, she was determined to crush the reformers.

33

Fearing what the Empress Dowager might do, the Kuang Hsu Emperor ordered General Yuan Shih-kai, a supporter of the Reform Movement, to confine her in the Summer Palace. But Yuan Shih-kai promptly changed sides and revealed all to her. The Empress Dowager returned to the Forbidden City. That day six leading members of the Reform Movement were beheaded. Their heads were displayed in Tien An Men Square. If he could have known what sufferings he was to endure for the rest of his life, the Emperor might have welcomed the same speedy execution for himself.

Quite apart from his role in the Reform Movement, there was another reason why the Kuang Hsu Emperor had incurred the hatred of the Empress Dowager. He made no secret of his love for one of his concubines, Pearl Concubine, whom he preferred to his wife. His marriage to Honorific Abundance was never consummated, and the old Dowager must have appreciated only too well the irony of the title she had chosen for her niece.

'The Emperor being ill, the Empress Dowager has resumed the regency.' The laconic announcement in the *Court Gazette* of September 1898 did not disclose that the Empress Dowager had ordered the Emperor to be detained in the Empty Room, part of a small pavilion that stands on the Fairy Isle in the Forbidden City's West Lake.

The Empty Room. How well the simple words describe his small dark cell! It had no heating, no window, and the air was foul. Once or twice during the years to come he would be taken under escort to the Summer Palace, but the windows of his room there were also blocked up. It was torture to hear the lake water lapping and not be able to see anything beyond the walls of his prison.

The Empress Dowager's successful *coup d'état* was acclaimed by several newspapers published in the foreign settlements. The *Peking and Tientsin Times* likened her to Queen Elizabeth I of England. The Empress Dowager, it said, was a symbol of that unity which the imperial system of government had bestowed on the Chinese people. The *North China Daily Mail* praised her for suppressing the Reform Movement, with its dangerous talk of progress. China, the paper said, was not yet ready for such radical changes. One day, perhaps . . .

It is easy to understand how the foreign newspaper editors came to adopt such a patronising attitude towards China's rulers. The tone had been set long ago by the British prime minister, Lord Palmerston. Irked by the stubborn resistance of the Chinese emperor and his mandarins to the British opium traffic, he had declared that 'the Chinese must be taught a lesson'. And, in 1860, Lord Elgin had obliged him by giving orders for the destruction by fire of the Imperial Summer Palace. For more than a week a pall of black smoke lay over the capital. The Empress Dowager, then the Emperor's secondary consort, was spared the anguish of seeing her beloved palace burning, for she had fled with the Emperor to Jehol, beyond the Great Wall.

Having taught the Emperor a lesson, and having obtained the concessions they wanted, the foreign powers, which included Britain, France, Germany, the United States and Japan, were concerned to prop up the decadent Ching dynasty of the Manchus and to defend it against peasant risings. The last thing the foreign traders wanted was anarchy. In 1864 General 'Chinese' Gordon led a mixed force of foreign mercenaries and Chinese imperial troops to crush the Taiping rebels who had come close to bringing down the Ching dynasty.

In time the foreign settlers in treaty ports such as Tientsin, Weihaiwei and Shanghai grew accustomed to the martinet who had ruled over China as Regent for so many years. Thanks to the unequal treaties, foreign missionaries and traders enjoyed the privilege of being free from Chinese laws. Not having to suffer the attentions of her officials, they could afford to be tolerant of the Empress Dowager. Some British settlers even compared her with that other matriarch, Queen Victoria.

The settlers' tolerance of the Chinese matriarch was about to be put to a severe test, however. In the autumn of 1898 there was widespread drought followed by famine in northern China. The Society of Harmonious Fists (or Boxers, as the settlers called them), part of the ancient secret society of the White Lotus, rose up in revolt. Their ranks were swollen by

35

large bands of dispossessed peasants. At first the rebels' target was their traditional enemy, the Manchu court in the Forbidden City, and their banners carried the emblem *Restore the Ming*. But the astute Empress Dowager managed to divert their fury against the foreign devils. A notorious amazon named Yellow Lotus led an attack on the British concession in Tientsin, the river port eighty miles east of Peking. After a month-long siege, an international force under the British Admiral Seymour succeeded in rescuing the settlers.

It was Peking's turn next. There, over 800 foreign soldiers and residents, including many women and children, as well as 3,000 Chinese Christian refugees, crowded into the compound of the legations' quarter, a few hundred yards from the Gate of Heavenly Peace. For over seven weeks in the summer of 1900 they endured daily bombardments from the Boxers, whose cannons were mounted on the city's ramparts. All the while, the Chinese imperial forces and their generals looked on.

By August sixty-five foreigners had been killed and 142 wounded. Casualties among the Chinese refugees were even higher. An epidemic of typhoid fever broke out in the compound. Food and water were running dangerously low when at last Admiral Seymour's relief force reached the outskirts of Peking.

When she heard the sound of the foreign devils' guns, the Empress Dowager put her escape plan into action. She disguised as a peasant and instructed the eunuch-gaolers to bring the Kuang Hsu Emperor, similarly disguised, to the big well in the courtyard of the Palace of Tranquil Old Age, where two horse-drawn carts were waiting. Hoping that he might escape from her clutches at last, the Emperor begged to be allowed to remain in Peking. The Empress Dowager was adamant that he accompany her. Pearl Concubine, who was standing nearby, fell on her knees and pleaded for the Emperor. In a rage, the old Dowager ordered the chief eunuch to throw Pearl Concubine down the well. Two eunuchs held back the distraught Emperor. The splashing of water mingled with Pearl Concubine's despairing cries. Then the iron cover was placed over the well and her muffled cries grew fainter and died away.

An advance party of foreign soldiers had already reached the Gate of Heavenly Peace when the two peasant carts carrying the Empress Dowager, the Emperor and a few attendants trundled out of the Forbidden City. As the Dowager had foreseen, they escaped detection in the turmoil of the crowded streets. Making their way by stages, the imperial party finally reached the ancient capital of Sian, where they were joined by a few loyal courtiers and generals.

A little over a year later, in October 1901, the Empress Dowager made peace with the foreign powers that occupied Peking, and, escorted by General Yuan Shih-kai, returned in triumph to the Forbidden City. In her entourage, scarcely noticed by the crowds lining the route, was the closely guarded Kuang Hsu Emperor. When the procession entered the Great Within, he was conducted by his eunuch-gaolers to the Empty Room. To those who inquired after him, the old Dowager replied that he was too ill to give any audiences.

There was a price to be paid for the peace that China had been granted by the victorious foreign powers. They demanded a huge sum by way of indemnity, which the Chinese were to go on paying with interest for many years to come. Despite this penalty, the Empress Dowager surprised her courtiers by professing a new-found admiration for her former enemies, whom she now referred to as 'the mighty foreigners'.

In general, the mighty foreigners responded to her new sentiment with delight. But some of them, remembering the recent, barbaric siege of the legations' quarter which so nearly ended with the massacre of every foreigner in Peking, expressed doubts about the trustworthiness of the Empress Dowager. Others, like Sir Robert Hart, director-general of the Chinese Customs, wished that there could have been some recorded facts, some documentary evidence, to prove whether or not the Empress Dowager and her favourite, General Jung Lu, had sided with the Boxers.

Sir Robert's wish was soon granted. Sir Edmund Backhouse, oriental scholar, benefactor of the Bodleian Library at Oxford, candidate for the chair of Chinese at the University of Oxford, secret agent of the British government, and arms dealer, was obsessed by the Empress Dowager. With another oriental scholar, J.O.P. Bland, he published *China under the Empress Dowager*. The central feature of the book is the diary of Ching-shan, assistant secretary of the imperial household and a relative of the Empress Dowager. Ching-shan was murdered by his son during the Boxer rising and Backhouse claimed that he found the diary in Ching-shan's house in Peking, shortly after the allied troops drove out the Boxers in August 1900. The diary makes clear that both the Empress Dowager and General Jung Lu were pro-Western and did all they could to protect the foreigners from the Boxers. This view became the conventional wisdom among scholars. The *Encyclopaedia Britannica* (1926 edition) sums it up in these words: 'It was to General Jung Lu, father-in-law of Prince Chun, that the foreign legations owed their escape from extermination.'

China under the Empress Dowager was a huge success. Within a short time, eight impressions were sold out, and it was translated into many foreign languages. The *Times* called it 'a document more illuminating than perhaps any that has ever come out of China'. Here then were the recorded facts, the stuff of history, and generations of historians and their readers have savoured and disgested Backhouse's reproduction of Ching-shan's diary, unaware that they were being duped. For, as Hugh Trevor-Roper has revealed in his brilliant work, *A Hidden Life: The Enigma of Sir Edmund Backhouse* (1976), the so-called diary of Ching-shan was a skilful forgery, manufactured by Backhouse in order to show the Empress Dowager and her favourite, Jung Lu, in a good light.

With so benevolent a matriarch as the Empress Dowager ruling as Regent, foreign traders felt optimistic about their prospects. China, they said, was now really open to the outside world. Lord Elgin had once declared, in a speech to the British chamber of commerce in Tientsin, that he looked forward to the time when the commercial crusaders, as he called his audience, would be free to spread among the Chinese 'the elevating influences of a higher civilisation'. That time had come. The newspapers liked nothing better than to report on the rapid spread of foreign ways of living among the mandarins and the growing class of wealthy Chinese merchants. The *North China Daily Mail* was first with the story that the Wagon-Lits Hotel in Peking was under contract to supply European-style food to the Imperial Palace. It was to be served in the Dowager's private dining-room, which was equipped with knives and forks imported from Sheffield, England.

Outside the west gate of Peking's Tartar City foreign scientists had designed and organised the new Zoological Gardens, where the animals included lions and tigers. The Empress Dowager paid it a visit. She expressed astonishment at the spectacle. The Chinese liked to cage little birds. But a caged tiger!

In the last years of her reign, her fawning courtiers had formed the habit of addressing the Empress Dowager at audiences as 'Venerable Buddha'. The title, with its suggestion of immortality, was unhappily translated as 'Old Buddha' by a secretary at the British legation who had a dubious command of Chinese. It was a schoolboy howler, but the name caught on. It suited the newspapers. Soon, traders, soldiers, missionaries and their families could be heard using it. Over their whiskies and sodas English business men in the Tientsin Club talked about 'Old Buddha' as they might talk about 'dear old Aunt Edith' back home in Kingston, Surrey.

Towards the end of her life 'Old Buddha' was looked upon with a mixture of affection and morbid curiosity by the wives and daughters of foreign diplomats in Peking. They vied with each other for invitations to tea at the Palace of Tranquil Old Age. There, surrounded by a clutter of chinoiserie and foreign bric-à-brac, so typical of the vulgarity of the Manchu monarchs, they were charmed. They found 'Old Buddha' magnetic, alluring, gracious. On their way back from her palace to the Gate of Heavenly Peace, they would pause to admire the serene aspect of the Fairy Isle on the West Lake.

Shortly before her seventy-third birthday, the last of her life, the Empress Dowager received seven of these foreign ladies at her palace. She had a surprise for them. A yellow curtain parted, revealing the Kuang Hsu Emperor, supported by four eunuchs. He had been specially groomed and robed. After a brief introduction, the curtain was drawn. The Emperor was led back to the Empty Room. Tea was then served. Had her visitors been able to read the Venerable Buddha's mind, they would not have felt so relaxed that afternoon. For she hated them and their kind with the utmost loathing. Did they expect her to forgive the desecration of her Summer Palace? During the Boxer rising she had offered the rebels a reward of 50 taels of silver (about £8) for the head of each male, and 40 taels for the head of each female barbarian. Despite her recent show of interest in their ways, her hatred of the foreign devils had not diminished. Even as she smiled over her teacup at these ladies, she was probably wishing that she could sentence them, there and then, to the death by a thousand cuts. Lingering death. That was her forte.

The ladies took their leave of 'Old Buddha'. Afterwards the British minister in Peking reported home to Lord Salisbury that 'Her Majesty's courteous amiability has made a most favourable impression'.

On her triumphant return to the Forbidden City in October 1901 the Empress Dowager, concerned at the stories that were circulating about the murder of Pearl Concubine, had published an edict in the name of the Emperor. In it posthumous honours were awarded to Pearl Concubine, who was praised for her courage 'which led her virtuously to commit suicide when unable to catch up with the Court on its departure from Peking'. This piece of hypocrisy, which the Emperor was forced to confirm with his seal, made him even more terrified of the ruthless Dowager. Convinced that she was poisoning him, he scarcely touched his food. At night he would be wakened by the sound of chuckling behind the bed hangings. The Dowager! Frantically, he would tear at them, to find no one there. His only hope of survival, he knew, was to outlive his old tormentress. It became an obsession with him. Early in the winter of 1908 it seemed that his chance had come at last. On 3 November, during the week-long celebrations for her seventy-third birthday, Venerable Buddha had picnicked in a boat on the West Lake until late in the evening. She caught a severe cold. Worse still, at the picnic she had feasted

40

on a dish of crab-apples with a generous helping of clotted cream, this last a foreign touch. The next day she suffered an acute attack of dysentery and collapsed. Hearing that she was on the point of death, the Emperor bribed his eunuch-gaolers to let him pay a secret visit to her bedchamber to make sure she was dying. He drew back the hangings and, to his horror, found her sitting up, expecting him. Her hideous chuckles followed him all the way back to the Empty Room. In his delirium he could not be sure whether or not that last visit was only a nightmare.

Four eunuch-gaolers dragged the Kuang Hsu Emperor along a corridor to the Hall of Cloudless Heaven. There, he was made to kneel before the yellow curtain. A gong sounded. The curtain was parted to reveal Venerable Buddha seated on the throne. Beside her stood her favourtie, Li, who had succeeded An Te-hai as chief eunuch. The Emperor prostrated himself before the throne.

Every month for the last ten years this silent audience had taken place so that Venerable Buddha could look with sadistic pleasure on her wretched prisoner. Today's audience was to be the last. It was 13 November 1908, and Venerable Buddha had already decide that the infant Pu Yi should be the next emperor. The chief eunuch gave the order for the kowtows to begin. Helped by his gaolers, the prostrate Emperor raised himself to a kneeling position. He then bent forward until his head touched the floor in front of the throne. Slowly and painfully he repeated the kowtow nine times. His humiliation was complete as he performed the humble obeisance which, by custom, only he, the Emperor, was entitled to receive from his subjects.

It is difficult to believe that the Venerable Buddha did not feel some compassion for him, as she watched the dying Emperor kowtowing to her. She had seen him placed on the dragon throne when he was but five years old. Now, although he was only thirty-eight, this half-starved and unkempt creature looked like an old man of ninety. Venerable Buddha raised her claw of a hand. The gong sounded, the yellow curtain was drawn, and the Emperor was taken back to the Empty Room.

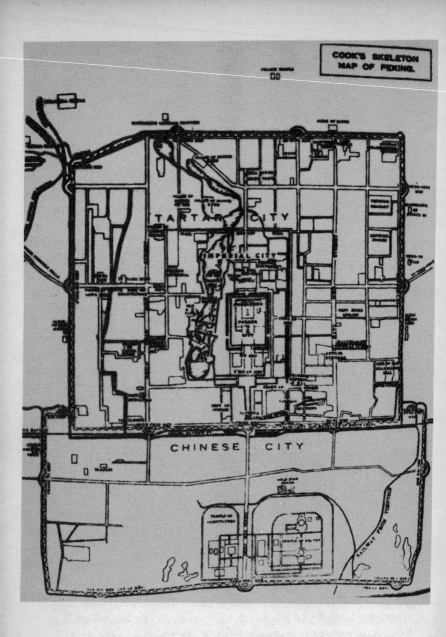

THOMAS COOK'S PLAN OF PEKING, *c.* 1900

Li, the chief eunuch, brought him writing materials for his last testament. He managed a few lines. It was General Yuan Shih-kai who had betrayed him, he wrote. He implored all the members of the imperial family to avenge the years of agony he had suffered.

That testament was the Emperor's fatal mistake. Within the hour the eunuch-gaolers came with his white burial-robes. There was a fierce struggle as he tried to fight them off. Just then Prince Chun, carrying Pu Yi in his arms, arrived at the door of the Empty Room. The gaolers hurried away, leaving the Emperor sprawled face downwards on his bed. He was wrapped in a long white shift. A white linen cap had been forced over his head, almost masking him. The other burial-clothes were scattered over the floor. Slowly and painfully the Emperor propped himself on one elbow and turned to face his visitors. No words passed between them.

Shocked at the sight of his brother, the Emperor, whom he had not seen for many years, Prince Chun lowered Pu Yi to the ground. Emperor and child stared at each other. Then they both screamed. Their screams became one, uniting them in their agony. Before its echo faded away, the child in Pu Yi had died and an old puppet's desperate cunning to survive, and his hatred of mortals, entered Pu Yi's soul. The Emperor sank back in his shroud.

At the Hall of Cloudless Heaven the yellow silk curtain was parted by an invisible hand to reveal the Empress Dowager and the chief eunuch, Li. As master of ceremonies he had served his mistress for over forty years, ever since the day when he had helped her to seize the imperial seal from the dying Hsien Feng Emperor. Prince Chun shuddered at this terrifying spectacle. Since he had last seen her, the old Dowager had shrivelled up. Under the dyed black hair with its silver and jade head-dress was the face of a skeleton, over which a thin yellow parchment of skin was drawn. A year before a stroke had left her mouth twisted. He was looking at the decay and death of the Ching dynasty of the Manchus.

With a mask-like grin, the chief eunuch motioned to the petrified prince to kneel and begin the nine kowtows. Holding on to Pu Yi with one hand, the prince made his act of homage. He worried that the child might make a scene, but it remained still gazing with fascination at the old Dowager. Although Pu Yi gave one or two sobs which irritated the Dowager, he did not shed a tear. There seemed to be no emotion left in him. The Empress Dowager raised her claw of a hand. Like the professional actor that he was, the chief eunuch performed with exactly the right gestures the dismissal at the end of the imperial liturgy.

The yellow curtain was drawn back to hide the throne. Surrendering the listless Pu Yi to the eunuchs of the presence, Prince Chun was relieved to be on his way. He was a trespasser here, he felt, and 'Her Sacred Majesty', the chief eunuch and the child Emperor-to-be were part of a mysterious rite not intended for mortals.

At six o'clock on the following morning, 15 November 1908, the Empress Dowager summoned a grand council. Announcing that the much-lamented Kuang Hsu Emperor had been borne on high by the dragon chariot, she decreed Pu Yi heir by adoption to her son, the late Tung Chih Emperor. By this piece of fiction she astutely nullified the legitimate claims of Prince Ching's family to the throne.

There were a few murmurs of dissent from the Ching supporters, including General Yuan Shih-kai, but the Dowager silenced them with a sharp rebuke. Pu Yi would become Son of Heaven at the forthcoming enthronement ceremonies, she declared. Nevertheless, she would have the final authority over him. She looked forward to many years of benevolent rule from behind the yellow curtain.

A special edict, issued in Pu Yi's name, elevated her to the rank of Dowager Grand Empress, the first to enjoy such eminence since the tyrant Chin founded the Empire in 221 BC. And the last. At midday the Dowager Grand Empress was about to sit down to a meal when, suddenly, she fainted. Her recent illness, which she had survived by an effort of will, had left her weak. The added strain of the last two days had been too much for her. On regaining consciousness, she had a premonition of death. Immediately she ordered the grand council to reconvene.

The dying matriarch informed the council that she had appointed Prince Chun as Regent, but that all his decisions were to be subject to the authority of the new Dowager Empress, Honorific Abundance. Yehonala had served her clan well.

Returning to her apartments in the Palace of Tranquil Old Age, the Dowager Grand Empress gave orders for her valedictory decree to be drawn up. When the grand secretary presented the draft to her, she studied it carefully and made a number of changes. Ever conscious of her image both at court and in the world outside the Forbidden City, she was determined that her last decree should reveal her as indeed Motherly and Auspicious. In the valedictory decree, which one of her foreign biographers was to describe as an impressive and 'nobly worded document', the old Dowager claimed that she was so overwhelmed with grief at the death of the Kuang Hsu Emperor that she could 'bear no more. And so I am come to the pass where no possible hope of recovery remains'. She ended it with the command that His Majesty, Pu Yi, 'must devote himself to studying the interests of the country . . . and hereafter add fresh lustre to the glorious achievements of his ancestors'.

At three o'clock in the afternoon the Dowager Grand Empress died. Her mind had been clear until the last moment of her life.

There were many at court and among her Manchu clansmen who found it hard to believe that the Venerable Buddha was really dead. For several years the chief eunuch and some of her senior officials had been encouraging her in the belief that she was immortal. A band of her disciples shared that belief. As the number of these disciples grew, it became necessary to join them if one was not to be suspected of treason.

The form of her immortality was that of a Bodhisattva. She was the incarnation of Kuan Yin, the Goddess of Mercy, it was said. At the many revels held in the palace grounds, the Venerable Buddha liked to appear in the costume of Kuan Yin, accompanied by her chief eunuch, dressed as an archangel. This was no mere charade. She believed in her role. There was one snag to the Venerable Buddha's claim to be the Goddess of Mercy. That august position was already filled. His Holiness the Dalai Lama of Tibet was held by all his

45

subjects to be Kuan Yin's incarnation. Moreover, many Buddhists believed that if two incarnations of the same Bodhisattva meet in one place, one of them must remove to another world. The Venerable Buddha's loyal disciples were not unduly troubled by this difficulty. Tibet was far away, and it was unlikely that the Dalai Lama would learn about his rival goddess, they thought.

Fate intervened, however, to upset their complacency. In 1904, at the instigation of Lord Curzon, a British force invaded Tibet and, after a bloody battle, marched into the sacred city of Lhasa. The Dalai Lama fled over the mountains into China. Slowly His Holiness, with a few followers and a train of camels and yaks, made his arduous way northwards. At last, in November 1908, this bedraggled procession from Tibet reached the Forbidden City in Peking, just in time for the Venerable Buddha's birthday celebrations.

One can imagine the embarrassment of the Manchu courtiers as they watched the two Goddesses of Mercy seated side by side in the throne-room of the Hall of Cloudless Heaven. The delicate topic of the dual Kuan Yin was carefully avoided, but the Dalai Lama was not deceived.

The festivities for the Dowager's birthday included theatrical performances, which went on for five days. On 3 November she was taken ill. The Dalai Lama presented her with a sacred image of Buddha. Provided the image was placed in her tomb in the Eastern Hills, he advised, she was sure to recover. Twelve days later she was dead. In her magnificent tomb the Dowager's body was laid in her bejewelled coffin under the waiting figure of the perpetually smiling Buddha.

The late Dowager's disciples refused to admit defeat. As soon as the Dalai Lama returned to Tibet, apparitions of their own Kuan Yin were reported. One of the Dowager's favourite pastimes had been to walk in the palace courtyards at dead of night, escorted by a company of eunuchs bearing lanterns and followed by other eunuchs playing eerie music on their reed-pipes and cymbals. When, after her burial, people spoke of having seen the Dowager processing with her eunuchs after dark in the Forbidden City, even the most cynical of officials quaked.

CHAPTER TWO

THE ARTICLES OF FAVOURABLE TREATMENT

At dawn on 2 December 1908, the Regent, Prince Chun, stood at the Altar of Heaven. A circular terrace, approached by flights of white marble steps, this high altar is open to the sky. To the north, east and south one looks out on to a vast plain. To the west, the skyline is broken by a range of dark, brooding hills; beyond those hills are the steppe lands and desert of the Interior. Incense was heaped on a piece of burning charcoal, and the smoke rose above the blue dome of the nearby Temple of Heaven, up into the fading night sky. Prince Chun bowed to the altar and the first red rays of sun behind it. On behalf of Pu Yi he made the Address to Heaven. He bowed again in the direction of the sun, and the brief ceremony was over.

The Regent's procession with its armed escort returned to the Forbidden City. As they made their way to the Hall of Supreme Harmony they passed a long line of noblemen and officials waiting, in order of seniority, for the ritual of the enthronement to begin. The court musicians on the upper terrace began to strike their stone chimes. The muted sound of the old musical stones, punctuated by intervals of silence, floated down to the waiting courtiers. These echoes of a past China had been composed in the days of the independent states, long before the Empire. A gong was struck and the

47

ancient music died away. The courtiers filed into the hall, each to his proper place marked on a flagstone. The eunuchs of the presence formed a rank behind the empty throne. All prostrated themselves. Pu Yi was placed on the dragon throne. A second gong sounded, and his subjects began the nine kowtows, ending in a kneeling position. Only then did they dare to look at the Son of Heaven.

Pu Yi's eyes were half closed. Over his thickly padded clothes he wore the imperial yellow silk robe embroidered with the five-clawed dragon. His arms were held out stiffly, and his legs were stretched out before him. Old Li, the chief eunuch, stood on the left of the throne. On the right was the yellow silk curtain. Some of the older courtiers kept glancing towards it. The Venerable Buddha used to sit behind that curtain, they thought. Was she there now? Why was the chief eunuch smiling to himself?

In front of the throne Prince Chun rose to read out the new emperor's name. Suddenly, Pu Yi gave a strangled cry. There was not a tear in his eyes, however. He jerked his arms and legs as if he were in a rage. Fearfully, Prince Chun stretched out his hand, but he seemed unable to touch the Emperor. After some moments of complete silence, Prince Chun recovered himself. In a high-pitched stammer he read out the reign title that the Venerable Buddha had chosen for Pu Yi. It was Hsuan Tung, which means Wide Horizon.

Celebrations were held in the Tartar City to mark the new reign. Even the shop fronts in the narrow lanes of the Chinese City were decorated with the yellow, dragon flag. The cannons of the Peiyang Army fired a salute. Alone in his study in the Northern Mansion, Prince Chun flinched at the sound of the guns. 'What is Yuan Shih-kai up to now?' he cried. Ever since his son's enthronement Prince Chun had been dreading the possibility of an army coup in favour of Pu Lun, the Ching prince. 'We shall be massacred,' he would wail. He remembered his mission to Germany seven years ago. Kaiser Wilhelm had given him some parting advice. 'Make sure that the command of the imperial army is in your own hands,' he said. 'You cannot trust a single general.' Now it was too late, and he greatly regretted not having heeded the Kaiser's words.

48

The Peiyang, or Northern Army, was the largest and best equipped of all the imperial forces. Although it had never won a battle, it had a reputation for being invincible. The main duty of this army was to defend the capital and its imperial palaces. In 1900, when the Boxers were besieging Peking, the Northern Army had remained well out of range of the cannon-fire. After the fighting was over, the Northern Army stood by while Peking was shamelessly looted by foreign soldiers and civilians as no city had been since the sacking of Constantinople by the Crusaders. When it was safe for the Empress Dowager to return to the capital, one of its regiments escorted her with fanfares to the Gate of Heavenly Peace. All the officers of the regiment were decorated for their gallantry.

Units of the Northern Army were sometimes sent on patrol to quell disturbances in the country surrounding Peking. Used to living in barracks and travelling by trains, the soldiers found these expeditions into the countryside an unpleasant and dangerous duty. A fiercely independent people with a traditional hatred of imperial officials, the peasants had a saying about soldiers which goes back to the time of the first emperor, the tyrant Chin: 'One does not use good iron to make nails.' The soldiers were despised not only for themselves but for their link with the imperial capital. Peking produced nothing. A million and more Manchu and Chinese officials, hangers-on, shopkeepers and soldiers lived and grew fat there, subsidized by the crushing grain tax on the peasants.

To the east and south of Peking the tall spears of *gaoliang*, a coarse maize that grows to a height of ten feet in the summer months, provided the villagers with excellent cover. At the first warning of the troops' approach, the peasants would hide their daughters and their livestock. Sometimes whole villages were evacuated. To have a company of the Northern Army billeted on one's village was worse than a death sentence. Rape and looting were sure to follow the arrival of the soldiers. It was not simply a case of wanton destruction. The soldiers behaved as they did through fear. Walking along the narrow paths between the ranks of *gaoliang*, the nervous soldiers would suddenly come on clearings where teams of sullen peasants, armed with machetes, looked less like harvesters than

49

guerrillas. A man hoeing a field, a young woman carrying vegetables to the market, who was to tell that they were not outlaws? It needed only one silent killing of a soldier for a whole company to be reduced to panic.

Even in the winter months when the *gaoliang* stalks had been cut down it must have seemed to the soldiers that there was no escaping the hated maize, for *gaoliang*, the staple diet of the northern Chinese peasant, was all the soldiers had to live on. In their barracks at Peking they were given millet and a weekly ration of rice to eat. Here, in the country, they had to put up with the bitter-tasting yellow *goaliang* gruel and harsh *goaliang* wine.

Apart from their arduous patrols, the soldiers of the Northern Army were called on to face an even more unpopular duty in the hostile countryside. To the north and west of Peking the *gaoliang* fields gave way to sand-swept plains and terraced fields backed by dry stone walls, rising to the hills, along the top of which ranged the Great Wall. This was outlaw country, and although the Northern Army made occasional forays into the plains, it seldom ventured into the hills except to relieve the garrisons which guarded the *yamen*, or headquarters of the imperial officials: governors, magistrates and tax-collectors who lived and worked in fortified compounds in the centres of towns. These hilltop towns and the wild country that surrounded them were the haunt of the ancient secret society of the White Lotus. The sworn enemy of the Ching dynasty, the outlaw leaders of the White Lotus had inspired many peasant risings, especially at times of calamity such as drought. Their first action at the start of a revolt was to attack the *yamen*, but their ultimate goal was to destroy that symbol of imperial rule, the Forbidden City.

In the market-places of provincial towns, and sometimes at the very gates of a *yamen* itself, the wandering story-tellers told of heroic concubines who were imprisoned and tortured in the Forbidden City, and they kept alive a hatred for that dark red citadel by re-enacting the history of how it came to be built. In 1368 Chu Yuen-chang, the beggar monk, led a peasant rising to defeat the mighty Mongol army and bring down the Yuan dynasty that Kublai Khan had founded a hundred years before. After his victory, Chu established himself at Nanking. He had no pretensions to be Emperor, but was content to rule over a small independent state with the title of duke. Like other members of the White Lotus, Chu dreamed of a return to that golden age when China was free from the burden of imperial officials and soldiers. In time, however, Duke Chu was prevailed on to become the first emperor of the Ming or 'Light' dynasty (a word taken from the creed of the White Lotus which praised as virtues the 'light' elements of nature: sun and moon, quickening fire, clear water, and searching wind). It was said of him that he would never allow officials to come between him and his peasant subjects.

On his death in 1398 Chu was succeeded by his sixteen-year-old grandson, the popular Kien Wen. Soon afterwards Yung Lo, an uncle of the young Emperor, gained control of the army, invaded Nanking, and claimed the throne. Yung Lo gave orders for the deposed Emperor, his nephew, to be murdered. The centre of Nanking was destroyed by fire and many innocent people were killed, but the young Emperor disguised himself as a monk and escaped from the burning city.

Haunted by the ghost of Chu, the first Ming emperor, and fearful of the White Lotus whose outlaw leaders had sworn vengeance on him, Yung Lo moved his capital from Nanking to Peking, where he built his fortress-palace on the site of Kublai Khan's former city. Imperial troops were sent on expeditions throughout China to hunt down Kien Wen, the rightful emperor, but he was never discovered.

Gate of Heavenly Peace. How the words continued to mock Yung Lo, who never spent a day free from anxiety in his Forbidden City! The court annals, followed ever since by both Chinese and foreign history books, salute him as 'The Illustrious Emperor and Great Builder'. Peasant legends revile him as the usurper who darkened the springtime of the Ming.

After the death of the Venerable Buddha, sensing that the end of the Ching dynasty of the Manchus was near, the leaders of the White Lotus were active again, and there were reports of

51

disaffected peasants massing near the Great Wall in the north-western province of Shensi. *Yamen* were attacked and several units of the Northern Army were ambushed on their way to relieve their garrisons. The task of the outlaws was made easier by the desertion of large numbers of Northern Army men, some of whom joined the rebels, while others made their way as best they could to the safety of Peking and Tientsin.

The commander-in-chief of the Northern Army, General Yuan Shih-kai, was a short, stout man with a neck that bulged out at the back, and a large, bullet-shaped head. Senior officers of the imperial armies were nearly always Manchus, but Yuan Shih-kai, an exception to the rule, was a native of Honan province in central China. A staff officer and a planner by training, Yuan Shih-kai was rarely seen with his troops in the field; he was more at home in the palace, where his weapon was the whispered word. The general was on good terms with the military attachés at the foreign legations. It was through them that he had acquired German-style uniforms and Austrian rifles for his men. He also had a British-style brass band. Sir Robert Hart, director-general of the Chinese customs, kept a brass band at his headquarters, and he had lent his Portuguese bandmaster to the Northern Army.

General Yuan Shih-kai was honoured by being granted the first private audience with the new Emperor. Pu Yi sat on the dragon throne. Around him were arranged the Empress Dowager, Honorific Abundance, the chief eunuch, the war minister, and the Regent, Prince Chun. The general wore a bright blue uniform with gold epaulettes. Considering his bulk, he performed the kowtows with remarkable agility. He was bidden to stand. With tears of emotion in his eyes, he declared that he wished for nothing but the privilege of serving the Emperor for the rest of his days. PuYi looked on with half-closed eyes. The general had a sudden inspiration. Perhaps His Imperial Majesty would like to hear his brass band one day? Pu Yi's eyes opened a little. Perhaps, the general went on, His Imperial Majesty would consider having a uniform made for himself? A blue one, with gold epaulettes? Pu Yi's eyes opened wide.

Honorific Abundance looked on with scorn at this mawkish

scene. The general had destroyed the Kuang Hsu Emperor. Although she had been estranged from her late husband for many years, she could not tolerate the general's insult to her family honour. His bluff charm was not going to prevent her from having her revenge. It had really been Prince Chun's duty to arrest the general, but, when approached, he could only whimper, 'What about the Peiyang Army? Suppose they open fire?' Honorific Abundance would have to act herself.

Within a few days of this audience it was announced in the *Court Gazette* that the general had been granted leave to return to Honan, where he would be able to have treatment for his ailing foot. In short, he had been dismissed.

Foreign manners and customs, which had been invading the Forbidden City, even began to infiltrate the liturgy of the imperial audience. Although it was held at dawn as usual, there were significant changes in the order of ceremony at Pu Yi's next audience. Instead of the entire court, only a few elderly courtiers and the officials of the highest grades attended the Emperor. When they had knelt and made the nine kowtows to him, they were permitted to stand. A new chief eunuch stood beside the Emperor. Li having retired, his place had been taken by Chang Yuan-fu. A handsome man, he had first come to the Forbidden City as one of a troupe of actors. He had stayed on to become the personal aide of Honorific Abundance. Now he was her favourite. There were some at court who claimed that Chang was not a eunuch at all.

At a signal from the chief eunuch, a grand councillor, who was also the minister for foreign affairs, entered the hall, followed by twelve men walking in file. They were dressed in European-style morning dress: black morning coats, striped trousers, starched white shirts, wing collars and white ties. Each carried a shiny black top hat under his left arm. They halted about fifty paces from the throne, formed into a single rank, and gave a well-rehearsed bow to the Emperor. His courtiers found it shocking that the foreign visitors did not kneel and kowtow to the Son of Heaven. In his high-pitched stammer, the Regent introduced them as the Minister of the United States of America and his suite. Pu Yi looked on as usual with half-closed eyes.

The American minister produced a document. It was, he said, a letter from President Taft. With the permission of His Imperial Majesty, he would like to read it. The letter was very long. Pu Yi's eyes became slits. When he came to the end, the minister bowed. An official interpreter read a Chinese translation. Mr Gale, a student interpreter with the American party, noticed that the Chinese version was much shorter than the original. It did, however, capture the essential point of the president's letter, namely that the United States would be pleased to help in putting China's finances on a firmer footing. The *North China Daily Mail* was to sum up the president's letter more crudely on its front page the next day: 'The era of dollar diplomacy has begun.'

It was now the Regent's turn to produce a document from his sleeve and read the Emperor's reply to the president. As he did so, several courtiers glanced nervously towards the yellow curtain hanging behind the throne. The Venerable Buddha would never have tolerated these long speeches when she was alive, they thought. The liturgy of silence had been replaced by a liturgy of words.

Throughout the proceedings Mr Gale had kept his eyes on the Emperor. His head and neck were so rigid, his arms and legs were stretched out so stiffly, that Mr Gale thought he looked like 'a mechanical toy'.

'Clear the city! Lock the gates! Light the lanterns!' The eunuch in charge of the watch gave his nightly warning cry. It was echoed by each of the eunuchs guarding the inner palaces. 'Clear the city . . . '

It was an hour before midnight. Nothing stirred. The half-moon was hidden by a cloud. The eunuch on guard outside the Palace of the Dowager Consorts stiffened. He could hear the sound of distant music. It was coming from the direction of the West Lake. Someone lit a lantern inside the palace.

Lustrous Concubine rose from her bed and put on a robe. Under the thin silk her firm breasts stood out as she fastened the clasp at her slim waist. Without hurrying, she walked along the terrace that led from her room to the Emperor's. The eunuch caught a glimpse of her tall figure. He could smell jasmine in the warm, spring air. Now he was certain it was she.

Lustrous Concubine was one of Pu Yi's mothers by adoption. Although she now held the rank of Dowager Consort, and Pu Yi addressed her as 'August Mother', she did not object to being called Lustrous Concubine by those concubines and eunuchs with whom she was intimate. The Dowager, Honorific Abundance, had appointed her controller of Pu Yi's household. She chose his food, her maids nursed him. She had been granted this honour because she was a close friend of Pu Yi's real mother, the Princess Chun.

The music sounded nearer. Reed-pipes and small, bell-like cymbals played in the rhythm of a stately march. The eunuch guard shuddered.

Pu Yi was with two young eunuchs on the terrace outside his room. They were looking out over the low marble balustrade. One of the eunuchs put his arm around Pu Yi's waist and said, 'Don't be afraid.'

Lustrous Concubine stole up behind them. A file of eunuchs, carrying lanterns, moved slowly across the courtyard below the terrace. Between the eunuchs, swaying as she walked, was the Goddess Kuan Yin. Now and again she would lean against a man who carried a staff and wore the head-dress of an archangel. The goddess put her scarlet lips to the archangel's ear in a long, lingering whisper. Chuckles followed by high-pitched laughter rose above the music for a few moments and then died away.

'Don't be afraid. It's only a masque,' the young eunuch repeated in a tremulous voice. Pu Yi did not seem in the least afraid.

The procession wound out of sight. Only the faint sound of pipes and cymbals could be heard. Smelling the rich scent of jasmine, Pu Yi turned round to face his August Mother. The eunuchs withdrew. Lustrous Concubine went inside with Pu Yi. Her maids were there, waiting to put him to bed. He was a strange one, she thought. The eunuchs took him to all the places that were haunted by the Venerable Buddha, but he disappointed them by showing not a trace of fear, only curiosity. He seemed far older than his years. Did he know the sounds that would follow Kuan Yin's procession?

55

From far away, beyond the Hall of Cloudless Heaven, came the first screams as the goddess tormented her archangel. Half asleep, Lustrous Concubine turned restlessly in her bed. The screams changed to chuckles, then laughter, cries for mercy, moans of pleasure. Then another scream, this time from the goddess as the archangel had his way. The sounds became more savage, like the wooing of wild cats as the lovers fought, troubling the sleep of many in the palaces. Now the screams no longer came from Kuan Yin and her angel, but from Honorific Abundance and her chief eunuch, Chang, as they played out the game of passion that the Venerable Buddha and her old eunuch, Li, had taught them.

Lustrous Concubine lay back, exhausted. People often asked her whether Chang was really a eunuch. Those three wives of his, the concubines who were brought to his bed, and this fierce, cat-like wooing of Honorific Abundance . . . But Lustrous concubine, who knew the truth, refused to speak about it.

Pu Yi, lay awake, his eyes wide open. A faint smell of jasmine lingered in his room.

Lustrous Concubine lay face downwards on her bed. The silk hangings had been drawn back. A maid poured oil of jasmine on her beautiful shoulders. Gently, the masseuse, Tsai Yu, spread the oil over her firm skin, massaging her from the nape of the neck to the hollow in the small of her back. Tsai Yu was not always so gentle. Those sensitive hands of hers could kill. On the instructions of the Venerable Buddha she had massaged an unsuspecting concubine who was pregnant by the Tung Chih Emperor. Suddenly her hands had wrenched the young girl's stomach, killing her unborn child. Lustrous Concubine hated this evil woman who knew too much about her.

Lustrous Concubine had been brought to the palace at the age of fifteen as a consort for the Kuang Hsu Emperor. Unlike most of the concubines, who matured early and soon became wizened, this voluptuous woman of thirty-six was still in her prime. Her face was not beautiful. Her mouth, which turned down a little at the ends, giving her a wistful look, was too large. Her eyes were heavy lidded. Although her legs were long and shapely, her knees were too bony. Her most beautiful feature was her back. Even those concubines who were jealous of her, marvelled at the flawlessly straight back that tapered down from her wide shoulders to her slim loins. When old Li, the chief eunuch, saw her naked for the first time, he could not help crying out, 'Her long body stands like jade.' He wrapped a blanket round her, carried her on his shoulder and laid her at the foot of the dragon couch. Hiding behind the drapings he watched, fascinated. She resembled less a column of jade than an uncoiling snake as she made her way slowly up the bed towards the waiting Emperor.

After the Emperor was sent away to the Fairy Isle, Li had thoughts about possessing Lustrous Concubine himself. But he was too afraid of the Venerable Buddha to try to do so.

'The Dowager Consort is beautiful today. She had better be careful or the chief eunuch will send for her,' the masseuse said, teasingly.

The maids in the room all laughed. Then one of them shrieked, pointing towards the door. It was wide open. Pu Yi stood there, solemn eyed. The masseuse dropped to her knees and began to kowtow. Lustrous Concubine lowered her feet to the ground and sat on the edge of the bed. Pu Yi turned and walked out on to the terrace.

Although Lustrous Concubine scolded her maids when they shrieked at the sight of Pu Yi, she was forced to admit to herself that there was something uncanny about his sudden appearances. He often played hide-and-seek with the young eunuchs and page-boys. She noticed that when the others came on Pu Yi hiding behind a curtain, they would run off, looking frightened. Sometimes the page-boys burst into tears when he startled them.

One day the eunuchs took Pu Yi to a small pavilion where the Venerable Buddha used to play chess. They told Pu Yi of the time when a eunuch of the presence captured the Venerable Buddha's knight. As he did so, he laughed triumphantly, saying, 'Your slave is about to kill this knight.' Furious, she ordered him to be dragged out and flogged to death. After hearing this story, Pu Yi, with a leer on his face, asked a young eunuch if he would like to play chess. The terrified eunuch fell ill and was absent from duty for a long time.

Lustrous Concubine remembered the first time she had seen Pu Yi smile. He had reported a eunuch for impertinence. The Empress Dowager ordered the culprit to be flogged. Pu Yi watched. As the bamboo rod struck the eunuch's bare back again and again, Pu Yi began to smile.

Lustrous Concubine realized that sooner or later the chief eunuch would send her a complaint about Pu Yi's treatment of his eunuchs. She also knew that with the complaint would come a summons to his awful presence. The chief eunuch, Chang, was no longer the handsome actor he had been when he first came to court. Fat and gout-ridden, he was carried about the Forbidden City in a sedan-chair, a privilege that used to be reserved for the nobility. This enormously wealthy man had amassed a fortune out of squeezes, as the commissions on palace contracts were called. Everyone at court feared him, and the Regent himself would quail whenever he saw the small, protruding eyes in Chang's toad-like face watching him from the sedan-chair. On one occasion the Duke Pu Shan, a cousin of the Emperor, had tried to defend an innocent man who was being assaulted by Chang's servants. One of them turned on the duke and flogged him with a horsewhip. The duke was advised by his fellow-noblemen to apologise to Chang.

The chief eunuch coveted Lustrous Concubine. He had only to see her walking on her terrace, to feel an uncontrollable lust for her. But she spurned all his overtures. For all his power, he could not force his attentions on her. That was until events outside the Forbidden city put her at his mercy.

In the autumn of 1909 an entire regiment of the imperial army was ambushed in the northern plain. The secret police believed that someone in the palace had given away details of the troops' movements to the outlaws. There was mounting evidence to show that the informer was Lustrous Concubine. One fact alone had always made her loyalty suspect. She was the sister of Pearl Concubine, who had been thrown down the well on the orders of the Venerable Buddha. Chang had witnessed the terrible scene at the well. Was it possible that Lustrous Concubine had forgiven that deed? The sisters had been close; both had been involved in the Reform Movement.

In 1900, when the court fled to Sian, Lustrous Concubine had remained in Peking. She was known to have paid many visits to the Chinese City, where she had friends. The Venerable Buddha had taken a risk when, a year later, she received Lustrous Concubine back at court. There was a theory, known to the secret police and to Chang, that Lustrous Concubine had died in the Chinese City during the Boxer rising, and that her place had been taken by Yellow Lotus, the notorious leader of the White Lotus society. Why else did Lustrous Concubine always wear a white jade ring, one of the symbols of the White Lotus?

Chang's fears and passions were roused by the thought that Lustrous Concubine might be Yellow Lotus. That exotic and mysterious woman, the only person of whom the Venerable Buddha had ever been afraid, had once been a prostitute in Tientsin. In 1900 she commanded the Boxers there. So great was her power, that even the imperial viceroy kowtowed to her. When Tientsin was relieved by foreign soldiers, she escaped in one of her clever disguises. Afterwards people claimed to have seen her in the Flower Market, the brothel district in the Chinese City of Peking.

The Chinese City was notorious as a meeting-place between Manchu traitors and outlaws who rode in from the northern plain at night. Both the secret police and Chang's own spies kept a special watch on the Golden Ship theatre in the Flower Market. Once the haunt of the young Tung Chih Emperor, the Golden Ship was now patronized by a few dissolute members of the Manchu nobility of both sexes. Sometimes, one or two senior government officials were seen to slink in through a side door. Inside, one could watch the lewdest of plays in the company of Chinese singing girls, actors and boy prostitutes. Afterwards one could enjoy the communal game of the loving cup. Chang remembered taking part in the loving cup when he was a young actor. Everyone, friends and strangers, sat round a large table. The woman on his right drank first. Then, mouth to mouth, she passed the wine to Chang. It was his turn to sip from the cup and, mouth to mouth, pass the wine to the young boy on his left. After each round, everyone changed partners and the kissing game continued.

The palace spies at the Golden Ship had been taking a special interest in a tall, masked woman who visited the place from time to time. One night, after a round of the loving cup, a boy prostitute, who was also a spy, saw her slip out of the room by the back door. She crossed the narrow lane and went into a wine shop. An hour later a man left the shop and rode away at great speed. The spies were certain that the masked woman had a lover to whom she gave secret information. Who was the masked woman. Was she an actor in disguise? Or was she Lustrous Concubine? Chang decided that the time had come to question her.

Chang received Lustrous Concubine in his lavishly furnished pavilion. He shrieked at her and threatened her with torture if she did not tell him the truth. Did she visit the Chinese City at night? Did she know any outlaws? Lustrous Concubine merely smiled contemptuously. As he watched her walking away, he decide to have her put to death. Yes, the masseuse would strangle that round, lovely neck. Then, in the next moment, he could not help picturing her in the room in the Golden Ship, drinking wine from the mouth of a complete stranger, and his lust for her returned.

That night a eunuch called on Lustrous Concubine with an invitation from the chief eunuch. She had been expecting it and was already dressed. Lustrous Concubine stood facing Chang. He was lying against the cushions at the head of his bed. She unfastened the clasp at her waist. Her silk robe fell to the floor. The long, jade-like body became a serpent as she made her sinuous approach up the length of the bed. Now she was beside Chang among the cushions. In a husky voice she whispered in his ear, telling him the erotic fantasies he ached to hear. When he could bear no more, he cried out, swearing that he would be her archangel, her slave . . .

In this way Lustrous Concubine survived. And with her, her secret life.

While Yuan Shih-kai sulked in his country mansion the armies he had left behind were being tested and found wanting. In the north-west a thousand peasants, led by an outlaw called the White Wolf, attacked the town of Ning Hsia, broke open the prison gates, and proclaimed the town's independence from Peking. Harried by the fast-riding outlaws and ambushed when they sought shelter in the villages, the Northern Army withdrew from the plains to the outskirts of Peking.

In central China, peasants in Honan province, angered by the heavy taxes imposed on them by imperial officials, rose up in revolt. Led by a group of outlaws called the 'Greens', they attacked and captured the ancient capital of Sian. From the distant south, reports reached the palace of a rising in Canton, where a number of government officials were killed. It was time for the supreme commander of the imperial forces to act. Prince Chun had assumed that post after the dismissal of Yuan Shih-kai. He agreed with the grand council that a bold stroke was needed.

The Regent's bold stroke was to send two royal princes, uncles of the Emperor, on missions abroad. Accordingly, Prince Tsai Hsun was sent on a naval mission to England, where he was graciously received by King Edward VII. He was piped on board the flagship of the home fleet in Portsmouth. The press paid him much attention. China, they said, intended to build a modern fleet on the lines of the grand fleet. The future of the British shipyards was assured.

When Prince Tsai Hsun returned home to the Forbidden City his most vivid recollections of his visit were of Windsor Castle and the wonderful furniture he had seen there.

Meanwhile, his brother, Prince Tsai Tao, had been sent on a military mission to Germany. He was warmly received by Kaiser Wilhelm, spent several days watching army manoeuvres, and took the salute at a huge parade in Berlin. China would model her new army on Germany's, said the papers.

Unlike his brother's naval mission to England, something practical did come of the prince's visit to Germany. A team of German military advisers and instructors was sent to Peking for attachment to the Northern Army.

There was bad news from the south. The trouble in Canton had developed into a large-scale revolt, led by a disaffected general. The rebels were on the march northwards. But Canton was a very long way from Peking, and there was no need for undue alarm.

Worse was to come, however. A rebellion broke out in Hankow and Wuchang, two cities close to each other on the banks of the Yangtze Kiang. Unlike the Canton rising, this one had been carefully planned by a revolutionary society. One of its members was Sun Yat-sen, the idealist and visionary who had long dreamed of a Chinese republic.

The grand council met and demanded action. The Regent could think of only one thing: send for General Yuan Shih-kai. When Yuan's reply came, the Regent's humiliation was complete. Yuan's foot had not yet healed, the message said. He hoped to be better soon.

The Hankow rebels began to march northwards. News reached the palace that Sun Yat-sen had arrived in Nanking and was about to proclaim a republic. This was ominous indeed, for Nanking was forever linked with the peasant leader of the White Lotus who had founded the Ming dynasty there.

Another message arrived from Yuan Shih-kai. His foot was better. Provided he was given supreme command and an office in the Imperial Palace from which to conduct the fighting, he would come to the rescue of the dynasty. There was a postscript: the army would need funds. He would like complete control over the imperial treasury.

His terms having been accepted, the general arrived with all his baggage, including his twenty concubines, and was installed in a mansion in the Tartar City. An office in the Forbidden City was also provided. He then directed some of the best regiments in the Northern Army to march towards Hankow and prevent the rebels from progressing any farther north. The two forces met, and remained locked in a stalemate.

Everyone at court was jubilant. The other regiments of the Northern Army could now capture the defenceless city of Nanking. The rebel leaders would then be brought to Peking in chains. The grand council considered a list of possible punishments for them. It would be nice to administer the death by a thousand cuts to Sun Yat-sen, but the more progressive of the foreign powers might be upset. A straightforward beheading, perhaps.

The days passed, and still the general made no move. Rumours began to spread about his intentions. Then an announcement came from his office which stunned the grand council. Yuan Shih-kai, it said, had detected some merit in the more moderate of the Republicans' principles. He hoped that an amicable compromise could be reached with Sun Yat-sen.

After the shock came panic. People besieged the railway station. The wealthy booked entire carriages, which they filled with their families and their possessions. On the streets there were long traffic jams of mules and carts, carriages and rickshaws. Within a week, over 300,000 people had fled from Peking. This was an invitation to the troops of the Northern Army to enter the Chinese quarter and loot the shops and houses. Some of them even tried to break into the Tartar City.

During the autumn of 1911 there was much secret parleying between the general and the visionary, none of which was disclosed to the imperial court. At length, the general's main condition for peace was accepted. China could have her republic, but its seat must be in Peking. Peking was the base of the Northern Army, and it went without saying that, once the Republican government was established there, Yuan would dominate it. He had won the day. All that remained was to deal with the imperial court.

Many Republicans would have preferred their government to be in Nanking, with Sun Yat-sen at its head, but the deciding factor in the general's favour was the backing of his foreign friends. Impressed by his apparent strength and decisiveness, they saw him as the future leader of China.

A year before, at the time of the Canton uprising, *The Times* of London had clamoured for Yuan Shih-kai's return to command, calling him 'the only man able to save the situation'. The general would soon repay that favour by appointing G.E. Morrison, the *Times* correspondent in Peking, as his political adviser.

Even more important than foreign opinion was foreign money. Huge loans were made to Yuan Shih-kai by a group of foreign banks. Twenty-five million dollars alone had been lent for the sole purpose of modernising the Northern Army. Against such forces, Sun Yat-sen's cause was lost. The era of dollar diplomacy had begun.

Pu Yi was in his schoolroom in the Palace of Mind Nurture when the large bell outside the Temple of Ancestors sounded the alarm. Soon, eunuchs of the watch were rushing from courtyard to courtyard, beating gongs and crying out 'Soldiers at the gate'. In the middle of all this din, a message arrived from the Dowager, Honorific Abundance, requesting Pu Yi's presence in the Hall of Supreme Harmony.

When he entered, Pu Yi found Honorific Abundance and General Yuan Shih-kai standing by the dragon throne. After Pu Yi was seated, the general marched stiffly to the centre of the hall, turned about, and made his kowtows to the Emperor. Honorific Abundance commanded him to approach. He came to the point at once. The Republican forces were gathering strength. With much regret, he had decided that it would be in the best interests of His Imperial Majesty if he were to abdicate . . .

Honorific Abundance shrieked 'No! No!' and then began to weep.

For the sake of national unity, the general continued, he would be prepared to take charge of a provisional government. There would be generous terms for the imperial family. His Majesty could keep his title and remain in the palace, and he would be given a salary of 4 million dollars a year. These and other terms were embodied in a document entitled 'The Articles of Favourable Treatment of the Great Ching Emperor' which the general had already signed. He felt sure that Honorific Abundance would like to discuss the matter with the grand council.

The general fell on his knees before the throne. A tear rolled down his cheek, then another. Honorific Abundance gave a loud sob. In a moment, both she and the general were crying unrestrainedly.

Pu Yi looked at the sobbing general with great interest. The eunuchs had been telling him about the general's twenty concubines, how he could not sleep at night because he worried that they might be seduced by other men. Two of the concubines were Korean and one was a Japanese. The general had tried to buy a White Russian girl in Peking, but she had gone off with a merchant. There was always fighting and shouting going on in the general's house, because he could not keep his concubines under control. What he needed was a eunuch to run his household.

When the tearful general looked up, he saw that Pu Yi was smiling.

The grand council's chamber was near the eastern gate. When they assembled, they could hear the sound of officers shouting orders and soldiers drilling.

The ministers of state and other senior officials were in favour of the Emperor abdicating. The Manchu nobility, who were in the majority, were against it. Honorific Abundance declared that she was for a fight to the last. If they fought bravely, there was a chance that the foreign soldiers in the legations would help them. Were they not the Emperor's allies? Did their treaties not say they would come to his aid?

The Manchu princes listened in awe to this defiant woman. As she spoke, all the primitive, tribal instincts of their race seemed to rise up again in her. The minister of finance coughed apprehensively and begged to be allowed to state another view. He was Yuan Shih-kai's strongest advocate. They should remember, he argued, that the general had the financial support of the greatest foreign powers. In the interests of national unity...

He was interrupted by a loud knock on the door. A eunuch entered the chamber with an urgent message for the Dowager, Honorific Abundance, from the deputy chief of staff of the Northern Army. The message could not have been more blunt. General Yuan Shih-kai's patience was exhausted. If the grand council did not decide immediately, his troops would occupy the Imperial Palace.

On 12 February 1912 Honorific Abundance issued an edict annnouncing the abdication of the Emperor.

CHAPTER THREE

THE COURT IN WONDERLAND

One summer's day in the third year of the Republic eight
eunuch guards, armed with ceremonial spears, marched in
file towards the Palace of Mind Nurture. Behind them, a team
of bearers carried Pu Yi in the yellow palanquin. When this
procession, which took place morning and afternoon on every
school-day, reached the entrance to the palace, two junior
eunuchs of the presence escorted Pu Yi to the schoolroom. It
was simply furnished with a few tables and chairs. A vase of
flowers and some hanging character scrolls were the only
decoration. There was also a large foreign clock with a
pendulum. The ritual in the schoolroom never varied. Pu Yi
sat at his own table, facing southwards, as an emperor always
should. The two eunuchs stood like figurines, one on either
side of him. 'Call them,' said Pu Yi pointing towards the door.

The eunuchs went to the door and ushered in a second
procession. First came a eunuch carrying a pile of books, then
came an imperial tutor, and last of all, Pu Yi's fellow-pupils.
They were his brother, Pu Chieh, and Yu Chung, son of
Prince Pu Lun who, by every right, should have been
emperor. Pu Chieh and Yu Chung knelt before Pu Yi and
then went to sit at a table with the tutor, leaving Pu Yi to sit by
himself.

It was time for the English lesson to begin. The tutor rose

and handed round copies of their only English textbook, *Alice in Wonderland*. Facing each page of the story was a Chinese translation, the work of an earnest missionary. Pu Yi became fascinated by the adventures of Alice. He saw her as a young English concubine who had fallen down a deep well into the underworld of the Forbidden City. Unlocking gates and parting curtains, Alice dared to enter the hidden palaces and gardens of what was also called the Purple City. There she met frog footmen who, clearly, were eunuchs in disguise. To her horror, she was confronted by the Venerable Buddha. Sometimes the Venerable Buddha was the Duchess, who beat her little boy mercilessly for sneezing; and sometimes she was the Queen of Hearts, who walked in processions and sentenced people to death for the slightest offence. 'Off with her head,' the Queen of Hearts cried when Alice failed to kowtow to her. Both the Duchess and the Queen of Hearts left Pu Yi in no doubt that the young eunuchs and concubines of this underworld court were there to be beaten and tortured.

Ants were not mentioned among the creatures in Alice's book, but Pu Yi felt sure that the long lines of yellow and black ants that he saw every day in the palace grounds must have marched as soldiers in the Queen of Heart's processions. Chen, the senior imperial tutor, who was an authority on insects, was gratified to see Pu Yi taking such a keen interest in the ant family. In order to amuse and instruct his pupil, he began to compile an illustrated album on the habitat and behaviour of the different kinds of ant.

After school one day Pu Yi received a special visit from his family. He had not seen his mother since that morning eight years before, when he was taken to the Imperial Palace. With her were her husband, Prince Chun, Pu Yi's brother, Pu Chieh, and his sister. In their sedan-chair, on the way through the courtyards, the prince remarked to his wife how little the palace had changed since his retirement three years ago. Eunuchs and bowing officials thronged the terraces, just as they did in the old days of the Empire.

The family met in a stateroom adjoining Pu Yi's apartments. Pu Yi was sitting on a divan, attended by two eunuchs of the presence. The princess was struck by her son's haughty manner. He might have been receiving a group of officials in audience, she thought. He allowed his parents to kneel to him as if he were a great monarch such as the Chien Lung Emperor, and not a boy of ten. It seemed absurd when one considered that China was now a republic. Lustrous Concubine was right. He was a strange one, and far older than his years. Pu Chieh, who had come to know his brother's moods in the schoolroom, took care to kneel to him. His sister, however, jumped on to the divan to sit beside Pu Yi. That piece of impertinence earned her a scowl. Prince Chun mumbled an apology and told his daughter that she must kneel to the Emperor.

Now the princess felt a deep fear. Those stories that Lustrous Concubine had told her about Pu Yi and the young eunuchs must be true. How he flew into a rage when they failed to kowtow to him, and how he had them flogged for the smallest breach of etiquette. Lately, Pu Yi had taken to flogging the young eunuchs and page-boys himself. One of the imperial tutors had the courage to complain to Lustrous Concubine that the Emperor had flogged seventeen eunuchs in one week for the most trivial offences. Even more sinister than these accounts of floggings was the story about the puppet show. A eunuch who was an expert puppet master gave excellent performances of Punch and Judy in the Chinese version. Lost in wonder, Pu Yi demanded encores. He could not have enough of the villainous Punch who killed his child in a fit of temper, then bludgeoned his wife to death, and ended by hanging the executioner.

One day, during a command performance of Punch and Judy, Pu Yi went behind the miniature stage to watch the eunuch manipulating his puppets. When he emerged at the end of the play, Pu Yi was unusually quiet. (In later life he admitted to having had 'an evil inspiration'.) Shortly afterwards he presented the puppet master with a cake as a special reward. The delighted eunuch did not know that Pu Yi had made a hole in the cake and filled it with iron filings. Pu Yi's nurse, a member of Lustrous Concubine's staff, happened to see Pu Yi preparing the cake. Just in time, she

69

intervened to save the eunuch. 'I only wanted to see what his face looked like when he swallowed some of it,' Pu Yi said with a laugh. Puzzled and frightened, the puppet master did his best to retain his composure, but he did not appear on duty again for a long time.

The Chun family gathering was obviously a dismal failure. The princess was wondering how it might be brought to an end without giving offence, when Pu Yi suddenly came to life and asked his brother and sister to play hide-and-seek with him. The three of them rushed into Pu Yi's bedroom and drew the curtains. In the dark room the young girl shrieked with fear when Pu Yi sprang out at her from behind a curtain. The prince and princess glanced at each other in alarm. Then they heard laughter, and all seemed well.

While the children were playing, Pu Chieh raised his sleeve, and Pu Yi noticed that it was lined with yellow silk. The imperial yellow! Only emperors might wear that colour. He began to taunt Pu Chieh. Then he shouted at him, saying that he would have him flogged.

The Chun family took their leave of the Emperor in silence. The eunuchs of the presence, who had been on duty in the stateroom throughout this scene, ushered them to their sedan-chair. The princess was never to see her son, Pu Yi, again.

The deputy chief of staff of the Republican Army requested the honour of being received by His Imperial Majesty. Pu Yi pointed towards the door. 'Call him,' he said to the grand secretary.

A general entered and saluted. He wore a blue-grey German-style uniform. On his arm he carried a coat-hanger, from which hung a parcel wrapped in paper. Having handed his cap and the parcel to a eunuch of the presence, the general performed the kowtow with admirable precision.

Pu Yi lifted his hand. The general approached with his parcel and unwrapped it. A bright blue uniform with gold epaulettes! Pu Yi's eyes showed his pleasure.

'His Excellency Yuan Shih-kai, provisional president of the Republic of China, hopes that you will find the uniform satisfactory,' the general said. 'Should Your Imperial

Majesty wish to be photographed wearing it, I shall gladly make the arrangements. The Republican Army band will be playing outside the Presidential Palace this afternoon. We have a new, British bandmaster. If Your Imperial Majesty would care to attend the performance, it might be a suitable occasion on which to wear your uniform.'

Pu Yi nodded in assent. What a good day this was turning out to be!

Yuan Shih-kai had decided that the time had come to be magnanimous. No one could say that his Articles of Favourable Treatment of the Great Ching Emperor – how well that phrase was worded! – no one could say that he had not been generous. Nevertheless, there were a few extra things he could do to improve his relations with the imperial family. In coming to that view, he had been helped by his political adviser, Morrison, the *Times* correspondent, or 'Morrison of Peking' as he liked to be called. 'Your Excellency should take steps to improve your image,' Morrison was always saying. At last the point seemed to have sunk in.

The president's next step was a disaster. He sent a framed photograph of himself in full-dress uniform to the Empress Dowager. The day after she received it Honorific Abundance collapsed and died. Her attendants said that she was 'full of rage and grief'. At her feet lay the picture of the commander-in-chief of the Republican Army. None of her Manchu courtiers doubted that the photograph had killed her.

The dilapidated building that was now the Presidential Palace stood in the southern part of the Forbidden City, among the outer courts. It had once been the office of the board of punishments. Although Yuan Shih-kai's duties obliged him to be at the palace during the day, nothing would persuade him to spend the night there, so close to the dimly lit courtyards haunted by the Venerable Buddha. Even in the daytime, when walking with his armed escort in the palace grounds, he would stop, all of a sudden, and mop the cold sweat from his brow, convinced that he had heard her devilish chuckles. Then he would hurry into the safety of the building. On one occasion he woke up in his sedan-chair, and found, to his dismay, that he was being carried past the Fairy Isle. For months he had tried to blot out the memory of that place. Now here he was, close to the small pavilion with its willow trees set like green jade on the silver waters of the lake. Somewhere hidden in that pavilion was the Empty Room. He shuddered. There were people in the palace who believed that in his dying moments the Kuang Hsu Emperor had scribbled two characters on a peice of paper: *Kill Yuan*. The paper had been smuggled out of the room, they said.

There was yet another reason why Yuan Shih-kai avoided the Forbidden City as much as possible. During the abdication crisis there were strong rumours of a plot to assassinate him. Inquiries by the secret police led them to the Palace of the Dowager Consorts, but they got no farther.

No, the Forbidden City with its ghosts and its plots was no place to be. And yet, when he saw the sun glinting on the yellow tiles of the Hall of Supreme Harmony where emperors had reigned for 500 years, he found himself hoping that one day he might conquer his fears and even sleep at ease under its curved roofs.

Having displayed their magnanimity, Yuan Shih-kai and 'Morrison of Peking' now had more businesslike matters to attend to. Elections were held for the first parliament of the Republic. Despite the intimidating presence of Yuan Shih-kai's troops, who surrounded the polling stations on the pretext of keeping order, the party to win most seats was not Yuan Shih-kai's faction, but the Kuomintang or Nationalist Party, as the foreign newspapers called them. The founders of the Nationalist Party had been inspired by the spirit of American republicanism, and their leader was Sung Chiao-jen, a close friend of Sun Yat-sen. The victorious Sung was on a visit to Shanghai when he received an invitation to meet Yuan Shih-kai in Peking to discuss the formation of a government. As Sung was boarding his train in Shanghai railway station, he was shot down by a group of Yuan Shih-kai's gunmen.

Sung had been on good terms with a number of army

commanders who thought highly of him. When they expressed their concern at his killing, Yuan Shih-kai's reply to them was prompt. They were dismissed and replaced by his own men. Swiftly following up that move, Yuan Shih-kai sent an army to besiege Nanking, which fell on 1 September 1913.

Within the next three months he declared the Nationalist Party illegal, dissolved parliament for good, and set up a council, drawn from his closest supporters. In January 1914 Yuan Shih-kai's council made him president for life. No one could say that China's leader was lacking in strength and decisiveness.

There was jubilation in the foreign legations' quarter, where parties were held to celebrate Yuan Shih-kai's presidency. Nor was his adviser forgotten. 'Morrison of Peking' was the guest of honour at a reception in the Wagons-Lits Hotel. Tributes were paid to his diplomatic skills. In proposing the toast, the editor of *The Peking and Tientsin Times* declared that Morrison was 'no ordinary newspaper correspondent'. It was a masterly, if unconscious, understatement.

Few correspondents can have received so much acclaim and so little deserved it. Lord Curzon had praised Morrison's 'intelligent anticipation of events'. Yet, while he was in China, Morrison had completely missed two momentous events: the Boxer rising in 1900, and the revolution in 1911. On both occasions he had been away, shooting wildfowl, and *The Times* had had to make do with reports from that eccentric arms dealer Sir Edmund Backhouse. The extraordinary Morrison had the unique distinction among journalists in China of being totally ignorant of the Chinese language, written or spoken. Nor was that all. He was proud of that ignorance and had not the slightest intention of doing anything about it. Apart from a few eminent personages such as the Venerable Buddha, whom he called 'that grand old lady', he had no interest in the Chinese people. China was but an arena in which various imperial powers played the 'great game' of competing for supremacy. Military might would decide the victor. Of one thing he was certain: the British Empire would, in the end, overcome all the other empires and govern the world. Proud of his part in the recent elevation of Yuan Shih-kai, he let it be put about that, henceforth, he would not be averse to being called 'Morrison of China'.

In Tien An Men Square a mounted escort of Carabinieri with drawn swords trotted in front of an open carriage pulled by shaggy Mongolian ponies. Inside the carriage his excellency the Italian minister sat beside his first secretary, Signor Daniele Varè. Opposite them their ladies, who were in court dress, chatted animatedly about their coming audience with the president of China. 'They say he looks just like Monsieur Clemenceau,' said the minister's wife. Signor Varè, who had been studying the Mongolian ponies, smiled and said, 'Yes, I'm sure you are right.'

At the Gate of Heavenly Peace the carriage and its escort came to a halt. The minister and his companions were transferred to two sedan-chairs and carried into the Forbidden City. The Carabinieri exchanged salutes with the guard of the Northern Army and then trotted away.

In the Hall of Supreme Harmony twelve generals of the Northern Army stood behind the dragon throne, six on each side. A row of foreign-style opera-chairs was arranged in front of the throne. The president's aide-de-camp motioned to the Italian party to be seated. After a short pause everyone rose as Yuan Shih-kai marched briskly on to the dais. He bowed to his visitors and then sat on the edge of the throne. He was wearing his bright blue uniform with gold epaulettes. His left hand held the hilt of the new sword he had been given by the British minister. Signor Varè was enthralled by the scene: the huge incense burners, the bronze cranes and phoenixes, and there, on the dragon throne, Yuan Shih-kai looking very much the emperor.

The first of the speeches began, but so carried away was Signor Varè that he did not listen to a word. His mind was on loftier things than Sino-Italian trade. Truly, he thought, the imperial stystem was the natural form of government for the Chinese. The word republic could have little meaning for the peasants who still looked to a Son of Heaven to pray for them. Perhaps Italy herself might one day give the world another great empire.

After their audience the Italian party stood on the upper terrace and gazed at the yellow sea of curved roofs. 'It's strange to think', said the minister's wife, 'that somewhere hidden in this maze of palaces, there is a little court in miniature where the old liturgy goes on with gongs, incense, eunuchs and an emperor who, I'm told, is a child . . . '

'Oh, do stop,' said Signora Varè. 'You've made my blood turn cold.'

Yuan Shih-kai had been reluctant to hold his audiences in the Hall of Supreme Harmony. But his council persuaded him that the shabby stateroom in the Presidential Palace was hardly a suitable place in which to receive the growing number of foreign deptutations. He felt uncomfortable sitting on the huge black and gold lacquered dragon throne, surrounded by bronze phoenixes. Nor could he quite forget that, standing by this throne, he had sworn allegiance to Pu Yi. At one audience, when the Dutch minister was delivering a congratulatory speech, Yuan's eyes wandered to the side of the throne. There, only a few paces away, was the yellow curtain. With great difficulty, he managed to control himself until the audience was over. Then, unable to contain his anger, he ordered his aides to get rid of the curtain and any other trappings left over from the former dynasty.

As audience followed audience, his self-control increased. A member of his council told him that he resembled the great Kang Hsi Emperor who had reigned for sixty-one years. To his surprise, he found that he was no longer afraid of being in the Forbidden City. He would walk through the courtyards for long distances. One night he even dared to sleep in his bedroom in the palace. There was an armed guard at the door, but Yuan passed an undisturbed night in the four-poster bed, draped with hangings, and did not have to call the guard once.

Some senior members of his council began to talk about a new dynasty. He brushed them off with a laugh, but inwardly he glowed with pleasure. He consulted 'Morrison of China', although he knew his opinion well. It was a law of nature, said Morrison, that only an imperial system of government could preserve national unity. For a second opinion, Morrison introduced him to Professor Goodnow, a distinguished

75

American political theorist. After exhaustive research, the professor gave his findings at a full assembly of the council. The Chinese, he said, were fundamentally unsuited to a republican form of government. If she were to continue as a republic, China would slide into anarchy, just as Mexico was sliding into anarchy today.

It was a skilful performance. With meticulous care, both the professor and the council members had avoided any reference whatever to 'the little court in miniature' hidden among the courtyards of the Forbidden City. The council had heard enough. They clamoured for an emperor. Yuan Shih-kai must found a new dynasty. They arranged for 'people's representatives' to be elected, who voted unanimously that Yuan should accept the throne. After a suitable show of reluctance, Yuan agreed to obey the people's will. It was now December 1915. He would be Emperor early in the new year.

Before daybreak in the depths of the winter of 1915 an armoured car with a machine-gun mounted on top trundled out of the Forbidden City through the Gate of Heavenly Peace. Gathering speed, it crossed the square on its way to the Temple of Heaven. A group of officers were waiting by the steps of the great open-air altar. The armoured car drove up, the iron hatch in its side was opened and a wooden step was placed under the opening. All the officers saluted as Yuan Shih-kai, assisted by his aide-de-camp, clambered out. In the first murky light of dawn Yuan Shih-kai carefully mounted the icy stone steps to the Altar of Heaven, and offered sacrifice so that the gods might favour his new dynasty.

Even as he performed that ceremony, Yuan Shih-kai knew, as did his officers, that the rubrics of the imperial liturgy forbade him to sacrifice at the Altar of Heaven until the dawn of his enthronement day, a few weeks off. But he had not been able to wait any longer, so consumed was he by his passion to be the Son of Heaven. He had anticipated the great event in other ways. A silver dollar had been minted, bearing his head, surrounded by a laurel wreath. It was already in circulation in several cities. A title had been chosen for the new regime: 'The Chinese Empire'.

Yuan Shih-kai's twenty concubines and their children had also anticipated the great event by moving into the Presidential Palace. They squabbled and fought, creating a deafening noise, while the military aides worked desperately to prepare the guest lists for the enthronement day reception.

An incident took place in that chaotic building which was to have dire consequences for the Emperor-elect. Tuan Chi-jui, the veteran general of the Northern Army, called to pay his respects. In the stateroom he encountered Yuan Shih-kai's eldest son lolling on a sofa. Although the kowtow had gone out of use since the abdication of Pu Yi, and, in any case, would never be given by an elderly man to a young imperial prince, the arrogant youth made the old general perform all the nine kowtows. The humiliated Tuan left the palace declaring that he had had enough of this upstart dynasty.

As the day of the enthronement drew nearer, dark clouds appeared on the southern horizon. The 'Green gang' of peasants began another rising in Yuan Shih-kai's own province of Honan. They were joined by those regional commanders whom Yuan had offended at the time of the assassination of the Nationalist leader in 1913. Another peasant rising broke out in the north-west, where the White Wolf was active again. Within a short time his guerrillas were in control of parts of the provinces of Shansi, Shensi and Kansu.

Peasant risings had brought down many dynasties, but never before had a dynasty been attacked on the very eve of its coming into being. Humiliated by these setbacks, Yuan Shih-kai turned to his old friends, the Northern Army generals for help. He had only to look into General Tuan's face and observe his aloof bearing to know that all hope was lost.

Ill and dejected, Yuan Shih-kai withdrew into the Forbidden City. His armoured car, which was parked in the courtyard, made the Presidential Palace look like a fortress. A handful of loyal guards remained to protect him. They spent much of their time trying to keep order among the concubines so that their master could have some peace. All the old ghosts returned to haunt him, and he would wake in the night screaming for help. He developed a high fever, and several foreign specialists were sent for, but none could diagnose his illness. When they tried to speak to him, he just mumbled something about the Empty Room. On his last day alive the attendants heard him cry out, 'It was that demon's fault. He betrayed me.'

That night he heard the Venerable Buddha whispering and chuckling behind the hangings around his bed. Frantic, he tore at them, but the chuckles sounded even louder. Early the next morning his aides found him dead. His face was contorted with fear. One of his hands still clutched the hangings which surrounded him like a shroud.

The official cause of death, put out by his doctors and published in the papers, was that Yuan Shih-kai had died suddenly, 'made ill by shame and anger'. Pu Yi received the news seated on his throne in the Hall of Cloudless Heaven. Near the end of his report, the grand secretary quoted Yuan Shih-kai's last words: 'It was that demon's fault. He betrayed me.' No one could tell, the grand secretary continued, who the demon might be. At this point he looked up. Pu Yi was smiling.

'The traitor is dead!' Wildly excited eunuchs rushed about the courtyards, shouting the news. Gongs sounded everywhere and the bell outside the Temple of the Ancestors began to peal. In the Tartar City there were celebrations, and the imperial dragon flag was hung on the gates of some of the larger houses while the Republican police looked on tolerantly. But there was a subdued atmosphere in the foreign legations' quarter, where ministers called on each other in anxious efforts to find out what was happening. Once again 'Morrison of China' had failed to anticipate events.

Parliament assembled. The mild-mannered Li Yuan-hung was elected president, and General Tuan Chi-jui was made premier. The appointment of this veteran of the Northern Army dampened the spirits of the 'Young China' group in parliament, but the majority of members shared the heady feeling of optimism. With the ogre gone, relations between the Republican government and the palace could not have been better.

In a friendly gesture the president returned a number of ceremonial spears which Yuan Shih-kai, of dreadful memory, had commandeered from the palace. The Emperor showed his gratitude by conferring honours: the yellow waistcoat and the right to ride on horseback in the Forbidden City, on some members of parliament. Not to be outdone, the president awarded military decorations to a long list of courtiers. Comfortably placed between palace and parliament, the corps of civil servants looked on with benevolence at the new-found concord. The heads of all the departments were pleased to receive honours and decorations from both their masters.

A number of changes were made at the palace which seemed to fit the happy mood of the time. Pu Yi approved the new office of grand guardian. The first to hold that rank was Chen Pao-shen, the senior imperial tutor. The dowager consorts were promoted to high consorts. The chief eunuch was allowed an increase in his staff, bringing the number of eunuchs up to 1,500. Twenty-five ladies in waiting (the word concubine had been dropped) were recruited.

The high consorts noticed, with relief, that Pu Yi was fully occupied with his favourite hobby, the study of ants. He was carried in the yellow palanquin all over the palace grounds. And, when his eunuch attendants saw ants, he would alight and observe them. Yellow ants, brown ants, black ants and red ants, all were of equal interest to him. Only one thing spoiled his delight. There were no white ants. The grand guardian informed him that white ants were to be found in Africa, but there were no reports of any being seen in China.

As part of the festivities to mark the revival of the Republic, the president graciously invited Pu Yi to be the guest of honour at a concert given by the Republican Army band in the grounds of the Presidential Palace. Pu Yi, in his bright blue uniform with gold epaulettes, sat on a platform with the president and General Tuan, the veteran soldier whom Yuan Shih-kai's son had insulted and who was now the premier. Other members of the cabinet and distinguished foreign guests were also present. On one side of the platform, half hidden by shrubs, was the late Yuan Shih-kai's armoured car.

Bandmaster Giles, late of the British army, had taught his

Chinese bandsmen a new number in honour of the Emperor. Having saluted his audience, he turned to face his brass band, raised his baton, and, to a count of four, launched them into the military march:

> It's a long way to Tipperary,
> It's a long way to go . . .

Faltering from time to time, the band blared out every verse at a funereal pace. Pu Yi's eyes began to close until they were slits. As the music droned on, he happened to turn his head, Slowly, his eyes opened. There, on the path in front of the armoured car, was a long line of red ants. Fascinated, he watched them march with precision until they disappeared into the shubbery. The last flat note of 'Tipperary' died away, and the bandmaster turned to salute his audience. He was gratified to see that His Imperial Majesty was smiling.

Bemused by the latest turn of events, when the new Chinese Empire they had been hailing suddenly ceased to exist, the heads of the foreign legations lapsed into an embarrassed silence. There was one last courtesy they could pay to their Chinese friend and ally. Led by Sir John Jordan, doyen of the diplomatic corps, they turned out in full force to watch the funeral cortège of Yuan Shih-kai as it left Peking for his native Honan.

Following the coffin on the long journey southwards was a procession of carriages and sedan-chairs which bore his concubines and their children. Behind them came mule-drawn carts, piled high with furniture. Signor Varè counted no fewer than 200 vehicles as they trundled past him, looking like an army in retreat. Was this really the end of the Empire? Jordan, the British minister, was right, he thought. They would have to wait and see. Perhaps another powerful general would take Yuan Shih-kai's place as China's ruler.

The foreign communities in the treaty ports were shocked by the sudden passing of Yuan Shih-kai, the champion in whom they had invested so much. The *Peking and Tientsin Times* published an obituary on him which filled an entire page. Relations between Yuan Shih-kai and Sir John Jordan had been close. Sensitive as to what might appear in the obituary, Sir John had taken the precaution of sending a telegram to the editor, H.G.W. Woodhead, asking him 'as a personal favour' not to criticise Yuan Shih-kai's plot to become Emperor. Honoured at being taken into the minister's confidence, Woodhead was glad to oblige him. No word of Yuan's vainglorious ambitions emerged in his lengthy obituary; on the contrary, he was depicted as 'a humble and dedicated soldier' whose death was a tragedy for China. Like Sir John Jordan, Woodhead was at a loss to explain why the massive support for Yuan Shih-kai had crumbled in the face of two relatively small-scale peasant revolts, one in the south and one in the north-west. Woodhead consulted 'Morrison of China', but he was equally mystified.

In common with most foreigners in China, these three influential members of the British community, Jordan, Morrison and Woodhead, knew next to nothing about the peasants and the part they played in Chinese history. As for the many thousands of displaced peasants who flooded into the foreign concessions in cities like Tientsin and Shanghai, those who became servants in foreign households were more often than not treated with amused condescension by their employers. But by far the greater number became coolies or beggars, and they were regarded as the illiterate dregs of society. For centuries Chinese history books had been written by scholar-officials for scholar-officials. These mandarins were concerned only with people who mattered, and they dismissed the peasant rebels in the countryside and their outlaw leaders as bandits who had not even the right to exist and, therefore, were unmentionable. It is significant that the Chinese character for bandit, *fei*, means, literally, a non-person.

Foreign experts on China, depending as they did on official Chinese history books, adopted the attitude of the mandarins. They even adopted the mandarins' dress. In the seventeenth century the great Jesuit missionary Father Ricci, in his flowing beard, tall mandarin's hat and long gown, was a well-known figure among scholar-officials in Peking. An odder

81

example is Sir Edmund Backhouse, 'The Hermit of Peking', and arch-forger of *China under the Empress Dowager*, who, in 1921, startled the passers-by in the streets of London when he appeared there dressed as a Chinese mandarin, complete with long white beard.

The mandarins' studied indifference to the lower orders and the peasants hardly changed over the years. In 1943 the Library of Congress in Washington published *Eminent Chinese of the Ching Period* (1644-1911). It was written by a team of sinologists (as Western experts liked to be known) in collaboration with some Chinese scholars. A widely known work, Woodhead found it an indispensable source. Its preface claimed it to be 'The most detailed and the best history of China in the last 300 years that one can find anywhere today. It is written in the form of biographies of 800 men and women who made that history.'

Among the 800 may be found, for instance, Chien Chien-yi, a scholar-official who had been president of the board of ceremonies at the end of the Ming dynasty. When the Manchus invaded China in 1644 Chien did not die like his emperor and empress, but, with the resilience of a civil servant, shifted his allegiance to the Ching dynasty of the Manchus and so kept his position at the board of ceremonies, suffering only a slight reduction of his status to vice-president. Another of the eminent 800 was a scholar-official who had spent forty years taking one imperial examination after another, before ending up as secretary to the grand secretariat in the Forbidden City. Such were the so-called 'makers of China's history'. On the White Wolf and his raiders in the wild country west of Peking, on Yellow Lotus, the woman leader of the secret society of the White Lotus, and on any of China's peasant millions, for that matter, *Eminent Chinese of the Ching Period* is, of course, silent.

Not all foreign men of learning followed the mandarin's example of ignoring the peasantry. The hardy few who ventured into the countryside, discovered among the peasants a wisdom, a deep historical mindedness, and a nobility of spirit in the sense of serving the oppressed, that went back to pre-imperial times. That great American scholar, H.G.

Creel, has said: 'It is a widespread view of experts on the Far East, that the Chinese, except for officials and scholars, are a mass of illiterate people. In accord with this theory, it has been assumed that in order to control China, one need only to cultivate the favour of officials or pay bribes to a few war-lords. The people in general could be ignored. I am ashamed to say that as a young man, before I had lived in China, I shared this impression . . . ' Creel came to realize that the market-place in village or town was a school where peasants bringing their wares for sale, hawkers, vagrants, coolies and household servants learned about China and its history from the wandering story-tellers and the talkers of books.

Teilhard de Chardin, the Jesuit priest, made more than one scientific expedition to the Ordos desert plateau in the Interior, the White Wolf's territory. In a *crie du coeur* from the Ordos, Teilhard said: 'Of China I have seen the hard life, the desolation, and the immense layer of dust over people and things. I possess neither the knowledge of the language and the past that would open the hidden treasures for me – nor the magical intuition that would enable me to perceive the secret beauty . . . ' He, for one, was in no doubt that the essential spirit of China, the hidden treasure, was to be found not in the cities, but among the peasants, 'the sap that flows in the age-old human branches', as he called them.

Esson Gale, the student interpreter with the American delegation who had been received in audience by the three-year-old Pu Yi, was another who discovered that the masses of ordinary Chinese were anything but illiterate. In the smallest country villages, he found boys and girls reciting passages from the Book of Mencius, the fourth-century BC sage. And in his town house, as he quaintly puts it: 'I observe closely the reading habits of the lower orders: cooks, gardeners, household servants, coolies, messengers . . . I invariably find them reading a well-thumbed book! I examine the little volume, often taking it from their hands unexpectedly. What do I usually find? Some entrancing thirteenth-century thriller of warlike prowess or palace intrigue!'

After the collapse of Yuan Shih-kai and his abortive Chinese Empire, Sir John Jordan had counselled his colleagues in the various foreign legations to wait and see whether another strong ruler might take control of China. He does not seem to have attached any importance to the Republican government, or to that 'court in miniature' hidden in the Forbidden City. One foreign power, however, had no intention of waiting. Japan was expanding her empire. In 1914, when the Great War broke out in Europe, Japan, who was Britain's ally, had seized the large territories and seaports of Shangtung province which Germany had formerly occupied. She now began to extend her domain in Manchuria, where she had long had a foothold.

In the autumn of 1916 the fiery Manchu Prince Su, known as the 'Mad Prince Su', an ardent champion of the Ching dynasty, led a Loyalist army against the Republican forces in Manchuria. The prince, who was backed by a Japanese bank and whose officers were Japanese trained, planned his attack with the help of the Japanese garrison commander in Tientsin. At the same time the Mongol chieftain Bajobab, an ally of the prince, invaded northern China to attack the Republicans at Kalgan. The aim of both these offensives was to topple the Republican government in Peking and restore the Ching dynasty with Pu Yi on the throne. After severe fighting, the Mad Prince Su and Bajobab were defeated.

The happy truce between palace and parliament had lasted for nearly a year. Now the first clouds had arrived to darken the scene. On 16 June 1917 a Loyalist general, arrived in the Forbidden City, urgently seeking an audience. The grand guardian, who was an admirer of the general advised Pu Yi to receive him. General Chang Hsun strode in with much bustle, and kowtowed. A short, stocky, middle-aged man with bow-legs, bushy eyebrows, large whiskers and a greying pigtail, he looked like a battle-hardened pirate. In a rasping voice he declared that he had come to restore the great Ching dynasty and save the Chinese people. The Republicans would be kicked out and Pu Yi would once more be the Hsuan Tung Emperor with full powers. The general produced a memorial on the subject, which he and his officers had drafted. His troops, sixty battalions of them, were marshalled outside the gates of the Forbidden City. Pu Yi had only to say the word.

Pu Yi looked at the grand guardian, who stepped forward and said that His Imperial Majesty would consider the general's request. The general kowtowed and then charged out, cannoning into a eunuch of the presence on his way.

The grand guardian lost no time in giving Pu Yi his opinion. Heaven, he said, had sent this fine warrior to avenge the indignities suffered by the dynasty. Chang Hsun was the general who had captured the undefended city of Nanking in 1913 and killed many Republicans there. He and his men still wore the pigtail as a mark of their loyalty to the Manchus, although the pigtail had gone out of use everywhere since the founding of the Republic. The more Pu Yi heard, the more delighted he became. His pigtailed army would make him Emperor again, he thought; no longer would he have to share the Forbidden City with the president of the Republic. The gallant general's offer was accepted.

Before that day was over, the imperial dragon flag was to be seen all over Peking, including the Chinese City. The shops did a roaring trade in artificial pigtails made of horsehair. People appeared in the streets wearing their old Manchu gowns and court dress as if they were taking part in a pageant.

Pu Yi issued an edict renouncing the abdication decree of 1912 and restoring the dynasty. Each day the grand guardian brought further edicts for Pu Yi's approval. Hundreds of people came to the Imperial Palace to kowtow to the Emperor and to congratulate him. It was all very enjoyable. Only one thing annoyed Pu Yi and his grand guardian. The wretched President Li would not go away. This was intolerable. A message was sent to the president suggesting that he might care to commit suicide. But he took no notice and remained sulking in his corner of the Forbidden City, defended by the solitary rusting armoured car. It was the pigtailed general who thought of an answer. His men let off a cannon outside the wall of the Presidential Palace. Within minutes President Li was fleeing to the safety of the foreign legations' quarter.

Five days passed, five days of edicts, audiences and celebrations. Then, on the fifth day of the restoration, cannon-fire was heard in the east. Reports came in of a Republican army which was fast approaching Peking. It was called the Army to Punish the Rebels, and was commanded by none other than General Tuan. When the grand guardian heard that name, he trembled. In vain he tried to laugh it off, protesting to Pu Yi that there were still sixty battalions of pigtailed troops dedicated to his defence. Pu Yi's eyes were almost shut. In that mood he might well say yes.

That afternoon a military aeroplane appeared in the sky and circled slowly over the Forbidden City. Pu Yi was in the Palace of Mind Nurture when the plane dropped its three bombs. One fell in to the West Lake; one landed with a thud in the grounds and failed to explode; the third bomb exploded outside the Temple of the Ancestors, wounding a bearer of the yellow palanquin. When the sound of the explosion died away, there was a silence, then utter confusion. People flung themselves on the ground. Pu Yi hid himself in the schoolroom cupboard and refused to leave it for a long time. A number of eunuchs fled from the Forbidden City and were rounded up later by the police, over a mile from the Gate of Heavenly Peace. But there was one eunuch whom they did not round up. Chang, the chief eunuch, urging on his bearers with curses, was carried in his sedan-chair to the Eastern Gate. There, he mingled with the crowd of bewildered soldiers and passers-by, and was last seen hobbling towards the Chinese City.

Leaving his troops to give themselves up or escape as best they could, the pigtailed general found refuge in the Dutch legation. For several weeks his hosts were embarrassed by this swaggering, drink-sodden brute whose rasping voice could be heard all over their compound. At last they managed to pack him off to the British concession in Tientsin.

The restoration was over. All smiles and bows, the grand guardian assured an emissary from the president that the Emperor wanted only harmony and peace between the palace and parliament. The grand guardian hoped that the president had enjoyed his brief holiday and asked that his respectful wishes be conveyed to him.

The next day President Li resigned. The events of the last week had been too much for him. It is just possible that the grand guardian's 'respectful wishes' were the last straw. The grand guardian drafted an edict of abdication on Pu Yi's behalf. The restoration had been an unfortunate mistake, said the edict. It was the fault of the pigtailed general. Nor would it have happened if it had not been for 'the Emperor's tender years' and the fact that 'we live deep in the Forbidden City'.

A new president was elected. Hsu Hsih-chang was a former scholar-official and a moderate Republican. He took a lenient view of the attempted restoration and assured the palace that the Articles of Favourable Treatment of the Great Ching Emperor still stood. Many members of parliament thought that the president was too servile in his attitude towards the palace; they accused him of wishing to act as a sort of regent on behalf of the young Emperor. But there were other, more important, matters to occupy them. In 1917 Britain and the United States had persuaded China to abandon her neutrality and declare war on Germany. Now, in the autumn of 1918, the war in Europe was near its end. The Chinese government had high expectations that the parts of Shantung province once occupied by Germany and later seized by Japan would soon be returned to China. President Wilson had assured China of his support.

The war in Europe ended, and negotiations began at Versailles to agree a peace treaty. The Chinese delegation was led by the foreign minister, Lou Tseng-hsiang. A scholar-official of meek disposition, he was the author of *Ways of Confucius and of Christ*. The cabinet decided that Lou Tseng-hsiang should be accompanied to Versailles by a political adviser. Who better than 'Morrison of China'? The arch warmonger who preached the need for a fight to the finish in Europe, had spent that war in the peace and quiet of a Chinese seaside resort. He had not been entirely idle, however, for he had written some articles defending Japan's military presence in Manchuria.

When Morrison left for Europe, he took with him the loot he had acquired during the allies' plunder of Peking after the Boxer rising. The prize piece in his collection was a book of Chinese prayers, encased in jade and gold. It had been stolen from the Venerable Buddha's bedroom. At Versailles, Morrison did most of the talking when the Chinese petition was presented. The conference listened politely, but took no action. Japan was allowed to remain in possession of the Shantung peninsula. It later transpired that Britain, France and Italy had agreed secretly not to support China's case.

After this abject failure, the sensitive Lou Tseng-hsiang retired to the Benedictine monastery of St André in Belgium, where he joined the community. Morrison settled in London, never to return to China. In his drawing-room was displayed the Venerable Buddha's prayer-book in its jade and gold case. He would point it out to his visitors and say, with a pleasing tone of nostalgia in his voice, that it gave him something by which to remember 'that grand old lady'.

CHAPTER FOUR

THE GREAT ESCAPE

Pu Yi sat at his imperial table in the schoolroom of the Palace of Mind Nurture. 'Call them,' he said. The eunuch in charge of books was ushered in, followed by the new imperial tutor and the two princes, Pu Chieh and Yu Chung. The new tutor strode up to Pu Yi's table and gave a stiff bow. When he stood erect, there was a distinctly superior air about him. Pu Yi looked into the pale blue, staring eyes and flinched. He had seen foreigners at a distance in the audience hall, but never had he been so close to one. The blue-eyed foreigner had a ruddy complexion, cleft chin and brown hair that was greying at the sides. He had the sturdy build of one who has been an athlete in his youth. Although he was but forty-five, Pu Yi thought he looked an old man.

The eunuch handed the tutor four copies of *Alice in Wonderland* and then backed away, unable to take his eyes off the foreigner's clothes: the dark grey suit and waistcoat, the knife-like creases in the trousers, the white starched collar, the dark blue tie dotted with white crowns, and strangest of all, the spats and the highly polished leather shoes.

The tutor glanced at the books and frowned. 'Is this the only book we have?' he asked in English.

Everyone stared at him, blankly. He tried again, this time in Chinese, delivered with an Oxford accent. Pu Chieh nodded.

'Well, it will have to do for today, but I think we must have a change,' said the tutor, brusquely.

Pu Yi was puzzled. *Alice in Wonderland* was full of treasures. Why should they have to change?

The tutor brought Pu Yi his copy. As he walked across the floor, the heels of his shoes made a sharp, metallic noise. When he reached the table, Pu Yi could smell a strange scent on him.

Returning to his place, the tutor began to read out a passage from the English text of *Alice in Wonderland*: 'The King and Queen of Hearts were seated on their throne with a great crowd assembled about them – all sorts of little birds and beasts, as well as the whole pack of cards: the Knave was standing before them, in chains, with a soldier on each side to guard him ... '

It was clear that his pupils did not understand a word he said. They could follow a smattering of their old Chinese tutor's English, but not this blue-eyed man's. As he read on, the new tutor glanced from time to time at the two eunuchs of the presence who were gaping at him, wide-eyed. His ruddy cheeks turned purple with irritation. Good God! he thought. Are they going to stay for the whole two hours?

Reginald Johnston, the new imperial tutor, was a native of Scotland. He had the finest of credentials, having been doubly educated: first at Edinburgh University, and then at Magdalen College, Oxford, that finishing school for Scots with high ambitions. In 1898 he joined the British colonial service and was posted to Hong Kong, where he became secretary to the governor. In 1904 he was transferred to Weihaiwei as a district officer and magistrate. The port of Weihaiwei, with its fine, natural harbour on the northern coast of the Shantung peninsula, was an important British naval base. Together with 300 square miles of hinterland, the port had been leased to Britain at the time of the unequal treaties. During the fifteen years he spent in Weihaiwei Johnston, a bookish man, became something of a recluse. He developed an interest in Confucian philosophy and made frequent visits to the shrine of Confucius at Mount Tai in Shantung. This convert to Confucianism found an outlet for his new fervour in bitter attacks on his former Christian faith. In 1911 he wrote, under the pseudonym of Lin Shao-yang, a book called *A Chinese Appeal to Christendom concerning Christian Missions*. Full of scorn, it ridiculed the missionaries of all Christian denominations. It was a work that he would live to regret. As magistrate, Johnston had given some help to the Marquis Li, a Manchu courtier who had fled to Weihaiwei from Peking in 1911 to escape the Republicans. In the winter of 1918, the president, who took a paternal interest in Pu Yi, persuaded the reluctant high consorts that it was time for the Emperor to have an English tutor. The Marquis Li recommended Johnston for the post. Sir John Jordan, the British minister in Peking, was consulted, the colonial office in London was approached, Johnston agreed, and early in 1919 he was seconded to take up his new duties at the Imperial Palace.

At the end of his first day's teaching, when he had recovered from the experience of reading *Alice in Wonderland* to the Emperor, the princes and their attendant eunuchs, Johnston wrote a long report in which he lamented the fact that the young Emperor had no knowledge whatever of English, nor much desire to learn any. This report was to be followed by many others. It seems that the release from his many years as magistrate and Confucian recluse had given Johnston an irresistible urge to communicate. Opinionated, supremely confident and pompous, he sat in almost daily judgement on the decadent life of the Forbidden City.

A new era began in the schoolroom of the Palace of Mind Nurture. *Alice in Wonderland* was put aside, and Pu Yi and his companions tried to follow Johnston as he read out passages from *The Lives of English Monarchs*. He thought it best to begin with the Tudor dynasty, the dawn of the modern age in Britain, as he called it. Pu Yi's eyes remained half closed and opened only with occasional flickers of interest during the reigns of Henry VIII and Queen Elizabeth I.

Johnston liked to intersperse his readings with touches of philosophy. In his most solemn voice he informed his class one day that the true Confucian had the qualities of an English gentleman. It was an idea that he had formulated after years of contemplation. He was about to explain it, when, to his surprise, Pu Yi put up his hand. After weeks of plodding, here at last was a question. He looked expectantly at Pu Yi. 'Yes, Your Majesty?'

'Have you ever seen a white ant?'

The eunuchs of the presence gaped. It was all Johnston could do to control himself.

There was no doubt that Pu Yi had become used to the staring blue eyes, and was regaining his confidence.

Johnston reached the reign of James I, and with it his favourite character, Sir Francis Bacon. This model of an English gentleman, he explained, was a great scholar-official, orator, scientist and lawyer . . . He looked up to see that Pu Yi had emptied his leather jewel pouch on the table and was arranging his pearls in a straight line. In desperation, Johnston consulted his fellow-tutors. The Emperor's personality, they explained, had long contained the quality of *fou*, which means to float, to be volatile. In his next report, Johnston wrote that he detected signs in the Emperor's nature of 'something like a permanent cleavage, suggesting the existence within him of two warring personalities'.

King James I gave Johnston an opportunity of telling his class something of his native Scotland. He recited a list of romantic traditions and bombarded them with words such as clan tartan, bagpipes, kilt and haggis. But all he could draw from his pupils were glazed looks. Then, one day, without thinking much what he was doing, he produced a picture magazine. It was a special issue devoted to the Prince of Wales. Pu Yi turned the pages and his eyes opened wide. There were photographs of the prince in kilt and glengarry, standing in the heather by a Scottish loch, in full Highland dress when taking the salute at Edinburgh Castle, in flat cap, tweed jacket and plus-fours when playing golf at St Andrews, in Oxford bags with a cigarette in a corner of his mouth . . . At last Johnston had broken through. From now on, Pu Yi paid attention to everything Johnston had to say. When Johnston revealed that he had been to the same college at Oxford as the Prince of Wales, Pu Yi's respect for his tutor came close to veneration. To think that this man had trodden the same immaculate lawns as the Prince of Wales, the wearer of all those wonderful disguises! Whatever Johnston's opinion, be it the benefits of the imperial system of government, his regret that China had abandoned the old imperial examinations for her civil service, his hatred of democracy and the growing American influence in China, his admiration for Mussolini who was doing so much for Italy, and, above all, his belief that China should have a constitutional monarchy on the lines of Britain, he could count on Pu Yi's total concentration.

There was a price to pay, however. The first signs of trouble came when Johnston marched into the schoolroom one morning to find Pu Yi reeking of eau-de-Cologne. He had discovered Johnston's scent, and his eunuchs, when dressing him, had sprayed him with large quantities of it. A few mornings later, Johnston arrived to find Pu Yi sitting at his table in a blue, foreign-style suit with a pink carnation in the button-hole. On the table was a bowler hat and a pair of gloves. Below the table could be seen a pair of pink spats and polished shoes. When he had recovered his composure Johnston informed Pu Yi that he could not conduct his lesson until Pu Yi was dressed in his proper, Manchu gown. He then marched out, leaving the eunuchs gaping. Pu Yi was baffled. His eunuchs had gone to a lot of trouble, including two visits to the theatrical costumiers in the Chinese City, to find an outfit that the Prince of Wales would have been proud to wear.

Undeterred, Pu Yi went on trying to please his foreign tutor whom he had come to see as the King of Hearts in the Forbidden City's Wonderland. One day he sent Johnston a poem he had composed in Chinese. As a finishing touch, he signed it with the new pen-name he had devised: 'Luminous Unicorn'. But Johnston turned purple and objected that the pen-name was undignified for an Emperor. This King of Hearts was proving difficult to please.

As Pu Yi was leaving the schoolroom one afternoon he was surprised to see his father waiting outside. The prince, whose eyes were red from weeping, broke the news that the Princess Chun had died that morning after a brief illness.

Pu Yi's journey to his mother's funeral was the first time he had left the Forbidden City since he was brought there at the command of the Venerable Buddha thirteen years before. The princess's open coffin stood on the small stage in the Northern Mansion's theatre. The strange, still figure in the long white robe looked as if it were taking part in a play. Alive, he had never known her, but now Pu Yi felt a bond with his lifeless mother.

By 1922, when he had been an imperial tutor for three years, Johnston was in a commanding position at court. The grand guardian deferred to him; his imperial pupil awarded him the black button of the highest grade of mandarins, and the Order of the Sable Gown. On the whole, Johnston was pleased with Pu Yi's new-found interest in the Prince of Wales; with careful management, his young charge might be given an interest in constitutional monarchy itself. Johnston was disturbed, however, by the Emperor's unhealthy physical life. Pu Yi was now sixteen years old, yet he continued to be dressed and undressed by his eunuchs. They also washed and combed his hair, and sprayed him with perfume. At sixteen, the average English schoolboy would be taken up with playing games, but Pu Yi's only outdoor activity was the observation of ants, and even then he was carried to the nests in his yellow palanquin.

Deciding that life at the palace must be reformed, Johnston put forward a number of recommendations, which met with instant opposition. The high consorts, led by Lustrous Concubine, had never accepted this meddling alien. They rejected all his proposals. Johnston was not unduly troubled by the old ladies' resistance. His real enemies, as well he knew, were the eunuchs. Aware that Johnston detested them, the eunuchs retaliated by coining a nickname for him, which quickly went the rounds of the Forbidden City: 'Old Foreign Buddha'.

Every weekend Johnston would retire to a small house he had acquired in the Western Hills outside Peking. He called it the Cherry Glen. There, he would write his reports and pace up and down the garden path, brooding over Pu Yi's career and the decadent life of the Forbidden City. Now and then his retreat would be disturbed by thoughts of the eunuchs. 'Old

Foreign Buddha' indeed! If only he could think of a way of getting rid of them.

Johnston had underestimated the high consorts. At the very time when he was wondering how to tempt Pu Yi away from his ants and make him more like an English schoolboy, the high consorts were considering a plan which was to change the Emperor's life. They decided it was time for Pu Yi to marry. When Johnston was given the news, he went off to sulk at the Cherry Glen. A confirmed bachelor, he always felt uncomfortable in the presence of women. The idea that his young pupil of sixteen should marry upset him. He had grown fond of Pu Yi and sometimes wrote of him as 'my young fledgling'. He was even more upset when he heard the arrangements for the choice of a bride. The high consorts gave Pu Yi a number of photographs of Mongol and Manchu ladies. He was asked to select the one he wished to be his wife. The outstanding beauty in the pack was the Lady Wan Jung, Beautiful Countenance, a Mongol girl of high breeding who was descended from the great Chien Lung Emperor. She was the choice of Lustrous Concubine. Pu Yi looked through the pack of photographs and chose Wen Hsiu, Elegant Ornament, a chubby little girl of thirteen. His choice displeased the high consorts, who invited him to try again. He chose again, correctly this time, and Beautiful Countenance was declared Empress. As a consolation, the high consorts decided that Elegant Ornament should be the Emperor's secondary consort. Johnston fumed. This was bigamy. 'Don't they realise we are in the twentieth century?' he wrote in his report. But Lustrous Concubine, who must have wondered what all the fuss was about, had her way.

The ever-solicitous president gave Pu Yi an imaginative engagement present. The Republican government paid the cost of converting one of the palace theatres into a cinema. The first film to be shown was a Harold Lloyd comedy, and he quickly became Pu Yi's favourite star.

On a bitterly cold November day the Lady Beautiful Countenance arrived by train from Tientsin, where her family lived. At dawn the next day she was carried in the phoenix chair to the palace. Following Manchu custom, the secondary consort had arrived in the palace the night before so as to be present to greet the Empress. After the long wedding ceremony the Empress, accompanied by her ladies in waiting, went to the bridal chamber to await her lord. When Pu Yi arrived, he found his beautiful bride lying on the dragon couch, clothed in her red robe. He sat on a stool, talking to her for a while. Suddenly he fell silent. There, just beside the stool, was a small piece of moon cake that had been dropped on the floor. A black ant was carrying a crumb in its jaws, and was making for the door. Soon a procession of ants was coming and going between the door and the cake. Tiptoeing to the door, so as not to disturb the ants, Pu Yi opened it gently and followed their trail out on to the terrace.

The forlorn Empress lay back on her pillow. She had lost her Luminous Unicorn.

One day, in a rare moment of frivolity, Johnston invited Pu Yi to pick from a list of English names the one he liked best. Pu Yi chose Henry for himself and Elizabeth for his Empress. The newspapers pounced on these foreign names. To Johnston's annoyance, the *Far Eastern Times*, a paper with Republican sympathies, reported the forthcoming wedding reception of Mr and Mrs Henry and Elizabeth Pu Yi.

Except for members of the imperial family, only foreigners were invited to the reception, which was held in the Hall of Supreme Harmony. Ling Su-hua, the young daughter of the Republican mayor of Peking, managed to smuggle herself into the reception by disguising herself in foreign clothes. In the Hall of Supreme Harmony, the imperial couple stood at the foot of the throne, receiving their guests. Pu Yi was dressed in a morning coat with a pink carnation in the button-hole, striped trousers, buff waistcoat, and a starched white shirt and collar. It was his version of what the Prince of Wales might have worn on such an occasion. There was one extra touch, however, that Pu Yi had borrowed from the silent film star, Harold Lloyd: a pair of large horn-rimmed spectacles.

Eunuchs and page-boys, carrying trays laden with glasses

of champagne, made their way through the crowd of guests. Johnston took Pu Yi by the arm and led him here and there, while the Empress followed them. Ling Su-hua saw Johnston propel Pu Yi towards the British minister, and then a few minutes later turn him round to face the Italian minister. 'He made Pu Yi look just like a mechanical doll,' she recorded in her diary. A French journalist, commenting on the scene, thought that Johnston had succeeded in making Pu Yi into 'an English dandy'.

On the terrace outside the hall, the band of the Republican Army performed under the baton of bandmaster Giles. As the newly wedded couple left the hall, waving goodbye to their guests, the band struck up their special number, 'It's a Long Way to Tipperary'. It was a long way indeed. Johnston, wearing a shiny, black top hat, stood alone at the edge of the crowd. He looked sad.

Each day brought Johnston fresh honours from his young Emperor, but he was not a happy man. His one aim had always been to turn Pu Yi into a Confucian gentleman, one who respects parental authority. To this, Johnston would have liked to add a judicious blend of the English love of a healthy, outdoor life. But the ever-present eunuchs who bowed to Johnston and then, behind his back, leered at him and called him 'Old Foreign Buddha', reminded him every day how difficult an aim that was. He knew that he must get rid of the eunuchs. But how?

As he paced up and down the garden path at the Cherry Glen one day, the answer came to him in a flash. A committee of inquiry! Of course. A committee to examine the accounts that the eunuchs were supposed to keep. Then, surely, they would be exposed for the lying thieves they were. The experience he had gained from so many years in the civil service should have given him the answer sooner, he admitted in his report. But there was still time to act. 'No longer', he wrote, 'would the vampires drain the life-blood of the dynasty.'

His committee was composed of two staff officers from the President's Palace, some senior government officials and himself as chairman. The officials joined only with reluctance. Civil servants and eunuchs had always co-operated in the running of the palace; they had learned to tolerate each other. Besides, who was to know what the committee might uncover? But Johnston, who had the support of the president, overcame their fears.

Johnston's first target was the Palace of Established Happiness. In its vast hall were stored many treasures, including those that had been sent from the palaces at Jehol and Mukden in 1912 when the Republic was founded. For some time past, Johnston had suspected the eunuchs of selling palace treasures to a ring of dealers in the Chinese City. Now he delivered his master-stroke. The committee instructed the eunuch of the treasury to provide an inventory of all that was contained in the palace. Before dawn on the next day the temple bell sounded the alarm, and the eunuchs rushed about the grounds shouting 'Fire!' The Palace of Established Happiness was alight. In a few hours it burned to the ground; all that remained of it was charred wood. In the afternoon the eunuch of the treasury gave the committee an estimate of what had been lost. The treasures included 2,685 gold buddhas and many thousands of priceless books and scroll paintings.

This was open war. Johnston raged. His purple face was to be seen everywhere in the palace grounds, shouting orders at all who encountered him. He saw the president. He sought an audience with Pu Yi. An edict was issued, banishing all the eunuchs from the Forbidden City. The expulsion of the eunuchs was conducted like a military operation. Eighteen days after the fire a regiment of Republican troops under the command of General Wang surrounded the Forbidden City. A second regiment took up positions around the courtyard of the Palace of Established Happiness. All the 1,500 or more eunuchs were rounded up and marshalled in the courtyard. The edict of expulsion was read out to them, and they shuffled away in silence.

Once they were outside the walls of the Forbidden City the eunuchs were allowed to return in small groups under military escort to collect their belongings.

It had taken strength and decisiveness, Johnston later said, to bring to an end a tradition of 2,000 years at a moment's notice. But his war against the eunuchs was not quite won. He had reckoned without the high consorts. They now appealed to Pu Yi. Life would be impossible without the eunuchs, who performed such vital services for them, they claimed. Pu Yi yielded, and fifty eunuchs were allowed to stay. Also on the staff were about fifty page-boys who had not been affected by the purge.

The burning of the Palace of Established Happiness gave Johnston an unexpected consolation. When the rubble had been cleared away, a large open space was left, just the right size for a tennis-court. With the help of some British Legation staff, Johnston had a court marked out and Pu Yi was encouraged to try his hand at lawn tennis. The first game was a men's doubles – Pu Yi and Pu Chieh against Jun Chi, the Empress's brother, and Johnston. It was not a great success, but at least it was a start.

Johnston was soon to have another chance to introduce Pu Yi to an outdoor life. In the spring of 1924 he was appointed warden of the Summer Palace, about ten miles outside Peking. Walking among the pagodas on the wooded hill slopes or browsing in the pavilions by the lakeside so loved by the Venerable Buddha, he wished that his fledgling could be there to share all that beauty with him.

His wish was to be granted when a message came from the palace to say that the Emperor and Empress would be arriving on the following day by motor car. It was the first time since his mother's funeral that Pu Yi had left the Forbidden City, and Republican troops were on duty outside the Gate of Heavenly Peace to keep back the inquisitive crowd which had gathered there. When the imperial car drove up, Johnston was relieved to see that Pu Yi was wearing the orthodox Manchu gown and black skull cap. There was one odd touch, however. A cane dangled from Pu Yi's arm, evidence that he had been watching a Charlie Chaplin film. But at least he had not come dressed for the Scottish Highlands. Johnston did not notice what the Empress was wearing.

An elderly and voluble guide showed the imperial party

around one of the many temples. They then went down to the shore, where stood the Hall of the Waters of Rippling Jade. After passing through a courtyard they entered a small, airless room. In the middle, standing on the tiled floor, was a throne. All the windows were blocked up with bricks. They were in the Kuang Hsu Emperor's holiday prison. Pu Yi stiffened. His arms straightened, pointing at the throne. The cane fell to the floor with a clatter. Johnston picked it up. He looked anxiously at Pu Yi and felt that there was something sinister in his expression.

When they emerged into the daylight, Johnston took Pu Yi for a row on the lake in an attempt to relax him, but Pu Yi remained tense, and when at the end of the afternoon he was ushered into the imperial automobile, his movements were mechanical and lifeless.

In the late spring the *Court Gazette* announced the sudden death of the high consort, Lustrous Concubine. She was in her early fifties. Long ago she had withdrawn from the court affairs, appearing only briefly to arrange Pu Yi's marriage. The news of her death revived the legend that she was the immortal Yellow Lotus. Could so beautiful and mysterious a woman die? The story-tellers knew that she was on a journey to the Interior. She had gone back to the people she came from, the outlaws of the steppes. She bequeathed her jewels, including her favourite – a white jade ring – to the Empress, Beautiful Countenance. But a eunuch of the high consorts' household betrayed her trust and handed her jewels to Pu Yi.

Pu Yi, accompanied by Johnston, went to pay his respects at Lustrous Concubine's coffin. As they were leaving the temple, Pu Yi undid the strings of his jewel bag, groped inside, and held up Lustrous Concubine's white jade ring. Without a word, he thrust it into Johnston's hand.

During his five years in the Emperor's service Johnston had been tutor, reformer and warden. He now spent more and more time as Pu Yi's unofficial political adviser. When Johnston looked beyond the Forbidden City at the wider scene of Chinese politics, he did not like what he saw. The Republic was in disarray. In the south, Sun Yat-sen had begun another revolt. In the north and in the Yangtze valley region, war-lords, each with his independent army, were on the march. They found arms easy to come by. Since the end of the Great War in Europe cheap surplus weapons had been flooding into China. Cash, too, was available to the war-lords. The Japanese backed Chang Tso-lin, the war-lord of southern Manchuria. Britain, France and the United States backed Wu Pei-fu, who was based in central China. Russia backed the 'Christian war-lord', Feng Yu-hsiang, who controlled the north-west.

Rumours began to circulate in Peking and Tientsin of another plot to restore the Ching dynasty. The editors of the leading newspapers paid court to Johnston, begging him for information and for his views. 'Johnston of the Forbidden City' had become 'Johnston of China'. Those editors who had backed Yuan Shih-kai, now championed the cause of Pu Yi, the 'boy Emperor'. The *North China Daily Mail* declared that 'Republicanism in China had been tried and found wanting.' A leading article in *The Peking and Tientsin Times* said: 'It is probably a moderate estimate to suggest that ninety per cent of the Chinese population would favour the return of the boy Emperor.'

Not all the newspapers pleased Johnston, however. 'That radical rag', the *Far Eastern Times*, reported the existence in Peking of 'A monarchist plot, as great as any formulated two hundred years ago in Europe on behalf of Bonnie Prince Charlie.' Johnston might be incensed by those lurid words, but Pu Yi was thrilled. Bonnie Prince Charlie! Had Johnston a picture of him?

More details of the restoration plot began to emerge. The Manchurian war-lord, Chang Tso-lin, was reported to have visited the Japanese garrison commander in Tientsin. Chang had acquired an ally, none other than the pigtailed general! Their plan was to seize Peking, take Pu Yi off to Manchuria, and set up the Ching dynasty in its ancient tribal homeland.

The president of the Republic, who had painful memories of the last restoration, found all these reports depressing enough. But the news that the pigtailed general was on the march again was too much for him. He resigned, quit Peking, and fled to the safety of the British concession in Tientsin.

Whatever plans Chang Tso-lin and the pigtailed general may have had were thwarted when, in the summer of 1924, two major war-lords, Wu Pei-fu and Feng Yu-hsiang, joined forces and prepared to attack Chang Tso-lin at Shanhaikwan on the Manchurian border. Feng's role was to hold the pass near Jehol, north of the Great Wall, while his ally, Wu, launched the main attack. Suddenly, without any warning to his ally, Feng withdrew his army, moved it southwards, and seized the undefended city of Peking. It was a clever and treacherous coup, worthy of Yuan Shih-kai himself, that archetype of all the war-lords.

The pigtailed general had fought his last abortive battle. Leaving his troops behind in the field – many of them were to turn to banditry – he returned to his haven in the British concession in Tientsin, where he gave himself up to a dissolute life. Within a few weeks he was dead. His magnificent funeral procession, attended by foreign dignitaries, took over eight hours to wind its way through the city. It was matched by a lengthy obituary in *The Peking and Tientsin Times* entitled 'The "Tiger" passes in a blaze of glory'.

If ever there were a paper tiger, it was the pigtailed general, but his escapades on behalf of the imperial cause won him acclaim in high places. Johnston was an admirer. And, shortly after the pigtailed general's funeral, Pu Yi, the Son of Heaven, bestowed on him the highest honours, a posthumous title of canonization.

Johnston the civil servant and contemplative Confucian was comfortable when viewing events from a distance, but the sight of Feng Yu-hsiang's troops in their Russian-style uniforms lounging about in the streets of Peking alarmed and outraged him. Hurrying off to the foreign legations' quarter, he urged the British minister to send for troops from Tientsin. It was intolerable that Feng Yu-hsiang, the Red Christian, should be allowed to occupy the capital, said Johnston. The British must lead an allied crusade against him and his Bolshevik comrades.

The idea of a crusade against the Bolsheviks appalled the staff at the British Legation. They and their colleagues at the other legations remembered with acute embarrassment the last such attempt only a few years before, in 1918, when trainloads of British, French, Italian, American and Japanese troops had been sent from Tientsin to fight the Bolsheviks in Siberia.

The president and commander-in-chief of the Far Eastern Republic of Siberia was the tsarist Admiral Kolchak. His soldiers, who now included the allied expeditionary force from Tientsin, were not popular in the railway towns of Siberia. One of Kolchak's senior commanders, the Cossack ataman Semenov, so terrorized the town of Chita, east of Lake Baykal, that the people of that region called him 'The ogre of Chita'. The allies, too, found him a menace. During their eighteen months in Siberia, they were to spend much of their time guarding their trains against Semenov's marauding Cossacks who were supposed to be on their side.

The expedition was a disaster. Kolchak's only experience of command was as an admiral of the Russian Baltic fleet. And the task of organizing an allied army, largely confined to the single track of the Trans-Siberian Railway, while he tried to keep his unruly Cossacks in order, proved beyond him. Nor was he helped by the arrival on the scene of a Czech army of 50,000 men who were trying to make their way eastwards by train to Vladivostok, *en route* for America.

After suffering their first reverse at the hands of the Bolsheviks in western Siberia, many of Kolchak's units mutinied and laid down their arms. The allies soon found themselves caught up in an undisciplined retreat. Harried by the rapidly advancing Bolsheviks and anxious to make good their escape from Siberia, the allies surrendered their leader, Kolchak, to the Bolsheviks, who shot him. After that shameful event, which led to bitterness and recrimination, it was every man for himself, as each contingent of the allies entrained for the safety of northern China.

Thousands of White Russian refugees from Siberia tried to follow the allied troops as best they could. Having no trains, they came by carts or on foot. Some of them settled in

Manchurian railway towns such as Harbin and Mukden. The hardy ones reached Tientsin, where they were treated with polite disdain by the other foreign residents. Most people felt that the expedition to Siberia was an adventure best forgotten.

Some years later Daniel Varè, who had been first secretary and then minister at the Italian legation in Peking, broke the diplomatic silence over the Siberian campaign when he described what he called 'a characteristic incident' at the campaign's end. The Italian contingent were holding a section of the Trans-Siberian Railway near Krasnoyarsk when they were ordered to retreat to Tientsin. Hearing that the Italians were about to leave, eighty Russian women, who were legitimate wives of Italian soldiers, sought out the Italian commander and asked to be allowed to accompany their husbands. The commander, Baron Eduardo Fassini, explained to the women that they could not possibly travel with the troops in the battle conditions, but, to their intense relief, he graciously offered them a reserved carriage at the rear of his special train. Just as Fassini's train was about to start, the couplings were undone and the carriage with the eighty wives was left behind.

On Fassini's return, Varè asked him if this story were true, but Fassini only laughed and would not confirm or deny it. Varè goes on to say that 'In lieu of the wives they left behind them', the soldiers of the Italian contingent brought back a bear, which was presented to Varè, the well-known animal lover. The bear became a great favourite in the Varè household in Peking. With this touch of light relief, the urbane Varè ends the story of the deserted Russian wives, which he recounts in his book called, aptly, *Laughing Diplomat*.

Johnston was not given his crusade against the Bolsheviks, but he continued to pester the British, Dutch and Japanese ministers with reports that the Emperor's life was in imminent peril. Hardly a week passed without the sight of Johnston's staid, black limousine, driven by a uniformed chauffeur, trundling into the foreign legations' quarter. In the back seat the portly figure of Johnston could scarcely be seen under his tartan rug, for he imagined that every group of soldiers in the streets was out to capture him, and every pedestrian was a Russian agent.

The various heads of legations did their best to soothe Johnston. They informed him that they had received assurances from Dr C.T. Wang, the respected Chinese foreign minister, concerning the Emperor's safety. After all, the British minister added, the foreign legations had no right to interfere in the internal affairs of the Republic of China. By now the staff at the British legation had had enough of Johnston. The first secretary regarded him as 'a scandal-monger and meddler' whose only official position was warden of the Summer Palace, but who behaved as if he were an old-style regent of pre-Republican times.

It was true that the warden of the Summer Palace now spent most of his time in the Forbidden City, where he saw Pu Yi almost daily; and it was more than likely that Johnston's viceregal manner was encouraged by Pu Yi's bestowing on him the most lavish of gifts, a large two-storeyed pavilion, set in the most beautiful part of the Imperial Garden. It was called the Lodge of Nature Nourishment, and Pu Yi had it decorated and furnished at enormous expense in the European style, specially for Johnston. As Johnston himself said of the gift, it was 'a mark of favour which according to the palace officials was unique in the history of the dynasty'.

Every evening Johnston held court in his grand pavillion. He lectured to his audience of one, Pu Yi, on the evils of Feng Yu-hsiang, the Red Christian, whom the missionaries had the cheek to style the 'Cromwell of China'. Even Sir John Jordan, the former British minister, saw Feng as an Old Testament prophet, complained Johnston. The present British minister was no wiser, for he refused to acknowledge that the Red soldiers and spies, who ringed the Forbidden City, were after Pu Yi's blood and his treasures. So he droned on, and Pu Yi's eyes would close. Until one evening Johnston arrived, at last, at his inevitable conclusion. He had the answer to all their problems. Escape! Pu Yi's eyes opened wide. Escape! Bonnie Prince Charlie in kilt and glengarry would escape from the 'Cromwell of China'. It was a wonderful idea.

First, preparations had to be made. Johnston visited Tientsin where he opened a bank account for Pu Yi. A house was bought for Pu Yi in the British concession in Tientsin. It stood in Gordon Road, close to where the former president of the Republic was living in retirement. Day after day, crates of treasures were taken from the Imperial Palace and sent by train to Tientsin, where they were deposited in bank vaults. The Red Christian's soldiers, who loitered in the streets of Peking, seemed to have taken no notice of all these comings and goings from the Forbidden City.

Details for the Emperor's flight from his palace were worked out. Johnston favoured a dash by car on a moonless night through the Gate of Spiritual Valour. The palace guard were carefully and secretly rehearsed for the operation. All was going smoothly when the Red Christian upset Johnston's dramatic plans. On 5 November Feng's troops disarmed the palace guard and took over the Forbidden City. The imperial family were asked to pack their personal belongings and leave. They were shown every courtesy. A motor car was provided for Pu Yi and, escorted by one of Feng's colonels, he and the Empress were driven to the Northern Mansion, where they were warmly received by Prince Chun. At last Pu Yi had come home.

Elegant Ornament, Pu Yi's secondary consort, was given lodgings in the Tartar City. The two remaining high consorts refused to leave the palace, declaring that they would rather die. Impressed by their courage, and uncertain how to manage the fierce old ladies, Feng relented and allowed them to stay. Not long afterwards Prince Ching, the legitimate head of the dynasty, persuaded them to go and live in his house in the Tartar City.

Deprived, in one simple stroke, of his fledgling, his grand pavilion, and his post as warden of the Summer Palace, Johnston sulked at the Cherry Glen in the Western Hills.

Feng's next step was to revoke the Articles of Favourable Treatment of the Great Ching Emperor. The title of emperor was abolished. Henceforth, Feng said, Pu Yi would be treated as an ordinary citizen of the Republic. Pu Yi's annual salary was reduced from 4 million to 500,000 dollars; a not

106

ungenerous arrangement for an ordinary citizen.

The near-hysterical Johnston rushed back to Peking when he heard the news. At the British legation he demanded protection for the Emperor. He was sure, he said, that the Red Christian's next foul deed would be to massacre the entire imperial family, just as the Bolsheviks had massacred the Romanovs in 1917. Pu Yi must be helped to escape from the Northern Mansion.

The British minister gave this outburst a cool reception and suggested to Johnston that he was over-reacting. Johnston crossed the road to the Japanese legation. Mr Yoshizawa, the minister, assured Johnston that Japanese troops were on constant patrol in the vicinity of the Northern Mansion. In his opinion, Pu Yi was perfectly safe there. The minister did say, however, that in the unlikely event of the Emperor and Empress coming under attack, he would be glad to offer them the hospitality of his own house in the foreign legations' quarter. During all the alarms and discussions about the Emperor's safety Mr Yoshizawa seems to have been the only individual who gave any thought to the well-being of the Empress.

In the meantime the Manchurian war-lord Chang Tso-lin arrived in Peking. He granted Johnston an interview, received from him a signed photograph of Pu Yi, and promised that Pu Yi would have his protection.

With all these assurances from so many quarters, there seemed no point in Johnston's continuing with his plans for the great escape. But he refused to change his mind; he had decided on an escape, and an escape there would be. His fledgling was not going to be left to the mercy of that Red Christian and his comrades. Johnston, the fervent Confucianist and upholder of paternal authority, would not even listen to the pathetic pleas of Pu Yi's father, Prince Chun, who was strongly opposed to his son leaving Peking. Striding into Prince Chun's study in the Northern Mansion one day, he brandished a copy of the Chinese newspaper *The Shuntien Times*. 'Look at this!' he shouted, pointing to a headline: 'Reds Advocate People's Self Rule.' The cowering Prince muttered something inaudible. Johnston flounced out.

His mind was made up. There must be no more delay. He and his fledgling must fly.

On 29 November Johnston arrived unannounced at the Northern Mansion. He had brought with him the only person he could trust, Chen Pao-shen, the former grand guardian who was living in retirement in the Tartar City. They must leave at once, Johnston informed Pu Yi. The escape was on! Pu Yi must bring no belongings whatever, for that would give the game away if they were stopped and searched. The old grand guardian was worried. He thought they should let Prince Chun know what they were doing, but Johnston flatly refused to do so. There must be complete secrecy. Neither Prince Chun nor the Empress Beautiful Countenance must be told.

Warning the gatekeeper to say nothing, they got into their waiting car. Pu Yi, in fur coat and hat to match, looked more like a Siberian trapper than Bonnie Prince Charlie. As the chauffeur was cranking the engine with the starting handle, Johnston noticed a bulge in Pu Yi's coat. He tapped Pu Yi on the shoulder and pointed to the bulge. Looking sheepish, Pu Yi produced a large bag. It was full of jewels. He had not been able to resist them. It was too late to go back, and Johnston took the bag for safe keeping.

Off they went. At every street corner, Johnston saw Red spies. Convinced that they would be pursued, he had laid a false trail. They drove first to a photographer's shop just inside the foreign legation's quarter. Pu Yi was thrilled. Although they were only pretending to shop, Pu Yi wondered if he might have his photograph taken. He had adopted the practice of sending signed pictures of himself to eminent people. No, His Imperial Majesty may not, replied Johnston. There was no time. Too late, Johnston realized his ghastly mistake. He had used the imperial title by force of habit and had been overheard. A shop assistant slipped outside, and within minutes a crowd of people were at the door, all curious to see what the Emperor looked like. They saw little, however, for Pu Yi quickly put on his dark glasses.

Making their way through the excited crowd, the escapers changed cars as planned, and were driven at high speed to the

German hospital. There, Pu Yi went through a mock consultation with Dr Dipper, a friend of Johnston's. They were now only a few hundred yards from their destination, the Japanese legation. In Johnston's eyes, not only Red spies but the whole of the 'Cromwell of China's' army seemed to be lining the route. At last they reached the Japanese legation. Looking across the road at the British legation, Johnston felt peeved at the way his own side had treated him. Scandalmonger indeed!

Mr Yoshizawa, the Japanese minister, smiled and bowed from the waist as only the Japanese can. He listened to Johnston's formal request for asylum for the Emperor, and gave his gracious consent. On behalf of the Emperor of Japan, he said, it was an honour to receive under his roof the Great Ching Emperor.

While Johnston and Pu Yi celebrated their successful escape in Mr Yoshizawa's house, the deserted Empress did her best to comfort the old prince in the Northern Mansion. Two days after Pu Yi's disappearance she discovered his whereabouts through a newspaper report. She decided that the honourable thing to do was to join him. But a cordon of troops had now been thrown around the Northern Mansion. She managed to smuggle a message to the Japanese legation. When Mr Yoshizawa read her pathetic note, he behaved chivalrously and sent a car to fetch the Empress. Johnston welcomed her with a glacial smile.

When Pu Yi and his Empress had been in the Japanese legation for about a month, a group of Manchu princes, led by Pu Yi's father, were allowed to pay them a visit. The great General Tuan Chi-Jui, now chief executive of the Republic, had promised Pu Yi every assistance, they said. Would he not return home to the Northern Mansion? Pu Yi turned to Johnston. The answer was no.

During the next two months Pu Yi left the legation only once.Escorted by Japanese secret policemen, he went one evening as far as the moat outside the Gate of Heavenly Peace. Over the dark red battlements he could see the yellow tiles of the myriad palaces. The Forbidden City was empty. Johnston had promised to bring him back here one day. Then he would

109

sit in triumph on the dragon throne.

A last despairing letter came from the Prince Chun, imploring Pu Yi to come home, but it was ignored. Spending most of his days in the study among his books, the old prince lived peacefully in the Northern Mansion until his death in 1951. No such peace lay ahead for Pu Yi.

PART TWO

THE FORD OF HEAVEN

CHAPTER FIVE

THE COMMERCIAL CRUSADERS

At about eleven o'clock on the night of 23 February 1925 a regiment of Japanese troops cordoned off all the approaches to the railway station at Tientsin. A dust-storm was blowing, and many of the soldiers wore face-masks. Shortly before midnight a guard of honour of Japanese marines, their bayonets glistening in the light of the station's two old lanterns, took up their positions on the arrival platform for the train from Peking. The train was late. General Ueda, commander-in-chief of the Japanese garrison, marched briskly up and down the platform, followed by his staff officers. Every time the general passed him, the station-master saluted and bowed. Behind the guard of honour a group of distinguished guests, including a few eminent Ching Loyalists, waited with the Japanese consul-general, Mr Shigera. Among them on this historic occasion was Woodhead, editor of *The Peking and Tientsin Times*.

A few minutes after midnight the train's long and melancholy whistle could be heard. The station-master's handbell clanged out its warning, and the train came in, panting and hissing. The guard of honour presented arms, buglers sounded a fanfare, and all the civilians removed their hats as a thin young man of twenty descended the steep steps. He wore a long, black Manchu gown, a black skull-cap, and

113

large horn-rimmed spectacles. A bamboo cane hung on his left arm. When the young man walked along the front rank of the guard of honour, Woodhead noticed that his arms and legs jerked in an odd way. Pu Yi, once the Dragon Emperor of China, had come to the Ford of Heaven.

While the welcoming ceremony went on, Woodhead rushed to pay his respects to Johnston, who was clambering down the carriage steps. Dressed in a large fur coat and cap, on which was pinned the button of the highest order of Mandarins, Johnston looked cheerful. He had accomplished his mission. The journey had been uneventful, thanks to the Japanese secret service, Johnston told Woodhead. With Peking under the control of the Red Christian, it was out of the question for His Imperial Majesty to remain there. The Empress? . . . The pale blue eyes turned to ice. No, she was not with the imperial party. He would say no more.

In the deserted station square, Pu Yi, Johnston and their entourage of courtiers were ushered into motor cars and driven at high speed through the Italian concession, across the Austrian bridge, through the French concession, and on to the safety of the Japanese concession.

Pu Yi's new palace was called the Chang Garden. A spacious, two-storey mansion, it stood in Asahi Road at the centre of the Japanese concession. Its owner, a former official in the Forbidden City, had offered it to Pu Yi rent free. A seven-foot high wall enclosed the house and grounds. In the middle of the garden was a pond. On one side of the pond was a summer-house. and on the other was a big circular cage, in which were kept a pair of Manchurian cranes. Facing the Chang Garden, across the road, was Kasuga House. It was occupied by Japanese secret service agents under the command of Staff Major Mino, who was responsible for the security of the Chang Garden. Japanese police were on patrol outside the Chang Garden throughout the day; at night the patrol was doubled.

No sooner was the former Emperor installed in his new palace than a long list of former courtiers and generals applied for audiences with him. Some of them had fled to Tientsin when the Republic was formed in 1911; others had sought refuge there after the failure of the restoration plot in 1917. The large reception-room on the first floor of the Chang Garden was converted into a throne-room, and there Pu Yi, assisted by the grand guardian, received the kowtows and declarations of allegiance from the repentant officials who had deserted him. The old grand guardian, Chen Pao-shen, who had been called out of retirement by Johnston to assist in the great escape from the Northern Mansion, had been released from his duties, and his place was taken by Lo Chen-yu. The new grand guardian, who wore a white goatee beard and a pigtail, was a scholar-official, dedicated to the cause of restoring the Ching dynasty. Acting on the advice of his predecessor, the grand guardian had steeped himself in the study of ants: not only could he answer all Pu Yi's questions on the subject with assurance, but he even added some illustrations to Chen Pao-shen's work on the parasol ants of the Atta family.

One of the grand guardian's duties was to preside over a cabinet of five senior ministers who supervised the day-to-day running of the imperial government in exile. By far the busiest member of the cabinet was the finance minister. A growing number of war-lords, including former generals of the Northern Army, presented themselves at the Chang Garden with offers of military help in exchange for cash. Most of these offers were eagerly accepted, and it was the finance minister's task to pay their advances to the soldiers of fortune.

Judging from the procession of Ching Loyalists who attended his court and the amount of military aid he had bought, Pu Yi had every reason to hope that his restoration to the dragon throne was not far off.

One day a sedan-chair borne by a team of eight servants in scarlet livery, and escorted by Japanese policemen, arrived at the Chang Garden. The gate was opened at once. The distinguished visitor was carried up the long flight of steps that led from the garden to the reception-room on the first floor. Pu Yi sat on his red lacquered chair, which served as a throne. His visitor performed the nine kowtows and then raised his grinning, toad-like face. It was Chang Yuan-fu, the chief eunuch, who had fled from the Forbidden City on the day it was bombed by the Republican aeroplane. Pu Yi stared wide-eyed at him. The grand guardian shivered. The notorious case of the concubine's murder was being talked about all over Tientsin. The chief eunuch lived in a magnificent mansion in the British concession. Recently one of his young concubines, who could no longer bear his cruelty, had fled to seek protection at the British police station at Gordon Hall. The police had escorted her back to the mansion and handed her over to the sadistic chief eunuch. That night he tortured the wretched girl and beat her to death. No action was taken against him.

Having expressed his pleasure at seeing the Emperor again, the chief eunuch begged His Imperial Majesty to do him the honour of visiting him at his mansion, where he had a theatre and an excellent troupe of actors. His Imperial Majesty would be quite safe there, for nearby, only across the road, were the house of the British consul-general and the Anglican All Saints' Church. British soldiers were always marching by. On Sundays they paraded, fully armed, at the church, where they sang warlike hyms which could be heard a long way off. Truly there was no better defence against revolutionaries and outlaws than to live close to a British church.

The chief eunuch peered about him at the sparsely furnished room. It was pitiful to see the Emperor without a single eunuch or page-boy in attendance. If His Imperial Majesty lacked anything, his slave, the chief eunuch, would be delighted to provide it, he said. Eunuchs of the presence, page-boys and concubines of the highest quality: His Imperial Majesty had only to ask.

As he watched this monster, the fascinated grand guardian remembered only too vividly the incense-laden atmosphere of the old court in the Forbidden City when the Venerable Buddha walked in her ghostly procession and the night silence was broken by screams of desire and agony.

The chief eunuch inquired after the Empress. He hoped that she and the secondary consort would arrive soon from Peking. No court was complete without the presence of beautiful ladies, he added with a leer.

Pu Yi and the grand guardian glanced at each other. It was

a relief to know that Johnston was now in Weihaiwei. What a scene there would have been, if he had come marching in to find the 'Archangel' of the eunuchs here!

As if he could read their thoughts, the chief eunuch asked Pu Yi to convey his respects to the imperial tutor, Johnston.

Johnston stood at the rail of a small Japanese steamer, the *Tokiwa Maru*. For the last two hours she had been lying off Taku Bar at the mouth of the Sea River, waiting for the tide. To the south, looming over the desolate mud-flats, he could see the ruins of the four Taku forts which the guns of the British and French fleets had pounded before sailing up-river to capture Tientsin in 1860. His return to Weihaiwei had been a bitter disappointment. There had not even been time for a visit to the shrine of Confucius at Mount Tai. For the last three months he had been engaged in the humiliating task of handing over Weihaiwei to the Republican government of China. It was all the Americans' fault. The Washington Treaty of 1921 had compelled Britain to give up Weihaiwei. 'Morrison of China' would never have tolerated such an abject surrender, thought Johnston. Now, in 1926, the Chinese, supported by the Americans, were accusing Britain of being so sluggish over her withdrawal as to break the treaty.

In his report to London, Johnston insisted that a number of administrative matters remained to be settled before he could recommend the immediate abandonment of so important a naval base. His old enemy, the *Far Eastern Times*, attacked him for using 'the typical stalling tactics of a colonial civil servant'. The endless wrangling had exhausted Johnston. It came as a relief when he was invited to attend the celebrations in Tientsin to mark the enthronement of Crown Prince Hirohito as Emperor of Japan.

The ship's engines started up and she weighed anchor. Slowly she made her way up the winding Sea River. Apart from one or two willow trees, all Johnston could see were mud-flats and salt marshes. It was hard to believe that, hidden in those marshes, was a maze of creeks teeming with the sampans of the nomadic boat people. A dreary journey lay ahead of him. Tientsin was forty miles up-river; in ancient times it had been on the coast, he reflected. That was before the Sea River and its tributaries had brought down all this silt from the high plateaux of the Interior. There was a popular belief among the northern Chinese that one day the desert would cover the whole world. He had to admit, that, in this bleak estuary, at any rate, the desert was indeed conquering the sea.

At five o'clock in the afternoon, four hours after the steamer had crossed Taku Bar, Johnston saw the first building on the north bank of the river. The steamer slowed to thread her way through the cluster of sampans and junks in the channel. A number of creeks entered the Sea River here. A little farther up, the river was crossed by the Grand Canal, which reached all the way to Peking, eighty miles to the west. Because this stranded inland port at the meeting of the waters gave travellers a way across them to the celestial city of Peking, it was called Tientsin, the Ford of Heaven.

Now Johnston could see the onion-shaped dome of the Orthodox church in the Russian concession. The sight of it always irritated him. The British and the French had taken Tientsin and established concessions on the south bank by treaty. But by the turn of the century no fewer than six parasite nations, preying on that success, had managed to wheedle concessions out of the Chinese – the Russians, Italians, Belgians and Austrians on the north bank, and the Germans and the Americans on the south bank. True, the Japanese also had a concession on the south bank, but that great Asiatic empire, which acted as a peacemaker and a check on Russian expansionism, could hardly be counted a parasite.

The engines of the steamer stopped, and she veered towards the British bund. Beyond the rows of godowns, Johnston could see the Customs House. Beside it was moored the gunboat HMS *Hollyhock*. The *Tokiwa Maru* tied up just beyond her. As the gangplank was being lowered, Johnston noticed Woodhead of *The Peking and Tientsin Times* waiting on the quayside. Johnston frowned. The last thing he wanted was another interview.

Johnston left his luggage with the hotel porter, waved away the clamouring rickshaw coolies, and walked with Woodhead the 200 yards up to the Astor House Hotel. On the way there,

Johnston briefed the grateful editor on the Weihaiwei negotiations. Later, sitting on the veranda outside Johnston's suite of rooms, they sipped their whiskies and sodas while they looked out on the centre of the British concession. Below them ran Victoria Road, where the best shops were to be found. Across the road lay Victoria Park, its 200 square yards surrounded by iron railings. 'No Chinese allowed' said the notice on the gate. In the middle of the park was a small pavilion with a curved Chinese roof and red pillars. The band of the Loyal East Lancashire Regiment had just taken their seats in the pavilion. The bandmaster raised his baton and launched them into a jaunty air from Gilbert and Sullivan's *The Pirates of Penzance*. Smartly dressed people sat on the benches near the pavilion, while others strolled along the paths between the carefully weeded flower-beds.

In the left-hand corner of the park, overlooked by the Tientsin Club, stood the war memorial to the British who had been killed in Europe during the Great War of 1914-18. A replica of the Cenotaph in Whitehall, London, it was surrounded by flower-beds laid out to resemble an English municipal garden. Looming over the right-hand side of the park was a dark grey building. A crenellated battlement ran between its two big towers. This was Gordon Hall, named after General 'Chinese' Gordon who, when he was a captain in the Royal Engineers, had surveyed and fixed the boundaries of the British concession in 1860. Both the hall and the park had been opened in 1887, the year of Queen Victoria's jubilee.

'This place always reminds me of a suburb of Manchester,' said Johnston, viewing the scene with disdain.

'Mad Mac, the travelling piano-tuner, says it reminds him of Edinburgh,' Woodhead said, and then blushed when he remembered that Johnston was a native of that city. 'Gordon Hall was designed by a Scottish missionary, you know,' he went on in a clumsy attempt to change the subject.

Johnston gave him an icy stare. 'It wouldn't surprise me in the least,' he said. 'There are more missionary headquarters and officers in the three square miles of the concession than in any other city in the world. And most of them are here, in

Victoria Road. Take the arch fund-raiser, the Reverend Jonathan Blunt, the man who had the nerve to christen Feng Yu-hsiang the "Cromwell of China". I suppose he's still here.'

The sun was setting behind the battlements of Gordon Hall, casting long shadows across the park. The band stopped playing, and the bandmaster turned round to salute the crowd. There was a ripple of applause. Johnston looked over the top of the pavilion to the far side of the park. He could see a little way up Meadows Road where the consul-general's house and All Saints' Church stood. Opposite them was a large house. Purple wistaria hung from its wall.

'Who lives in that big house by All Saints'?' he asked.

Woodhead gulped down some whisky. 'I'm afraid we've had some trouble there,' he said nervously. 'He's a Chinese by the name of Chang. All the war-lords living in the concession seem to be called Chang. It's very confusing. But this Chang used to be the chief eunuch of the Imperial Palace. . . .'

Johnston snorted, his face its customary purple. 'Why the devil. . . .? I suppose he bought his way in here. Probably through a missionary. That case of the concubine. A damned disgrace. It was splashed all over the Weihaiwei papers. I don't want him anywhere near the Emperor. That's final. I'll have to see the Japanese police about that. Our people are useless. Who's in charge of security here?'

'Peebles is chairman of the watch committee. Being leader of the municipal council, he's chairman of everything in the concession, of course.'

'Hopelessly weak,' said Johnston. 'Why can't they elect someone strong and decisive?'

'Then there's Captain O'Riordan, seconded from the army. A reliable man. His special duty is to liaise with the Japanese. The plain-clothes inspector, Kellaher . . . I'm not too happy about him. He's been here a long time, speaks Chinese. They say he's too familiar with the riff-raff, rickshaw coolies and the like. Drinks too much, if you ask me.'

'Are you going to bring His Imperial Majesty over to see us soon?' Woodhead asked, changing the subject. 'We keep getting letters from our readers asking about him.'

'The Japanese want him to lie low for a while, naturally, but I hope to bring him out next week, after the celebrations for the Japanese Emperor. Our consul-general is giving a small garden party. I'm sure you'll be asked. In the meantime you must come to tea at the Chang Garden. I shall be staying there tomorrow.' Johnston smiled for the first time that evening. 'You'll never guess what I'm giving His Imperial Majesty for a present. An English bulldog! Specially imported from Surrey. It's taken eight weeks to get here. I must collect it from the Customs House Kennels.'

'I'm afraid it will find some competition at the Chang Garden,' said Woodhead. 'General Ueda has presented the Emperor with a pair of Alsatians.'

The smile faded from Johnston's face. He looked down at the deserted park. About twenty crows, cawing loudly, circled over the row of small trees bordering the park. Near the cenotaph, Wang the park policeman was locking the gates. Johnston felt depressed. Tientsin always had that effect on him.

The Japanese park was much bigger than Victoria Park. A road ran through the centre of it. Hundreds of flags, white with a red sun, decorated both sides of the road to celebrate the new Mikado's accession. In the middle of the park a grandstand had been built for distinguished guests. Pu Yi sat in the front row. He wore a new pale blue uniform. His cap, which was of Austrian design, had peacock-blue feathers which hung down from the crown. Next to him was Johnston in a top hat and morning coat. On Johnston's other side was a thickset Japanese with a shaven head. He wore a drab, grey civilian suit of the kind worn by bank clerks. Johnston introduced him to Pu Yi. 'This is Major Mino of the Japanese secret service,' he said. 'I'm sure he will look after you when I go back to Weihaiwei.' Major Mino bowed from the waist. Throughout the parade, he kept his eyes fixed on the ground. Pu Yi wondered if he was interested in ants.

Sitting on his white charger in the middle of the parade, General Ueda took the imperial salute. '*Tenno Banzai*!' the crowds of Japanese shouted. The general rode up to the grandstand. With a flourish of his sword, he saluted Pu Yi. Johnston doffed his hat.

An open car drove up to the stand. Two orderlies helped General Ueda to dismount. He then invited Pu Yi to join him in the car. Escorted by four motor cycles in front, and four at the rear, the car drove slowly down the road. The many Japanese children lining the roadway cheered and waved their little rising sun flags. '*Banzai! Banzai!*' they shouted. Pu Yi, who was standing in the middle of the car with the general, raised his hand to his cap in salute. Now and again the feathers on his cap hung over his spectacles, and he had to brush them aside in order to see.

The car reached the end of the park and turned back. As it was nearing the grandstand, three Japanese air force planes flew low overhead, making a loud roar. To Johnston's dismay, Pu Yi disappeared from view. He had dropped to the floor of the car. The general tried to lift him up, but the Emperor's inert body lay flat, his hands covered his ears. As far as Pu Yi was concerned, the parade was over.

Johnston's return to the Chang Garden was not a success. Outside the summer-house he presented Pu Yi with Pongo, a fully grown bulldog. 'Ever since the reign of King Henry VIII the bulldog has been England's finest guard-dog. I like to think that it represents some of our finest qualities,' he said with pride. Gingerly, Pu Yi held on to the lead, as Pongo slobbered over his Manchu gown.

Johnston and Pu Yi, who dragged the reluctant Pongo behind him, walked to the stone steps leading up to the house. They posed on the second step with Pongo between them while the grand guardian took their photograph. Just then they heard growling noises coming from behind the summer-house. The growls turned into fierce barking as two Alsatians, followed by their two pups, appeared and raced towards the group on the steps. Yelping, Pongo took off, pursued by the Alsatians. 'Come here, Pongo!' Johnston shouted angrily, but the bulldog disappeared into the shrubbery at the far end of the garden. In the birdcage the cranes flapped their wings and squawked.

In the Chang Garden's entrance hall four page-boys bowed as Pu Yi led the way into the reception-room. At the door, Johnston turned to the grand guardian and said, testily, 'I didn't know there were any page-boys on the staff here. Where did they come from?'

The grand guardian smiled. 'We have so many audiences. If they are to be conducted properly, His Imperial Majesty needs the page-boys' help.'

The walls of the reception-room were lined with dark wood panelling. There was a parquet floor. At the far end, on a low dais, were a red lacquered chair and some long benches. The airless, dingy room made Johnston feel he was back in the Forbidden City.

Pu Yi sat beside Johnston on one of the benches. Two page-boys stood behind them. Johnston tried to explain to Pu Yi the procedure they must follow at the British consul-general's garden party on the next day. Pu Yi's eyes began to close. The presence of the page-boys irritated Johnston, and every now and again he would turn round and glare at them.

The grand guardian decided that he must do something to soothe Johnston, who was still smarting over the bulldog's panic flight. He sent a page-boy for the imperial album on ants and, when it arrived, he offered it to Johnston with an obsequious smile. Pu Yi came to life. 'You haven't seen the grand guardian's latest pictures of the ants' royal procession,' he said to Johnston. The grand guardian turned the pages until he reached a series of water-colours of the queen ant's nuptial flight. Three feet underground, long corridors opened at intervals into chambers of about a foot square. Slave ants, captured from another colony, were storing food along the sides of these chambers. The great queen struggled up the main corridor which led to the exit from the nest. Behind her came seven kings and many worker ants. When the queen reached the surface, she stretched out her wings, and workers swarmed all over her to clean and brush every part of her body. The queen shook them off and flew away, climbing slowly. In the air, each of the kings mated with her. She then descended in a long spiral to the ground. After cleaning her antennae, she scraped a hole in the sand with her jaws, and began to lay the eggs for her new colony.

Johnston was overcome by a feeling of nausea. Pleading tiredness after his journey, he went off to his room on the second floor. On the way he tried to console himself with the thought that tomorrow, away from this Alice in Wonderland world, he would take Pu Yi under his wing, and all would be well again.

He was crossing the entrance hall when the front doors were flung open, and in swept the Empress Beautiful Countenance followed by the secondary consort, Elegant Ornament, and a retinue of servants. At the rear of the party a lady in waiting was being pulled along by two Pekinese dogs which strained at their leashes. A page-boy carried their four pups, two under each arm. He set them down, and immediately the hall was filled with the sound of their infernal, high-pitched yapping. Johnston fled.

The Empress and her party, who had not been expected, had just arrived from Peking. Mr Yoshizawa, the Japanese minister, had kindly made the travel arrangements. When the Empress first learned that Johnston, with the connivance of the Japanese secret service, had taken her husband off in the middle of the night, she felt humiliated and angry. But when she discovered that they had gone to the Japanese concession in Tientsin, she was appalled. She knew her native city better than did Johnston or his Japanese friends. If a refuge were needed for Pu Yi at all, Tientsin was the last place she would have chosen. For many years the foreign concessions had been notorious as hiding-places for war-lords and corrupt officials on the run. In the concessions they were outside Chinese jurisdiction. These renegades were viewed with contempt by their foreign protectors and by the native Chinese. The proud Empress foresaw that life in the concessions would be a degrading form of imprisonment. She considered that the proper course for Pu Yi and herself was to remain in Peking with his father, Prince Chun. And yet her sense of honour obliged her to join her husband, that strange young man who lived in his own underworld. Sometimes, as she watched him tiptoeing after his ants in the garden, she felt sure that he was not an ordinary mortal, but a changeling left by creatures from another universe. People often laughed at Pu Yi; even the page-boys jeered at him behind his back when he floundered about as if his legs were wooden stilts. But the Empress Beautiful Countenance came to realize with a chilling fear that, while he played the fool, he had a heart of iron, and that his vacant smile masked a hatred for the mortals who surrounded him.

Soon after the Empress arrived at the Chang Garden Johnston brought Woodhead to tea there. Woodhead was not introduced to the elusive Empress, but he caught a glimpse of her feeding the cranes in the garden. She made an unforgettable impression on him, and he later described her as 'A lovely girl who resembles a piece of delicate porcelain'.

Woodhead found the Chang Garden 'a large, ramshackle mansion which seems to be overrun with Pekinese and Alsatians'. He was intrigued by the throne-room. Running along the wall of that room, said Woodhead, was a sixty yards' long silk scroll on which was painted the order of procession to the Altar of Heaven for the imperial sacrifices. The scroll depicted in minute detail the robes and the proper position of every one of the court officials.

Although this was their first meeting, Woodhead was known to Pu Yi through his writing. For several years the editor had been sending a weekly edition of *The Peking and Tientsin Times* to the Imperial Palace in the Forbidden City. Johnston used Woodhead's leaders as a model for Pu Yi's English lessons. Woodhead's style was a mixture of ornate prose borrowed from *The Times* of London, coy, old China hand humour, and sporting terms that he had inherited from 'Morrison of China', whose disciple he was. More often than not, his leaders contained the stock phrase 'not playing the game', a sin usually attributed to Republicans and bandits. The effect of this blend of styles was to leave Pu Yi tongue-tied whenever he was expected to converse in English. A short man with a pallid complexion, twinkling eyes, and unusually large ears, Woodhead put Pu Yi in mind of the White Rabbit in *Alice in Wonderland*; and when, with a twitch of his nose, Woodhead produced from his waistcoat pocket a large watch which he consulted, furtively, the picture of the White Rabbit was complete. Although he used such difficult words, Pu Yi found him much less frightening than he had imagined him to be. Within a year of their first meeting at the Chang Garden, Woodhead was able to boast that he was 'on intimate terms with His Imperial Majesty', The Empress, however, remained an enigma.

It must have eased the pain of Johnston's exile in Weihaiwei to know that so worthy a person as Woodhead was keeping an eye on his young fledgling. H.G.W. Woodhead, Commander of the British Empire, and Chevalier of the Order of Leopold II, was born in England in 1883. He came to China in 1901, the year after the Boxer rising and the beginning of the 'Golden Age' for foreign settlers in China. After working as a reporter on a Shanghai paper, he was appointed editor of *The Peking and Tientsin Times* in 1914. He also found time to edit an annual reference work, *The China Year Book*, which had the reputation of being the last word on Chinese affairs in the English-speaking world. Like 'Morrison of China', whom he greatly admired, Woodhead had championed the allied cause against Germany in the 1914-18 war. Week after week, from his office in Victoria Road, Tientsin, he urged the allied troops to fight on to the finish in the mud of Flanders. The militant editor was forced to fight a battle on his home front in Tientsin as well, for the British there were unenthusiastic about the war. The British and the Germans had fought side by side against the Boxers. Many British families lived, as did Woodhead himself, in the attractive residential quarter of the German concession, and they sent their children to German boarding-schools in Shantung province. Sitting with their German friends in Kiessling and Bader's café in Kaiser Wilhelm Strasse, far from the battlefield of Flanders, the British found the war unreal. They had so much in common with the Germans. After all, was not Kaiser Wilhelm, whose statue stood near the café, the grandson of Queen Victoria?

Against that lethargy, Woodhead waged a war of attrition in his editorials. He succeeded at last in getting his fellow-Britons to subscribe to the cost of an ambulance which served on the Western Front. For his tireless propaganda campaign,

Woodhead was made a CBE by the King of England, and a Chevalier by the Belgians. Woodhead now spoke with such authority on Chinese affairs that people no longer took much notice of the carefully worded pronouncements that came from the British consulate. It was Woodhead they listened to. When Japan seized the German occupied ports in Shantung province and refused to give them up to China, Woodhead defended her action. He believed, with Morrison, that the Japanese accepted the leading role of the British Empire and were willing to serve as a kind of police force to defend British interests in China. 'Japan, our trusted ally, is the Keeper of the Peace in the Far East,' Woodhead told his readers. 'What matters is that our Concessions are defended against any attempt to regain them by the Chinese. Japan can be counted on to do that.'

The war in Europe over, Woodhead was free to wage other crusades. The British Empire was his religion, and Empire brought with it responsibilities. If he had one creed, it was summed up in these words: 'Be a commercial crusader.' They were taken from the speech by the victorious Lord Elgin to the British merchants after the capture of Tientsin in 1860. How can we claim to be commercial crusaders if we allow gross injustices to go on in our concessions? Woodhead would rail in his paper.

The *Peking and Tientsin Times* ran a campaign against the employment of child slaves in the metal working sheds and carpet factories in the foreign concessions. These young boys were sold by peasants to the factory owners, the paper claimed. The boys lived in the same airless sheds where they worked. If a boy was maimed in an accident, he was thrown into the street and left to join one of the bands of professional beggars. The many British-owned import and export companies in Tientsin profited from that slave labour, Woodhead said, and he challenged the companies' directors to visit the factories and see for themselves the wretched condition of the child slaves.

Woodhead's paper also ran campaigns against the export of coolies in horrific conditions from Weihaiwei, and the spread of opium dens in Tientsin, many of which were owned by war-lords. Tientsin had become the vice centre of Asia, Woodhead claimed. Each year thousands of Chinese and Korean girls were sold into prostitution in the concessions. The *Peking and Tientsin Times* quoted the director of the Pasteur Institute, who said that the epidemic of syphilis among foreign troops in Tientsin was out of control. The American authorities admitted that the rate of venereal diseases among their soldiers in Tientsin was higher than in any other part of the world. It pained Woodhead to have to report that every Friday night there were disgraceful scenes in the British concession when the foreign soldiers, who looked so smart on their parade-grounds, were reduced to a drunken rabble fighting outside the brothels in Dublin Road.

During his investigations into the opium in Tientsin Woodhead discovered that the war-lords who had obtained money from Pu Yi in exchange for promises to fight for the restoration of the Ching dynasty were among the biggest opium-dealers and brothel-owners. Woodhead interviewed the grand guardian at the Chang Garden, and he confessed that he had been unable to contact any of the paid war-lords for a long time. It seemed unlikely that they had spent a copper of Pu Yi's money on equipping their troops.

CHAPTER SIX

THE SHOP OF CLAY FIGURES

The British consul-general and his wife received their guests in the garden of their home on the corner of Racecourse Road and Meadows Road. Like All Saints' Church across the road, the consul's grey brick house was modelled on Gordon Hall. A crenellated tower gave it the appearance of a fort. The spacious garden was darkened by the many tall bushes of rhododendrons which a former consul had imported from India. Near a herbaceous border the regimental band of the Loyals was playing a selection from the stately 'Henry VIII Dances'. Intended as a compliment to 'Henry' Pu Yi, this choice of music was the idea of Ogden, the consulate secretary. A graduate of Oxford University where he had obtained a PhD in oriental studies, the secretary liked to be addressed as Dr Ogden. Although it was not one of his official duties, he spent most of his time acting as aide-de-camp to the consul's wife. He did not get on with Johnston, who thought that the young secretary was too full of himself.

The consul's wife, with Dr Ogden in attendance, walked among her guests. She approached Mr Hume, the headmaster of the British school, who was standing with some members of his staff. 'Isn't it splendid?' she cried. 'People in Shanghai and Peking have always looked down on our little river port. And now we have the Emperor himself!'

129

'Yes, perfectly splendid,' said Mr Hume, who received a patronizing smile from Dr Ogden for his correct answer.

The consul's wife was talking to Mr Shigera, the Japanese consul, and Woodhead of *The Peking and Tientsin Times*, when two black cars containing Pu Yi and his entourage arrived. The crowd of beggars at the gate surged foward, and the police had to push them back as Pu Yi, Johnston and the Empress left their cars and walked up the garden path. Behind them, a lady in waiting and a page-boy struggled with the six Pekinese whose leads kept getting entangled. Some stray dogs in Meadows Road came running up, and the Pekinese started a yapping match with them. Johnston, who had failed to persuade Pu Yi to leave the dogs at home, was not in the best of humours. His humour did not improve when he heard the band strike up 'Highland Laddie'. Johnston was in no doubt that the number had been selected for his benefit by the impudent Ogden.

When Johnston had introduced Pu Yi and his Empress, the imperial party began their procession through the garden, which was thronged with guests. Dr Ogden, acting as equerry, led the way. Then came the imperial couple with the consul's wife. After them walked the consul, Johnston and Woodhead.

'Have you heard the latest news?' Woodhead asked his companions. 'Feng Yu-hsiang the "Red Christian" has just pulled his army out of Peking.'

There was a moment or two of awkward silence. Johnston tried to appear unruffled. He knew what the others must be thinking. With the 'Red Christian' out of Peking, the whole point of the Emperor's great escape had vanished. 'I wouldn't trust the "Red Christian" to stay away,' he said lamely.

Captain O'Riordan and Inspector Dan Kellaher strolled along the garden path behind the imperial party. Ahead of them a sturdy figure in a grey suit walked with the rolling gait of a sailor.

'Mino,' said Kellaher. 'He's never far from Pu Yi. I'd hate to fight him. He's a judo expert.'

'Don't forget, Dan,' said the captain, 'he's more than just a secret agent or a major in the army. He reports to Colonel

130

Doihara, head of the Japanese secret police in Manchuria and a member of the Black Dragon Society. They're dedicated to restoring the Ching dynasty in Manchuria as part of the Japanese Empire. That's a political matter and no concern of ours. We've got a job to do here, to protect Pu Yi when he's in our concession. I wish you'd get on better with the Japs, Dan. It would make life so much easier.'

'Do we take orders from Doihara?' asked Kellaher.

'Well, let's put it this way,' said the captain. 'Although he's rarely in Tientsin, he's a member of our watch committee, so we must work with him.'

'Will Pu Yi go off to Japan, do you think? There was talk of it a short while ago.'

'No, not yet. I think they'll wait and see how his brother Pu Chieh gets on. He and another Manchu prince have a Japanese tutor here, Takeo, a member of the Black Dragon Society. The plan is that Pu Chieh will go to the military academy in Tokyo. There's a complication, however. The Japanese diplomats are at loggerheads with their military high command. The diplomats don't think Pu Yi should leave this country. Shigera believes that Pu Yi should have stayed in Peking in peaceful retirement.'

'I gather Semenov is in town. One of my men saw him in the Russian concession,' said Kellaher.

'I don't think he'll bother us,' said the captain. 'The Japs will keep an eye on him. They know all about him. He does some work for the Black Dragon Society in Manchuria.'

The procession stopped by the band, and the consul asked Pu Yi if he would like to make a request for some music.

'March of the ants,' said Pu Yi in his best English.

The consul and the bandmaster were baffled. Johnston came to the rescue. He stepped forward and whispered to the bandmaster, who saluted, turned to his band and gave them some hasty instructions. They began to play:

> It's a long way to Tipperary,
> It's a long way to go. . . .

For the first time that afternoon Pu Yi looked animated.

At last the procession reached the gate, and farewells were exchanged. Kellaher found himself standing close to the Empress. She looked thin and pale; her eyes had dark shadows under them. He was touched by her beauty. Perhaps it was the high cheek-bones and the sad expression about her mouth. He could not tell. But he felt there was a disembodied, almost spiritual, quality about her beauty, as if it did not belong to her alone, but to all Chinese women.

When Kellaher walked away down Meadows Road, her face kept coming back to him, and with it a line of the Irish poet, Yeats. It was the only line of poetry he knew by heart: 'Eternal beauty wandering on her way.'

One half of the young man's face smiled; the other half was twisted in a sinister leer. Swiftly, the fingers moulded the wet clay: a black skull-cap, tinted spectacles, a black Manchu gown, a thin yellow cane, and the six-inch figure was done. The old hunchback sat on his heels and grinned up at Kellaher.

'Two minutes. You haven't lost your speed,' said Kellaher.

'You won't arrest me for this?' said the hunchback. The other *ni ren* makers, working beside him, laughed. *Ni ren*, which meant 'mud men' was their name for the little figures made out of different coloured clay mixed with water. People asked for what they wanted, an opera singer, mandarin or warrior; and within two or three minutes the figure would be finished. Zhao, the eighty-year-old hunchback, was the best of them all. He was especially good at making foreign soldiers. He would watch them parading in the streets, and in no time he could produce a lifelike figure of the commanding officer. Sometimes he got into trouble with the police over his caricatures. A figure of General Gordon wearing the imperial yellow waistcoat, a sign that he was a lackey of the Manchus, had led to the hunchback being banned from the market-place for a year.

'I'm sure you have more wicked figures of Pu Yi hidden in your Taku Road shop,' said Kellaher with a smile.

'Only this one,' The hunchback reached into a cloth bag and pulled out the figure of a child. Its face was impassive. The

132

eyes were slits. Under the yellow imperial robes its arms and legs were stretched out stiffly. 'They didn't invite the chief eunuch to the reception for Pu Yi yesterday,' said the hunchback. 'That was a pity. I should like to make a new figure of him.'

Kellaher frowned and cupped a hand over his mouth in embarrassment. He knew what the last remark meant. All over the concession the police were being ridiculed for not taking action over the concubine's murder. He himself was still in two minds about whether to resign from the force.

'You have come about the *Tokiwa Maru*?' the hunchback said. 'Nobody here, not even the story-tellers, can tell you anything about it. Can't the Wild One help you?' The Wild One was his nickname for Mad Mac, the piano-tuner.

'I'll try him,' Kellaher said with a sigh. The Japs would soon be pressing for action, he thought. But he could see that the raid on the *Tokiwa Maru* was going to be another insoluble case. During the consul-general's reception for Pu Yi, pirates had boarded the *Tokiwa Maru*, which was anchored off the British bund. They kidnapped the captain and four other Japanese, and took them in a sampan down a creek. Once they reached the network inhabited by the nomadic boat people, pursuit was hopeless. Whoever carried out the raid must have known the river and the creeks well. It was probably the work of the Society for Men of Rivers and Lakes, whose motto was 'Kill the rich, help the poor'. The society was made up of men who had been thrown out of work when the steamships came to the Sea River and the Grand Canal. There were reports that they had joined forces with the White Lotus. If that were true, it was ominous news indeed.

As Kellaher walked away across the market-place the hunchback called out, 'Try the Fool, but you will have to be quick to catch what he is saying.' The *ni ren* makers laughed.

In the middle of the packed square a cart pulled by a mule had come to a standstill, and the shouts of the carter mingled with the cries of the stallkeepers and pedlars calling out their wares. The air was thick with the smells of aniseed, garlic, soya and different oils. At the far side of the market-place was the high back wall of the old imperial granary. Although it was

133

now owned by various merchants, it still stored the rice which came up from the south of China. Kellaher noticed that someone had daubed on the wall in white paint the Chinese characters for the old slogan 'Restore the Ming'. In front of the granary wall the acrobats, story-tellers and conjurers performed. Many of them were intinerants. Travelling along the Grand Canal, they would break their journey to entertain the crowds at the main stopping-places. In the spring they would reach Tientsin. By November, when the river and the canal began to freeze, they would be on their way south again.

One of the story-tellers was known as the Fool because he spoke little, but mostly mimed his story. He came from a family who had passed down the art of reciting the ancient serial 'Outlaws of the Marshland' from father to son for several generations. The Fool performed on a small wooden platform which was pushed against the granary wall. He had a thick bamboo staff which he whirled and slashed about him as if it were a sword. Although he was lame in one leg, he would leap and fall on his platform like an acrobat.

When Kellaher reached the crowd standing around the Fool, he had just finished his performance, but the crowd refused to let him go. 'The hermit!' they cried, throwing coppers onto the platform. Kellaher saw Mad Mac standing among some coolies at the edge of the crowd.

The Fool opened a cotton shoulder-bag in which he kept his costumes. First he dressed in the flowing robes of a Buddhist monk, and walked up and down with a mincing step while he rattled his beads. Now and again he halted and, drawing a begging-bowl from inside his wide sleeve, he held it out for alms. Next he became a Confucian scholar, and strutted about in a tall square-topped hat and gown. Full of pomp, he unfurled a long scroll and muttered as he read it. Both these characters made the crowd laugh with delight. Then, sweeping off the hat and gown, and wearing only the rags of a peasant, the Fool seized his staff and pretended he was climbing a mountain. The crowd continued to laugh. Suddenly the Taoist hermit turned and made a menacing lunge; the bamboo staff had become a spear! There was complete silence. Even the stallholders, who must have seen this performance many times, stopped their cries and watched. Fear, excitement and anarchy were in the air.

More coppers were showered on the platform. The Fool stopped to pick them up. Then he limped away.

Kellaher went up to Mad Mac. 'Magic,' he said. 'Not so long ago he would have been beheaded for that in the Native City.'

Mad Mac laughed. 'He's a difficult man to catch. I saw the police trying to arrest him once. The crowd surrounded him and helped him to slip away.'

Kellaher and Mad Mac looked an oddly contrasting pair as they left the market-place together. Kellaher, a tall, dark Irishman from Cork, might have been mistaken for a Spaniard. Mad Mac was short, freckled, and bald except for a fringe of red hair about his ears. He came from the Western Highlands of Scotland. When he was a young boy, his family were evicted from their croft. Mad Mac made his way to Australia and then the west coast of America before crossing the Pacific Ocean to finish up in Tientsin. He became a travelling piano-tuner for Robinson's Piano Company in Victoria Road and was often sent to work in the country west of Peking, deep in the Interior, where he tuned the pianos of missionaries and war-lords. He was given his nickname because he was considered to have gone native. He could speak three Chinese dialects and would disappear for months on end in the countryside, where few foreigners ventured. When in Tientsin he lived in the back room of a Chinese shop in Taku Road.

They walked down the narrow, dusty Taku Road which smelled of horse manure and was thronged with mule-drawn carts and coolies swaying under the loads on their shoulder-poles. This old dirt road ran from the Native City through the Japanese, French and British concessions, and on to the estuary and mud-flats of Taku, forty miles to the east. On their left, Kellaher and Mad Mac passed the side entrance of Gordon Hall. Inside it were the law court and police station. They came to the iron railings of Victoria Park; over them they could see across the park to the Astor House Hotel, the Tientsin Club, and Whiteway & Laidlaw, the gentlemen's outfitters. On their right, the road was lined with godowns and many small Chinese shops. A Russian beggar in rags, and holding a tin mug, sat outside the old clothes shop run by Bogol, the Siberian Jew. A little farther on, they turned into the narrow doorway of a Chinese shop. The walls of the front room were lined with shelves, on which stood hundreds of small clay figures.

Mad Mac led the way to the small back room. 'We are expected,' he said, pointing to a jug of wine and three bowls on the table. On the wall hung an ink and water-colour sketch of a marshland scene with rushes and pools of water. The back door was open, and they could hear chickens clucking in the yard. A girl came in and greeted them. She was about twenty and wore a white shirt over her trousers. Unlike most Tientsin women, her feet were not bound. She must be of the boat people, thought Kellaher. 'He will come soon,' the girl said. She poured a bowl of rice wine for Mad Mac, and then waited beside Kellaher. He understood her gesture; there was an agreed code in the Taku Road district. If he accepted the wine, his visit would be deemed unofficial, and everything which was said in that room would be held in strict confidence. But if he refused the wine, he was at liberty to report what he pleased. Kellaher nodded, and the girl filled his bowl.

'Did you see that slogan on the granary wall?' asked Kellaher — '''Restore the Ming''. I wasn't sure whether to take it seriously or not.'

'It's the signature of the White Lotus,' said Mad Mac. 'I suppose you realize that it doesn't mean restore the dynasty, but only the first of the Mings, the one who refused to be emperor. He was the peasant leader of the White Lotus who brought down the Mongol Empire and tried to do away with the army of officials. Ming means light, and ''Restore the Ming'' really means bring back the springtime before the empires when the peasants were free from imperial soldiers, salt tax-collectors, grain tax-collectors, scholar-officials, magistrates, governors, the whole deadweight of the civil service. The officials have always been alarmed at the word ''Light''. During the last dynasty a poet was beheaded because of a line in one of his poems: ''Tomorrow at dawn I

136

shall enter the bright capital.'' The magistrate said it was a threat to the Forbidden City. You've been to Peking, Dan, and seen the massive wall around the Forbidden City, built to keep out the avenging peasants of the White Lotus. The walls around all the big towns in China were put up as defences against Chinese peasants, not against foreign invaders.'

The hunchback appeared in the doorway. 'The Wild One should have been a story-teller,' he said with a chuckle.

'It's the wine,' said Mad Mac.

The hunchback filled their bowls and sat on the bench beside Kellaher. 'There is one wall which was not built to keep the peasants out,' said the hunchback. 'The Great Wall of China. The official guides tell the visitors that it was built to keep out the barbarian invaders, but they don't tell them that the first of the emperors, the tyrant called Chin, had the wall built to stop the peasants leaving China for the steppe lands of the Interior. He couldn't afford to lose their skills, and he was afraid they might join the barbarians and return to destroy him.'

'Nor do the guides mention the price that was paid for the Great Wall,' said Mad Mac. 'The Emperor's soldiers rounded up masses of peasants and forced them to work on the wall. Few of them returned home. They were blinded by the sandstorms and frozen by the winter winds from the Gobi. Countless thousands died. Those who fell ill were buried alive in the foundations of the wall. When you stand on it, you stand on a tomb.'

'The first emperor,' said Kellaher, 'I've seen your puppet play about him.'

'Come,' said the hunchback, and led the way into the front room. On a shelf in the corner was a group of figures. In the centre was the hideous Chin in the imperial robes of yellow. On his right were Li Ssu, his grand councillor, and other officials wearing the tall hats of ministers. On his left were groups of eunuchs and concubines. Behind him were the imperial chariot and rows of soldiers.

'These figures were the models for the puppets in my play,' said the hunchback. He began to recite the play's opening lines: 'The Chin dynasty was without the True Way. It made the several dukedoms into one empire by treachery, intrigue and naked force. It burdened the people with taxation and exhausted their strength. Greed and vice came into being. The powerful counted their fields in thousands, while the weak had not even the space in which to insert the point of an awl. . . .'

As Kellaher listened, the figures came to life as they had done in the play. The grand councillor whispered in Chin's ear, 'You are the sacred Yellow Emperor, the Son of Heaven, and your reign will last for ever.' The other officials clustered round. Chin listened to them, and ordered all the books in the Empire to be burned. Police were posted at town gates, passports were issued to the citizens, officials were stationed throughout the Empire to do the Emperor's bidding. For all his power, the Emperor dreaded that his peasants might assassinate him. Each night his chariot carried him to a different palace. He fell ill and died. The grand councillor and the other officials kept his death a secret. They propped up his corpse in the chariot and surrounded it with rotting fish to keep up the pretence that the Son of Heaven was alive. . . . The hunchback spoke the closing lines. 'When at length, Chin was buried, his concubines were buried alive in his tomb. He left behind the system of officials which has continued to govern China to this day. Scholars of all nations praise him as the great unifier and upholder of the laws. The peasants curse him as the cruel tyrant who enslaved them.'

'Will you make a play about the last emperor?' asked Kellaher.

The hunchback laughed. 'The officials would still behave in the same way. I would have to put some foreigners in it. Perhaps after the Emperor dies.'

They went back to sit at the table. 'Do you think that Pu Yi's life is in danger?' asked Kellaher.

'Not from the White Lotus, if that is what you are thinking,' said the hunchback. 'After all, the legitimate heir to the Ching dynasty, Pu Lun, is living at his father's house in Peking, and they haven't even got a guard at their gate. If Pu Yi is in danger from anyone, then it is the Japanese military command. They want to use him, they care nothing for his life. And that goes for all the mercenaries who are flocking to the Chang Garden with promises to restore the "Great Ching" dynasty. They will turn against Pu Yi the moment it suits them. At present the foreign newspapers are all for Pu Yi, just as they were for Yuan Shih-kai, who took Pu Yi's throne from him. Watch them change their tune.'

'What of the Empress?' asked Kellaher.

'Beautiful Countenance? She will be destroyed,' the hunchback said. There was an unexpected tone of sympathy in his voice. 'She is too independent to be anyone's tool. At the same time, she is too honourable to desert Pu Yi.' He turned to Mad Mac. 'Your friend is a strange one to be a policeman. He cares more about people than laws.'

Mad Mac chuckled. 'It didn't take you long to see through him. He's an Irish barbarian.'

As he got up to go, Kellaher looked again at the picture on the wall. This time he saw something he had not noticed before. At the foot of the rushes, skilfully concealed by the artist's brush strokes, was a nest, guarded by a pair of wild geese.

Kellaher walked down Taku Road in the hot sunshine. He looked at his watch and was surprised to find that it was already three o'clock in the afternoon. Talking to Chinese like the hunchback always gave him a feeling of timelessness. Was there anywhere else in the world, he wondered, where one could discuss the events of 2,000 years ago as if they had happened only yesterday?

At the corner of Taku Road and Meadows Road he came to the chief eunuch's mansion, and tried hard not to think of that murderous villain gloating behind his high walls. Kellaher crossed over into Racecourse Road and walked by the consul's house. The stray dog van was parked outside All Saints' Church, and coolies carrying long poles with wire hoops on the ends were patrolling the street on the look-out for rabid dogs. After passing D'Arc's Hotel he reached the Empire Cinema. The poster outside advertised Charlie Chaplin in *The Gold Rush*. Just beyond the cinema the Empire Bridge spanned a creek that linked the Sea River to the Grand Canal. The creek bordered Dublin Road, the main brothel area. Kellaher stood on the bridge, looking down the creek and the row of small houses and bars. Many of the brothels were also opium dens. The nearest one to the bridge was called Fragrant Inn. A woman dressed in a kimono was sitting on the small veranda, knitting. She looked like a Korean, thought Kellaher. Recently the Japanese had exported hundreds of Korean women to Tientsin to work as prostitutes. Many had found their way to the British concession. The fruity voice of a crooner came from a gramophone on the veranda:

> 'O give me a home where the buffalo roam
> And the deer and the antelope play. . . .'

Dublin Road looked peaceful enough now, Kellaher thought, but by eight o'clock in the evening all its verandas would be filled with women ogling the troops in the street below. Then the fighting would begin; the British, Italians and others against the much better paid American marines. A tall, slender Chinese woman walked out of the front door of the Fragrant Inn and got into a waiting rickshaw. Something about her manner, a touch of elegance about her dress, caught Kellaher's eye. The Empress! Was it possible? He watched the rickshaw disappearing down Dublin Road, and wondered if the rice wine and the heat of the June sunshine had affected him.

One day, people walking in Romanov Avenue in the Russian concession were forced to leap for their lives when a large open car, with its headlights on and its horn blaring, raced at high speed down the avenue. Men in leather overcoats, brandishing revolvers, stood on the car's running-boards. In the rear seat, half hidden by his bodyguard, a Cossack general leaned back, smoking a cigar. Semenov, the Ogre of Chita, had arrived in Tientsin. At the bund, the car turned right and roared at high speed through the Italian concession, and across the Austrian bridge to the south side of the river. On it sped, through the French and Japanese concessions, until it stopped with a screech of brakes outside the Chang Garden.

Semenov was shown into the throne-room, where Pu Yi

was expecting him. He had come, he announced with all his bravado, to offer Pu Yi his private army to restore the 'Great Ching' dynasty which the Bolsheviks had destroyed. All the foreign military commanders in China regarded his gallant Cossacks as the spearhead in the fight against the Reds, he declared.

So eager were the grand guardian and the three other members of Pu Yi's inner cabinet to accept the services of the Cossacks, that they advised Pu Yi to pay Semenov a first instalment of 50,000 dollars for his services there and then. Seldom can Semenov have had so easy a picking.

Three times Semenov visited the Chang Garden, but the police did nothing to stop him and his gangsters as their car roared through the Russian, Italian, French and Japanese concessions at a recklessly high speed. Each time he came and went he was carefully watched by Major Mino of the Japanese secret service. On the last visit a formal pact was signed by Pu Yi and Semenov. It was called the Sino-Russian Anti-Bolshevik Convention.

Pu Yi was jubilant. His ministers congratulated him. He was now one of the world's leaders in the crusade against the Reds, they told him. Johnston was bound to be pleased.

As more and more war-lords offered to fight for his cause, Pu Yi's treasury began to run short of money. It was a welcome change, therefore, when the great war-lord from Manchuria, Chang Tso-lin, not only pledged his support for Pu Yi, but sent him a donation of 100,000 dollars. The marshal, as Chang Tso-lin now styled himself, invited Pu Yi to his residence in Tientsin's Native city. There, in complete secrecy, they could discuss the final plans for the restoration of the Ching dynasty.

The marshal's army was based in the south Manchurian railway town of Mukden, once the capital of the Manchus. Trains were as vital to the war-lords as horses had been to the Mongols, and control of railway junctions such as Mukden and Tientsin was an important element in their strategy. Several of the major war-lords had private trains in which they and their concubines travelled. The British-backed General Wu Pei-fu had a grand piano in his train. Mad Mac had been

141

out many times to tune it for the White Russian pianist who entertained General Wu and his concubines after dinner. But the marshal had the best train of all. Not only was it lavishly furnished, it was armour-plated.

The marshal had become increasingly independent of his former masters, the Japanese high command. He had annoyed them by denouncing Pu Yi's escape from Peking and Johnston's part in it, claiming that he had acted in collusion with the Japanese secret service. Some of the marshal's divisions were deployed around Peking, and their presence had led to the withdrawal of the Red Christian's forces. The Japanese were aware that the veteran marshal had come under the influence of his son, Chang Hsueh-liang, a young general with strong anti-Japanese feelings.

Late one night Pu Yi and the grand guardian slipped out of the Chang Garden. The marshal's car was waiting. They drove to the Native City, which bordered the west side of the Japanese concession. Unknown to Pu Yi, they were followed by a car containing Colonel Doihara and Major Mino.

In the courtyard of the marshal's house a guard of honour saluted Pu Yi. Inside the entrance hall the marshal knelt and kowtowed to his Emperor. To his surprise, Pu Yi found that the marshal was not the fierce warrior he had been expecting, but a thin, dapper little man with a moustache, and dressed in a smart foreign suit. He looked just like Adolphe Menjou, one of Pu Yi's favourite film stars who sometimes played the part of a hotel manager. The marshal put forward his plan. The old Manchu Palace Museum at Mukden would be restored as a palace and Pu Yi would be enthroned there. He would have the full protection of the marshal's army. When the time was ripe, Pu Yi would return to the Forbidden City. The grand guardian promised that His Imperial Majesty would consider the proposal.

Pleased with the way the meeting had gone, the marshal escorted Pu Yi to his car. The black reptilian eyes of Doihara watched from the shadows of the courtyard. He heard the marshal's last words to Pu Yi: 'You must not let the Japanese bully you. If they give you any trouble, let me know in Mukden. I shall be returning there soon.'

A week later the marshal left Tientsin in his armour-plated train. It was approaching Mukden station when there was a huge explosion and the marshal was destroyed, together with his train. The *Far Eastern Times* accused the Japanese secret service of assassinating the marshal. The *Peking and Tientsin Times* suspended judgement. General Tanaka, who had recently come to power in Japan, announced that his 'Army of pacification' would do all they could to find the marshal's killers.

After the loss of their commander some of the marshal's regiments stationed near Peking went on the rampage, looting villages in the countryside. Ninety miles north-east of Peking, in a pine forest surrounded by hills, were the eastern tombs of the Ching emperors and empresses. Among those buried there were the great Chien Lung and the Venerable Buddha. Using dynamite, the soldiers broke into their tombs and began to ransack them. Republican troops, who were responsible for guarding the tombs, arrived on the scene, drove off the marshal's soldiers, and took over the looting themselves.

When news of the desecration reached Peking, a group of Manchu nobles hurried to the tombs. When they entered that of the Venerable Buddha, they found it stripped bare. Gone were her gold and silver incense burners, her precious jade ornaments, and the jewelled couch on which her coffin had stood. The coffin had been smashed to pieces. Under one of its planks the naked body of the Venerable Buddha was lying face downwards. Gently, they turned the body on its back. 'The complexion of the face was wonderfully pale,' they later reported. 'But the eyes were deeply sunken, and seemed like two black caverns.'

The Venerable Buddha's tomb and its magnificent treasures had cost the state 8 million dollars, a bill which was paid for largely by an extra grain tax on the peasants of northern China. Now those treasures were swiftly passed through the shops of Peking to the dealers in Shanghai and Hong Kong. Long before the Venerable Buddha's black, cavernous eyes had turned to dust, the jewels which were meant to grace her resting-place were being bought and sold in the auction-rooms and shops of the world.

As soon as he heard the terrible news of the violation of the imperial tombs, Johnston took the first steamer from Weihaiwei to Tientsin. He arrived at the Chang garden to find it had become a place of pilgrimage for past officials and their families who had come to mourn the Venerable Buddha. A long line of these Ching supporters stretched through the garden, up the steps, and into the entrance hall, where they waited their turn to enter the throne-room. The grand guardian, bowing like a monk, ushered Johnston into the dimly lit throne-room. It had been converted into a temple. On an altar, surrounded by burning incense, the two ancestral tablets of Chien Lung and the Venerable Buddha had been erected. People knelt before them, praying. As Johnston approached the alter he saw to his horror two eunuchs of the presence in bright scarlet jackets standing by it. He knew both their faces. One of the eunuchs, who used to be on duty in the schoolroom of the Palace of Mind Nurture, smiled at Johnston. Furious, Johnston turned to the grand guardian. 'These eunuchs,' he said. 'They were expelled from the Imperial Palace. What are they doing here?'

The grand guardian put his finger to his lips. Johnston demanded to see Pu Yi. The grand guardian took him to a small study adjoining the throne-room. Pu Yi smiled wanly and held out a limp hand. When Johnston had greeted Pu Yi and expressed his condolences, he asked about the eunuchs, but Pu Yi would only look down at the floor sadly. 'His Imperial Majesty is in mourning,' the grand guardian explained.

'How long will the mourning go on for?' demanded Johnston.

'The state mourning and the funeral services in the throne-room are to continue until the eastern tombs have been repaired,' said the grand guardian.

On the second day of his visit to the Chang Garden Johnston found a different Pu Yi. The Emperor was in a rage. He had heard that some of the jewels from the Venerable Buddha's tomb had found their way into the possession of Chiang Kai-shek, head of the Nationalist government in Nanking. 'Those pearls on the Venerable Buddha's phoenix

1. *Prince Chun, father of Pu Yi.*

2. The treacherous General Yuan Shih-kai.

3. The Empress Dowager, Tzu Hsi (Motherly and Auspicious), with attendants at the Palace of Tranquil Old Age, in the Forbidden City, 1903. On the far right is the Empress Honorific Abundance (Lung Yu).

4. *Pu Yi, aged about 10 or 11, in the Forbidden City.*

5. *Pu Yi, dressed for a ball at the Astor House Hotel, Tientsin, c. 1927.*

6. *Pu Yi and the Empress Beautiful Countenance by the steps of the Chang Garden, Tientsin. Reginald Johnston is on the far right, third row. H.G.W. Woodhead is second from left, fourth row, and immediately below him is Nona Ransom.*

7. *The tragic Empress, Beautiful Countenance (Wan Jung): the sixteen-year-old bride in ceremonial dress, 1922.*

8. *Elegant Ornament (Wen Hsiu), secondary consort, divorced by Pu Yi after fleeing from the Chang Garden.*

9. *The Emperor as prisoner: Pu Yi in the Fushun detention centre for war criminals, 1956.*

10. *The Emperor remoulded as model cadre: Pu Yi with his new citizen wife, Li Shu-hsien.*

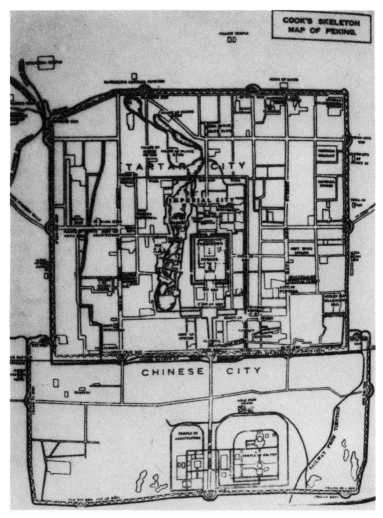

11. Thomas Cook's Plan of Peking, c. 1900 showing the sinister labyrinth of the Forbidden City.

crown,' Pu Yi cried out to Johnston, 'they have been fixed on to Madame Chiang Kai-shek's shoes!' Johnston had never seen Pu Yi so angry. He knew that Pu Yi had a passion for jewellery, especially pearls, and that he hated being parted from a single one of them, but he had not expected this violent reaction while the court was in solemn mourning. Johnston did his best to console his fledgling. He promised to get in touch with Colonel Doihara. If Chiang Kai-shek had any of the jewels, said Johnston, Doihara would be sure to recover them.

Johnston himself was feeling touchy on the subject of the imperial jewels. The *Far Eastern Times* had published a scathing attack on him for his part in removing many packages of jewels and other treasures from the Imperial Palace in the weeks before Pu Yi's departure from the Forbidden City. The paper supported Chiang Kai-shek's view that the palace treasures were not Pu Yi's personal property but belonged to the nation.

General Chiang Kai-shek, the southerner and leader of the nationalist government, had recently married the beautiful Soong Mei-ling. Both he and his wife, who had been educated in America, were ardent Republicans. A Christian who always carried his Bible into battle, Chiang Kai-shek was being hailed by some missionaries as another 'Cromwell of China'. Johnston regarded him as an even greater menace than the Red Christian, Feng Yu-hsiang. The Red Christian was a Bolshevik idealist, but Chiang Kai-shek was dangerously practical, and had declared it as his objective to abolish the foreign concessions, which he saw as an affront to Chinese pride.

In 1927 a Republican mob stormed the British concession in Hankow and destroyed the British war memorial and the Customs House. Within a month the British municipal council was dissolved, and the concession was meekly handed over to the Nationalist government. There was alarm in Tientsin. What was to prevent the same thing happening there? people asked. Woodhead rallied the faint-hearted. The principle of extra-territoriality was at stake, he declared in a leading article. That principle, enshrined in the Treaty of Tientsin, gave foreign powers the right to administer their concessions without interference from the Chinese, he reminded his readers. They must stand up to the Nationalists.

Encouraged by the events in Hankow, Chiang Kai-shek led his army northwards. Some of his troops actually entered the Native City in Tientsin, but they did not remain there long. The Japanese high command considered that northern China was their sphere of influence. They issued an ultimatum to Chiang Kai-shek. Either he withdrew or the 'Army of Pacification' would destroy him. Chiang Kai-shek withdrew to Nanking. There was rejoicing in the Tientsin Club, but it was somewhat tempered when, within a short time of Chiang Kai-shek's retreat, all the foreign powers, including Japan, followed America's lead and gave their official recognition to his Nationalist government.

In Johnston's view, the universal recognition of this second 'Cromwell of China' was a betrayal of the 'Great Ching' dynasty and of all that those early British settlers, the old China hands, stood for. It was, of course, the fault of the Americans and their anti-colonial policy. He was able to derive some consolation from the fact that although the new capital was Nanking, Britain kept her minister and his staff hundreds of miles away in Peking. Undaunted, Johnston would carry on his single-handed rearguard action to delay for as long as possible the surrender of the British naval base at Weihaiwei. It was time for him to return there.

Johnston was waiting in the entrance hall of the Chang Garden to say goodbye to Pu Yi when he heard a commotion on the first-floor landing. Elegant Ornament, Pu Yi's plump young concubine, came rushing down the staircase, followed by the two eunuchs of the presence. After them came Pu Yi. Screaming 'No! No! Take them away' the concubine, her hair dishevelled, fled through the front door with the eunuchs after her. The grand guardian and some mourners came out of the throne-room to see what was the matter. Pu Yi, all smiles, held a glass phial in his hand. It was full of squirming ants. 'What a foolish girl that is!' he said to Johnston. 'All I did was put a king ant and six workers on her pillow as a surprise, and she ran away, screaming for help.'

Johnston was too upset by the sight of the grinning eunuchs rushing about the house to bother about the ants. He hated the thought of returning to Weihaiwei not knowing what decadent games the eunuchs and the page-boys would arrange for Pu Yi's entertainment. One of the page-boys, who acted as Pu Yi's personal attendant, seemed to have a special hold over him. The boy's lofty air annoyed Johnston, but every time he tried to bring up the subject of this boy and the eunuchs, Pu Yi would lapse into an attitude of mourning, with his sad eyes fixed to the floor. Before taking his leave, Johnston felt in duty bound to try once more. 'The eunuchs . . .' he began.

Sharp, cracking noises at the glass panes of the front door interrupted him. Just then the concubine and the eunuchs rushed back into the house. 'Locusts!' one of the eunuchs yelled. A swarm of locusts, their wings whirring, flew into the hall and thudded against the walls. 'Quick! Shut the door,' someone cried. Johnston and Pu Yi went to the door and looked out. The sky was dark. A cloud of locusts was raining down on the garden. Hundreds of them were already on the ground, squirming over each other in a vicious and silent tangle as they fought to get at the grass. The grey-brown insects went on cracking blindly at the glass panes and dropping, half-stunned, in a tangled pile on the steps.

Johnston had seen many plagues of locusts before, but this desperately fierce swarm, which seemed determined to get into the house, frightened him. He looked anxiously at his young fledgling. Pu Yi was smiling. A ghastly thought struck Johnston. Was Pu Yi going to take up locusts as well as ants? Heaven forbid!

CHAPTER SEVEN

'BONNIE PRINCE CHARLIE'

People sitting at the marble-topped tables in Kiessling and Bader's café stopped chatting. Some of them stood up and began to clap. Herr Kiessling, a fat, double-chinned man, rushed with surprising speed towards the swing-doors, followed by Herr Bader. The trio of two violinists and a cellist, seated by some potted palm trees, faltered and then broke off playing. There was a buzz of excitement. 'The Emperor,' someone said. 'The Emperor!' people repeated down the length of the café. More people stood and joined in the clapping.

'This is indeed an honour, Your Imperial Majesty,' chorused Herr Kiessling and Herr Bader as they bowed and then collided with each other in their eagerness to usher their distinguished visitors to a table. At the head of the imperial party came Pu Yi in his Prince of Wales suit with a pink carnation in the button-hole. He was followed by the secondary consort, Elegant Ornament, with a Pekinese under each arm. After them came Woodhead, who nodded condescendingly to some friends, and last of all a lady in waiting with the four Pekinese pups. Herr Kiessling clicked his fingers at the trio. Their leader was Herr Schneider, a short, pale-faced Austrian with a small moustache and sad, dark eyes. He raised the bow of his violin, bowed to his

149

colleagues, and they continued with the Viennese waltz 'Gold and Silver'.

Woodhead gave the order, hot chocolate and pastries. Herr Kiessling repeated it to the head-waiter and his assistant, who raced to the kitchen. Herr Bader, a small, bald-headed man, hovered behind Pu Yi's chair, keeping a nervous eye on the Pekinese.

Woodhead addressed Pu Yi: 'The street we are in used to be called Kaiser Wilhelm Strasse,' he said. 'After the Great War it was renamed Woodrow Wilson Street. Kiessling's has always been our most popular café, and I hope that Your Imperial Majesty . . . ' He stopped when he realized that Pu Yi was not listening to a word.

'Charlie Chaplin,' said Pu Yi.

'I beg your pardon, sir?' said Woodhead, baffled.

Pu Yi was spellbound. He had always wished to meet Charlie Chaplin, and there he was, seated only a few yards away under the palm trees, disguised as Herr Schneider. No detail of Herr Schneider's technique escaped Pu Yi. The way, for instance, he closed his eyes during the most lyrical passages, and the way he turned the sheets on his music-stand with a flourish. But Herr Schneider was at his most fascinating during the intervals. When Herr Kiessling thought that his trio were taking a little too long over their interval, he would stand beside them with his hands behind his back and click his fingers. Herr Schneider would sigh, look up to heaven, take up his bow, place a small cushion on his shoulder, settle his violin on it, and begin to tune each string with infinite care in preparation for the next waltz. It was a masterful performance, thought Pu Yi. And when Woodhead at last persuaded him that it was time to leave, Pu Yi kept looking back over his shoulder to see what Charlie Chaplin's next act was going to be.

For Pu Yi's next outing to the British concession Woodhead arranged a visit to the Empire Cinema. It could not fail to be a success, for the leader of the cinema orchestra, a quartet, was none other than Herr Schneider. Pu Yi soon became the Empire's most enthusiastic patron. The imperial party, which included the secondary consort but never the Empress, sat in the front row of the stalls so that Pu Yi could see into the orchestra pit. The performance began with an unchanging ritual. When the musicians appeared in the pit, Fräulein Kluge sounded the key note on her piano while Herr Schneider and his colleagues tuned their strings. Herr Schneider would turn and glance up at the cinema manager who stood beside the film projector at the back of the gallery. It was his signal that the orchestra was ready, the lights could be put out, and the picture might begin.

Herr Schneider never spared himself. Whether it was a forest fire scene from *Tarzan of the Apes*, or a wild western in which a Red Indian horde galloped down from the hills to attack a white settlers' camp, he played with such passionate intensity that many in the audience felt carried away and unable to tell whether the music was following the story or the story the music.

Seated a few rows behind Pu Yi, Major Mino watched with amused interest the tactics of the cowboys and Indians. Still farther back, Kellaher waited for another kind of tactics to begin. When the Siberian boys from the French school were in the gallery, there was bound to be trouble. Sooner or later a shower of paper darts would land in the orchestra pit. The music would come to an abrupt stop. The cinema manager would switch on the lights and rush to try to catch the dart throwers.

On these occasions Major Mino would jump up, looking shell-shocked. But Pu Yi was not in the least disturbed. He would gaze with admiration at the heroic orchestra leader. Even when a direct hit had been scored on him, Herr Schneider behaved like a true artist. With the violin in his left hand and the bow in his right, he would hold his arms straight out before him and look up to heaven. When the commotion subsided he would bow to the pianist, and the whole meticulous procedure of tuning the strings would begin again.

Pu Yi enjoyed the Charlie Chaplin films most of all. Herr Schneider put his heart into them. He would pluck briskly at his strings in the funny parts of the story, and draw his bow gently over them in the sad parts, until Pu Yi wondered whether the real Charlie was playing in the orchestra or appearing on the screen.

Having introduced Pu Yi to the Empire Cinema, Woodhead was now faced with the problem of keeping him away from the wretched place. The Siberian riff-raff in the gallery and the drunken soldiers with their prostitutes in the back rows of the stalls were hardly fit company for an emperor. The cinema was not very safe, either. About a year before, a war-lord had been stealthily garrotted there, even though he was with his bodyguard. Fortunately for Woodhead, the answer to his problem was already on its way across the Atlantic — the talkies. Very soon the booming sound-track of voices and recorded music banished the silent film and with it Herr Schneider and his quartet from the Empire. The cinema with its dark and empty pit lost its magic for Pu Yi.

'We must help him to broaden his interests,' Johnston had said to Woodhead, before departing for Weihaiwei. Woodhead agreed whole-heartedly. If China were ever to have a constitutional monarchy on British lines, then her emperor must receive a balanced, modern education. Woodhead foresaw a difficulty: Pu Yi seemed more interested in style than content. He took a keen interest in the Prince of Wales's clothes, for instance, but that was as far as his interest went. If only he could learn to appreciate the importance of character.

Before the coming of Pu Yi, the social column in *The Peking and Tietsin Times* used to consist of a brief paragraph or two: a report on a dinner-dance at the Astor House Hotel, perhaps, or a review of a concert at Gordon Hall. Occasionally there were notes on some of the passengers who had arrived by steamer or train, more often than not *en route* for Peking or Shanghai. Now there was a complete change. Hardly a day passed without a long column on the exiled Emperor's social engagements; sometimes an entire page, illustrated with photographs, was devoted to him.

Thanks to the privilege that Johnston had procured for him, Woodhead was in the happy position of knowing Pu Yi's programme of engagements well in advance; he often arranged the programme himself. He was besieged by appeals for information from the editors of other newspapers. The Japanese police would not allow their reporters near the Chang Garden, nor could they get through on the telephone, they complained. Could Woodhead help? Woodhead sympathized with their plight, he told them. He would see what he could do. To the editor of his former paper, the *Shanghai Daily News*, who had once described Tientsin as 'That squalid little inland river port', he granted the odd sporting fixture, such as Pu Yi's attendance at the races; to his friend Green of the *North China Daily Mail* he allowed some concert engagements; but to the radical *Far Eastern Times* he gave nothing at all. 'The interests of security did not permit him to divulge . . . ' his curt note to the editor would begin.

The *Far Eastern Times* retaliated by continually referring to the imperial family as Mr and Mrs Henry Pu Yi, a form of address that infuriated Woodhead just as it used to infuriate Johnston. But the *Far Eastern Times* had yet to play its trump card. It published the very first photograph of Pu Yi's concubine, Elegant Ornament, on a shopping spree in Victoria Road. Woodhead had always taken the view that it was ungentlemanly to allude to the existence of the imperial concubine. 'This is simply not playing the game,' he spluttered over his lunch-time gin at the Tientsin Club.

The circulation of *The Peking and Tientsin Times* shot up as its readers feasted on the latest picture of His Imperial Majesty, Pu Yi. He was shown playing golf on the Russian concession links, wearing a tweed jacket, plus-fours and flat cap. In his Prince of Wales suit he attended the ceremony of Trooping the Colour at the British barracks on the King's birthday, and he was piped on board HMS *Hollyhock* at the bund. Sometimes the pale, mask-like face of the Empress appeared in these photographs with Pu Yi. And, now and again the more observant of Woodhead's readers noticed a thickset man with a shaven head, hovering in the background.

The Tientsin Country Club, which adjoined the racecourse, had a strict rule against admitting Chinese as members. But Woodhead managed to persuade the club to admit Pu Yi as 'a special Chinese'. Woodhead also tried to make Pu Yi a member of the Tientsin Club, which overlooked

153

Victoria Park, but the members, mostly British and American businessmen, could not bring themselves to accept even 'a special Chinese' as a member. The committee did, however, suggest that Pu Yi might be the club's guest of honour at its annual dinner.

The consul-general took the chair at the dinner, with Pu Yi on his right and Woodhead on his left. Behind them, hanging over the fireplace, was a portrait of Lord Elgin. 'You must tell the Emperor about your last posting in Africa,' Woodhead said to the consul as the soup was served. It was a fatal mistake. The consul, grateful for the lead, turned to Pu Yi and began to deliver a lecture on the behaviour of the African elephant in the Kenya bush. 'The cow elephants take charge of the herd,' said the consul, 'while the bull elephants . . . '

'Have you ever seen a white ant?' asked Pu Yi, interrupting him. The astonished consul confessed that he had not.

'The white ant kings can eat their way through walls and houses,' said Pu Yi.

A strange feeling of exhaustion came over the consul. The conversation had come to a halt, but he could think of no way to revive it.

The secretary called for silence for the royal toast. The consul rose. 'Gentlemen, the King!' he said, solemnly. 'The King!' chorused the members. The band of the East Yorkshire Regiment played 'God Save the King'.

Pu Yi's mind began to wander. Woodhead proposed the toast to the guest of honour. After a few witticisms he reached the kernel of his speech. It never varied, whether he was speaking at a wedding reception, a christening or a business function. Drawing himself up to his full five feet eight inches, he declared: 'As I stand here today, I call to mind Lord Elgin's famous words, "Be a commercial crusader . . . "'

Pu Yi was far away. Seven huge white ant kings, their wings whirring, rose into the air after their queen. One by one, they mated with her and then spiralled after her to the ground. While she began laying her eggs, the kings set off into the African jungle, carving a way through anything that stood in their path.

One morning all the traffic was stopped in Victoria Road. British families lined the park railings, and the verandas of the Astor House Hotel were packed with people waiting to welcome a new regiment of British soldiers to Tientsin. A ceremonial bamboo and paper arch had been put up. It stretched from Gordon Hall across Victoria Road to Whiteway & Laidlaw, the gentlemen's outfitters. The arch was covered with strings of small Chinese crackers. Just before midday Mr Peebles, chairman of the British municipal council, came out of Gordon Hall with his guest, Pu Yi. Behind them was a group of council members. There was a ripple of excitement when people in the crowd recognized the Emperor and pointed him out to each other. In the distance the sound of bagpipes could be heard. The sound grew louder, and someone called out 'Here they come!' 'Welcome, welcome' the cry went up. The drums and pipes of the Argyll and Sutherland Highlanders in their green and black tartan kilts came into view. As they passed under the arch, the Chinese crackers blazed away angrily against the shrill sound of the bagpipes playing 'Highland Laddie'. The colonel of the Argylls roared 'Eyes right!' and lowered his sword in salute. Mr Peebles raised his top hat and then placed it over his heart in the American manner. Pu Yi clapped his hands with joy. Bonnie Prince Charlie must have felt like this when his Highlanders marched to his rescue, he thought.

Mr Laidlaw, of Whiteway & Laidlaw, smiled and bowed as Pu Yi entered his shop. He was always pleased to see his most distinguished customer, the Emperor, especially when he brought no dogs with him. An imperial Alsatian had ruined the tweed trousers on one of his tailor's dummies recently. Mr Laidlaw had preserved a discreet silence, of course, but he would shake all over when he saw Pu Yi's dogs bounding down Victoria Road, dragging their page-boy attendant after them. Mr Laidlaw hoped that His Imperial Majesty had enjoyed the welcome for the Argylls. No, Mr Laidlaw was not a Highlander, he confessed. He was from Edinburgh, but he enjoyed reading about the romantic history of the Highlands. A kilt? Mr Laidlaw looked thoughtful. Perhaps His Imperial Majesty should consult Mr Johnston about that first. Quickly changing the subject, Mr Laidlaw trusted that the tweed jacket and plus-fours had proved satisfactory. They had looked very well in the newspaper photograph, he said. An evening suit of the kind the Prince of Wales might wear? Might he be bold enough to ask if His Imperial Majesty intended wearing it at the St Andrew's Society ball? He would be honoured to make it, and would have it ready in time, Mr Laidlaw said, rubbing his hands with pleasure.

Whiteway & Laidlaw was Pu Yi's favourite shop. Sometimes he would spend as long as half an hour standing outside, just looking at the tailor's dummies, which fascinated him. He would like to buy one of them, he thought. It would look good in the entrance hall at the Chang Garden. Perhaps the dashing young man with wavy hair in the double-breasted pin-stripe suit.

'Is there anything else, Your Imperial Majesty?' asked Mr Laidlaw, as he noticed Pu Yi hesitating.

PuYi pointed to the dummy. The pin-stripe suit? Certainly . . . The dummy as well! The smile left Mr Laidlaw's face. He was afraid . . . this was most unusual . . . he would have to consider . . . there were not many tailor's dummies to be had in northern China . . . he would make inquiries.

After Pu Yi had gone, Mr Laidlaw took a deep breath. What was Johnston going to think? He was already worried as to what Johnston might think when he saw the picture of the Emperor in plus-fours. Mr Laidlaw was beginning to realize that there were hidden complications in serving an emperor.

The St Andrew's Society were delighted when Pu Yi graciously accepted their invitation to be the guest of honour at their annual ball. They sent a delegation to consult Woodhead over the arrangements. Although only three in number, they occupied most of the space in the editor's small office. Woodhead was not in the best of tempers. He was wrestling with a long and involved editorial on the 'Cromwell of China', Chiang Kai-shek, and his sinister intentions towards the foreign concessions. 'The sword of Damocles hangs by a thread over the British Concession,' he had just written, when the simpering voice of Miss Stewart interrupted him in mid-sentence: 'Well, here we are. I do hope we are not disturbing you.'

While Mr Peebles, the chairman, smiled unctuously, and Captain 'Freezer' Frost, late of the Royal Scots, took notes of every word that was uttered, Miss Stewart, manageress of the Scottish bakery, asked Woodhead endless questions about the Emperor and the Empress. What might they wear? What did they prefer to drink? Who should be introduced to them? Did they speak English? There was an awkward pause as Miss Stewart reached the most delicate part of her mission. She blushed and asked, 'Will they be bringing other members of their family? The concubine . . . ?'

The very sound of Miss Stewart's voice irritated Woodhead. She often performed at the concerts in Gordon Hall. When she sang her maudlin ditties about the lochs and glens of the Highlands of Scotland, with her 'wee' this and her 'wee' that, Woodhead's ears would all but droop, and he would find an excuse to slip away. Now, however, he was trapped. And in his own office, too! One day, he thought, he would write an editorial exploding the whole myth about the romantic tradition of the Highlands. How the rigmarole of tartans and kilts and bagpipes, far from being part of Scotland's ancient heritage, had not been invented until the eighteenth century, and was later embellished for the Hanoverian monarch, George IV. How the reels they danced had been composed in the reign of Queen Victoria, and owed much to her patronage. How the green and black tartan worn by the Argyll and Sutherland Highlanders had been designed by a committee at the British war office in modern times. Yes, he would enjoy writing that editorial.

If Woodhead found Miss Stewart trying, he found Peebles impossible. An accountant by training, Peebles had risen to be chief executive of the British-owned coal-mines north of Tientsin. In Woodhead's view, Peebles was typical of that new breed of professional men who had begun to take charge of affairs in the outposts of the British Empire. He lacked the crusading spirit. When confronted by a problem, Peebles would say with cautious diplomacy, 'We must consult our American friends.' Woodhead could think of no surer way of undermining the Empire.

157

The arrival in Tientsin of a very important person brought some colour back to Woodhead's life and rescued him from the parochial concerns of the St Andrew's Society. A message arrived at Woodhead's office one day from the consul-general. His Royal Highness the Duke of Gloucester was on his way from Shanghai for a brief visit. In record time a special, illustrated number of *The Peking and Tientsin Times* was produced to commemorate the royal duke's visit. Woodhead was in his element. He expanded on the theme of the British Empire. Nor did he forget to mention all those Chinese people who yearned for an empire on the same constitutional lines as the British one.

The Duke of Gloucester expressed a wish to meet Pu Yi, and Woodhead was called in to help with the arrangements. The entire Japanese army seemed to be on parade outside the Chang Garden when the duke arrived. Apparently forgetful of his duty to be invisible, Major Mino strutted about outside the gates.

The scene in the garden was remarkably peaceful. The Alsatians and the Pekinese had been moved across the road to Kasuga House for the day. Only the amiable bulldog, Pongo, dozing at the foot of the steps, was left to greet the duke. Pu Yi was thrilled to meet the brother of the Prince of Wales in his throne-room. He handed a photograph of himself to the duke and asked him to give it to his father, King George V, when he returned to England. The photograph bore Pu Yi's signature; under it was the stamp: *Yamamoto Photographic Studio, Victoria Road, Tientsin*.

Some weeks later a letter arrived from the King, thanking Pu Yi for his photograph and enclosing one of himself, signed *George R.I.* Pu Yi had a large collection of signed photographs of famous people in his study. They included the King of Italy, Mussolini, Count Ciano and Harold Lloyd. Now a space was cleared for the photograph of George V, Defender of the Faith, King of Great Britain and Ireland, and Emperor of India. If only Johnston could see it, thought Pu Yi. Johnston, whose fondest dream was of a close union between the empires of Britain and China.

The ballroom of the Astor House Hotel was decorated with

tartan for St Andrew's Day. Pu Yi and his Empress sat on a dais with Peebles and Miss Stewart. Pu Yi was wearing his new evening dress suit of tails and a white tie. Near the dais the pipe major of the Argylls tuned up his bagpipes while the dancers took the floor for an eightsome reel. Off the dancers went, as the pipe major began to play 'Devil among the Tailors'. Trying to make herself heard against the whine of the pipes and the yelps of the dancers, Miss Stewart shouted in Pu Yi's ear, 'De'il amang the Tailors!' Pu Yi smiled. 'Very traditional,' he said. 'The Spey in Spate,' Miss Stewart shouted in Beautiful Countenance's ear as the tune changed. On and on went the reeling dancers, while the more senior ones among them barked out orders in the endeavour to keep some pattern in the chaotic movements. 'Over here, quick! Now turn your partner. No, not you!'

'Not enough rehearsals, I'm afraid,' Miss Stewart said to Peebles. The tune changed again. 'Sleepy Maggie!' Miss Stewart shouted in Pu Yi's ear.

At last the eightsome came to an end, and the pipe major marched off for a rest. The dancers went back to their tables. 'We're going to have a waltz next,' Miss Stewart said. 'We like to mix the modern with the traditional.' Pu Yi stiffened. A familiar sound was coming from across the room. A violin was being carefully tuned. Could it be Charlie? Miss Stewart answered his question for him. 'Herr Schneider and his trio are playing the next number,' she said. 'I hope you will enjoy them.'

Herr Schneider looked up to heaven. In a slow and melancholy waltz time, he led his trio in the Highland lament for Bonnie Prince Charlie:

> Will ye no come back again?
> Will ye no come back again?
> Better loved ye canna be,
> Will ye no come back again?

Pu Yi's evening was complete.

One morning Major Mino was alerted by one of his men. At

the end of Asahi Road, close to the border with the Native City, the major found two Japanese policemen holding a young Chinese girl. She was shivering with fear and hysterical. Drawing nearer, Major Mino recognized her as Elegant Ornament, the imperial concubine. This was the third time that Elegant Ornament had tried to escape in recent weeks. She had been giving a lot of trouble at the Chang Garden; often her screams could be heard in the street outside. The eunuchs of the presence could do nothing with her. The grand guardian believed that she would not have gone on behaving so badly if there had been a dowager living in the household. Elegant Ornament's complaints were never ending. She was jealous of the Empress who, she claimed, was always out shopping while she was forced to stay at home. She was terrified of the Alsatians who snarled at her every time she went into the garden. She kept finding ants in her room, and would spend hours watching in case they marched in through the gap under the door.

Eventually Elegant Ornament managed to bribe one of the pageboys, who helped her escape by hiding her in a cart. Once in the Native City, she went to the magistrate at the *yamen* and applied for a divorce. Pu Yi did not contest her case, but he issued an edict reducing her status from that of a consort to a commoner. Pu Yi's ministers and the Japanese secret service hoped that there would be no publicity over Elegant Ornament, but the ever-watchful *Far Eastern Times* disappointed them. Not only did the newspaper report Elegant Ornament's divorce case, but it published an article describing the macabre life that went on at the Chang Garden, where page-boys were flogged and screams were heard in the garden at night. Pu Yi's court in Tientsin, suggested the article, was as decadent as the Venerable Buddha's court in the Forbidden City.

'Life at the Chang Garden' was followed by 'Wild Extravagance of Mr and Mrs Henry Pu Yi', in which the *Far Eastern Times* revealed that Pu Yi had run up large bills at a number of shops in the British concession, which he could not afford to pay. There was, for instance, a bill for two pianos supplied by Robinson's Piano Company. The truth of the matter was, said the paper, that the court at the Chang Garden had paid out so much cash to war-lords, mercenaries and advisers of every kind, that there was nothing left with which to pay the household bills, let alone the shopping sprees in Victoria Road.

The Empress tried to detach herself from all this notoriety. At the social functions she attended, people noticed that, although her command of English was greater than Pu Yi's, she hardly ever spoke, but would sit, wan and aloof, while the chatter went on around her. Among the few visitors received by her was Nona Ransom, art mistress at the British school, who gave Pu Yi private lessons in English. One day Miss Ransom was with the Empress at the Chang Garden when the cook entered the room and announced that there would be no supper that evening because there was no food left in the house and he had run out of shopping money. The Empress was deeply embarrassed, but she managed a laugh and passed over the matter lightly. It was beyond the strength of the frail young Empress to endure her life in Tientsin without some support. She began to smoke opium as an escape from the squalor of the Chang Garden, and, within a year of her arrival in Tientsin, she had become an addict. Pu Yi, who knew of her condition, showed no concern. The Japanese secret service also knew about her visits to the opium dens. But the first inkling that anyone in the British concession had that she was a drug addict came when one day the Empress collapsed in the foyer of the Astor House Hotel. A doctor was called, and he found that she had been having morphia injections.

About this time the lonely Empress made the acquaintance of the Manchu princess, Yoshiko. She was the daughter of the 'Mad' Prince Su who had raised an army to fight for the 'Great Ching' dynasty against the Republicans in Manchuria in 1916. When her parents died, the princess was adopted by a family friend, Kawashima, a leading member of the Japanese Black Dragon Society. She was brought up in Japan and renamed Yoshiko, which means 'Eastern Jewel'. In 1927 Yoshiko married a Mongol prince, but they never lived together. In 1928 she went to Shanghai, where she became the lover of Tanaka, a senior officer in the Japanese secret service.

She took to wearing men's clothes and was sometimes photographed standing beside Japanese air force planes, wearing military uniform and jackboots.

The Empress was amused by Yoshiko and her tales of life in Japan and Shanghai. But she especially enjoyed hearing from Yoshiko about her travels in Mongolia and other parts of that region which used to be called Tartary. Like many Chinese, the Empress was fond of dreaming about the mysterious Interior and the ancient nomadic life that still survived there. At night, intoxicated by opium, she would recite to herself her favourite poem. It spoke of a woman who yearned for an imaginary island oasis in the desert where lived the lover of her dreams.

> Which is the road that leads to the Western Island?
> I'll ask the man at the ferry by the Bridge of Boats.
> But the sun is sinking and the orioles flying home;
> And the wind is blowing and sighing in the walnut tree.
>
> The sea shall carry my dreams far away,
> So that you shall be sorry at last for my sorrow.
> If the south wind only knew my thoughts.
> It would blow my dreams till they got to the Western Island.

'I hear Yellow Lotus has been seen again,' Kellaher said. He was sitting on the bench in Mad Mac's back room in Taku Road.

Mad Mac drank from his bowl of wine and made a face. 'Not as good as the hunchback's. This is mixed with *gaoliang*. Can you taste it?' He looked at Kellaher and said sharply, 'Some boat people came to the market-place and claimed they had seen her. Are you afraid?'

'In a way. It's remarkable that she never dies.'

'You only die when you are forgotten,' said Mad Mac. 'Have you heard of White Chrysanthemum?'

'The girl outlaw leader in Manchuria?'

'Yes. She's only eighteen years old. She led a raid against the Japanese garrison just north of the Great Wall. There has always been a White Chrysanthemum in the district, and the peasants won't let her die.' Mad Mac laughed. 'The Fool let one of his heroines die once. She was a character in *Outlaws of the Marshlands*. But the audience wouldn't allow it. He had to resurrect her in the next instalment. The Chinese must have the strongest sense of history of any people, but history for the peasants doesn't mean books written by scholars, it means the peasants' fears, hopes and dreams. The story-tellers give them what they want. As for the books, there has been such a doctoring of ancient historical texts by sycophantic officials that even the most learned scholars, Chinese or foreign, are at a loss to reconstruct them. Take the sayings of Confucius. The scholar-officials have succeeded in reducing that tolerant and humorous man to a smug and opinionated patriarch. All those moralizing anecdotes are the work of later historians. And see how they have used Confucius to justify the inferior status of Chinese women. You know about the Three Obediences, how a woman must be subject to the men of her family: before marriage to her father, during marriage to her husband and in widowhood to her son. Well, they even attribute that rigid social code to Confucius. But the story-tellers have always been the champions of woman.'

'Why is it always a woman who is immortal?' Kellaher asked.

Mad Mac got up and filled their bowls from a jug. 'Come and look at these,' he said. Two scrolls of Chinese characters hung on the wall above the *kang*. 'The hunchback's daughter painted them. They're Taoist, and full of reverence for women.' He read them out in his low voice:

> 'The Tao flows everywhere
> And nourishes all things.
> It does not try to possess them
> Or rule over them

163

'Water is the noblest element.
It gives life to everything,
Yet it is humble and flows
In places which people despise.
That is why water is so close to the Tao.'

'Tao means the way of nature,' said Mad Mac. 'And, to the Taoists, woman is very close to nature. She *is* water, the noblest element. The White Lotus Society are Taoist through and through, and here, in the coastal region, their leader has always been a woman, Yellow Lotus.'

'Not all the outlaw leaders are women, of course,' said Kellaher. 'There's the White Wolf, for instance, who led the peasant rising near Peking after the drought last year.'

'Another "Robin Hood" type,' said Mad Mac, 'just like the outlaws of the marshlands. He's immortal, too. Robs the rich and gives to the poor. The present White Wolf is a brilliant young man, son of a mandarin. He terrorizes the Republicans as well as the war-lords. I hear that no government official dares set foot in Pao An in the Yellow River valley, where the White Wolf has his base. The White Wolf has always been the scourge of the imperial armies.'

'That's what I'm afraid of,' said Kellaher. 'The watch committee thinks there's a growing link between the anti-Ching guerrillas of the White Wolf and Yellow Lotus and her outlaws down here.'

'Watch committee!' said Mad Mac. 'You mean Doihara. Have you ever wondered why we go to all this trouble to prop up the Ching dynasty, which is long since dead? All those years Johnston of the colonial office spent in the Forbidden City, and here in Tientsin all the fuss we are making over a pathetic young man who abdicated nearly twenty years ago. We like to think ourselves superior to the Japs, but we're behaving as if we are the tools of Premier Tanaka and his jumped-up colonels.'

'The Japanese military say there would be anarchy if they didn't police northern China, especially as there isn't an emperor to hold the nation together.'

'They'll never wipe out anarchy here. You may as well try

164

to wipe out nature. There's a long tradition of anarchy in China. And in Japan, too. The Samurai were the direct descendants of the Chinese ''Robin Hood'' type heroes.'

'The Taoists were anarchists, too, weren't they? That hermit character of the Fool's.'

Mad Mac laughed. 'You wouldn't like some of the Taoist ideas: ''Let the world go its own way. Abolish Law and Order, and people will learn to love each other again.'' Have you heard the Fool recite the sayings of the Taoist sage, Chuang Tzu? They're pure anarchy:

'''We do not see Heaven command the four seasons,
Yet they never swerve from their course.
So, also, we do not see the sage ordering the
People about, yet they spontaneously serve him.'''

Listening to those words from the age before the empires, Kellaher felt again a sensation of timelessness. This bare room with no furniture but a *kang*, a bench, and a straw mat on the floor, might have been a peasant's room of 2,000 years ago, he thought. The characters on the scrolls and their wisdom were even more ancient. Mad Mac also seemed part of this age-old scene. His bald head and his face were lined and weather-beaten, and the fringe of hair above his ears looked like a piece of the matting on the floor, straw coloured and frayed at the edges.

Kellaher crossed Taku Road and re-entered the world of time. In Victoria Park some children were having fun on the swings, watched by their amahs. The band of the Argylls was playing a selection from *The Love Parade*. The benches by the small pavilion were filled with people. He passed a group of Japanese ladies wearing kimonos and combs in their hair. At the foot of the steps leading up to Gordon Hall Miss Stewart, who was carrying a parasol, gave Kellaher a friendly wave and went on chatting to Peebles. The grey towers of Gordon Hall loomed over them. Its walls still bore the scars of that last battle in 1900 when Yellow Lotus had besieged it. One day, she had prophesied, she would bring that foreign building crashing to the ground. There were times when Kellaher himself wished that Gordon Hall and all that it stood for would come crashing down. They were usually after he had been drinking with Mad Mac in Taku Road. He felt ashamed of his lack of loyalty. Like many Irishmen in the forces, he was only a mercenary. 'Those whom I guard I do not love,' Yeats had said in a poem about an Irish airman who was shot down in the Great War. Those whom Kellaher guarded he did not love. When he saw the gangs of Siberian refugee boys roaming the back streets or hitch-hiking by sampan down the Grand Canal, he envied them. Riff-raff they might be, but they did not have to pretend to any allegiance; they were citizens of the world.

In the autumn of 1930, nearly ten years after Britain had agreed to return Weihaiwei to China, the Union Jack was hauled down at the naval port. Not even Johnston could do any more to prevent the final surrender. Johnston was posted home to England. Before leaving, he paid a farewell visit to Pu Yi. Time was short, and Johnston could only afford one night. It was arranged that Pu Yi should come to the Astor House Hotel, where Johnston was staying. This was just as well from Johnston's point of view, for he would hardly have enjoyed the scene at the Chang Garden, where the Alsatians bullied Pongo, the Pekinese yapped at the Alsatians, the Manchurian cranes squawked, and the grinning eunuchs of the presence hovered, ever attentive, in the hall.

Pu Yi and Johnston sat on the veranda outside Johnston's suite. They talked with nostalgia of the old days in the Forbidden City. Pu Yi had a special request to make. When they returned there in triumph, and he reigned once more from the dragon throne, could they have a band of drums and bagpipes, dressed in a special imperial tartan of yellow and purple? Johnston felt sad and helpless. He tried to explain that tartans and bagpipes were purely Scottish things and did not translate easily abroad. But, said Pu Yi, if Queen Victoria's consort, Prince Albert, who was a German, had designed a tartan, why couldn't he? For a moment Johnston was aroused. Woodhead had been talking to Pu Yi, he thought. That remark about Prince Albert ... Then he subsided again. He would take advice when he was back in London, he promised.

Early the next morning, 15 September, Pu Yi returned to the hotel by car to collect Johnston. They drove down to the British bund, where Johnston's steamer was waiting. They both went on board and remained talking in Johnston's cabin until the steamer's hooter gave a warning blast and Pu Yi left the ship. Before going ashore, Pu Yi gave Johnston a farewell present. It was a fan on which Pu Yi had copied a traditional Chinese poem of farewell. The steamer gave another blast, cast off its ropes, and chugged away down the Sea River. Johnston stood at the stern waving to Pu Yi, who was sitting in his car. The steamer rounded the bend by the Russian church, and Pu Yi was lost to sight. Johnston picked up the fan and read:

> Out of the city's eastern gate I go on foot. . . .
> Here it was that we parted, and my friend went away.
> I want to follow him across the river,
> But the river is deep and has no bridge.
> O that we were a pair of herons,
> That we could fly home together.

Inert and lifeless Pu Yi sat in his car, watching the steamer carrying Johnston away to those exotic places in the Prince of Wales's magazine: Balmoral, Windsor Castle, the blue Mediterranean. A long time ago Johnston had promised to take him to Windsor Castle, but the only British castle Pu Yi had seen so far was the dingy Gordon Hall. Pu Yi felt deserted.

Major Mino, who was parked a little way down the bund, behind Pu Yi's car, became impatient. He ordered his driver to signal Pu Yi's chauffeur, and, without waiting for the Emperor's orders, the imperial car drove off.

At the Chang Garden Major Mino recorded the exact time of Pu Yi's arrival. Two page-boys helped Pu Yi from the car. He walked jerkily into the garden. The cranes began to squawk. This annoyed Pu Yi, and he ordered the page-boys to silence them. The page-boys tried to hit the cranes with long

167

bamboo rods, but they flew about the cage squawking even louder.

Since Elegant Ornament's escape, security had been tightened at the Chang Garden. Fewer visitors were allowed in, and the house resembled a fortress. Pu Yi went less often to the British concession than he used to. When he did go there, he went alone, for the Empress had withdrawn from public life. The Emperor was not welcomed with the same enthusiasm at the big shops in Victoria Road, but he was still in demand for the occasional charity at Gordon Hall, where his quaint figure was an object of curiosity. 'There's the Emperor of China,' members of the audience would remark, pointing him out. 'They say he keeps concubines and eunuchs in his palace. The Empress is locked up there. She's an opium addict.' People now said things about Pu Yi that they would never have dared mention when his protector, Johnston, was still in China.

The loyal Woodhead accompanied Pu Yi on some of his engagements. Woodhead was not a musical man, but he knew the difference between good and bad, and the interminable concerts with their undeserved encores tested his endurance to the limit. There was, however, one form of music that he could not have too much of, the military brass band. He had only to hear the blare of trombones and the clashing of cymbals for his patriotic spirit to be roused. Like 'Morrison of China' and Johnston, Woodhead had never served in the armed forces, but had waged the Great War with words from China. Conscious of his civilian status, he had a deep respect for all things military. His manner, when in the presence of senior military officers, bordered on the servile. The businessman, thought Woodhead, might be a commercial crusader, but the military officer, strong and decisive, was the real, fighting crusader and the spearhead of the Empire. A small bronze statue of a Japanese soldier stood on the drawing-room table in Woodhead's house. His most prized possession, the statue had been presented to him by General Hayashi, then premier of Japan, in gratitude for Woodhead's loyal support. The general was specially pleased with some articles Woodhead had written in praise of the Kwantung Army.

The district of Kwantung, in the Liaotung peninsula of southern Manchuria, had been leased to Japan by China in 1898. Known as the Kwantung Army, the Japanese army in Manchuria had fought against the Russians in 1904. It was also engaged in a continuous series of campaigns against the bandits and outlaws who came down from the mountains to raid the railway towns in the Manchurian plain. With its battle-hardened and seasoned troops, the Kwantung Army was regarded as the *corps d'élite* of all the Japanese forces. Moreover, its generals had considerable influence on the government in Tokyo and on the imperial court. General Hayashi himself had been commander-in-chief of the Kwantung Army before being appointed premier of Japan. Woodhead was doubly honoured by the Japanese, for General Hayashi had also told him that the Emperor of Japan had expressed his pleasure at the award of the statue to Woodhead, 'that good friend of the Japanese soldier'.

Woodhead enjoyed escorting Pu Yi to military parades in the British concession, like the Trooping the Colour ceremony on the King's birthday, but he was disappointed to find that Pu Yi did not share his enthusiasm to the full. Pu Yi liked to see the soldiers' uniforms, but as soon as they began to march, his attention would wander and he would lower his eyes to the ground as if searching for something. At one parade, Woodhead was startled when Pu Yi asked why the soldiers did not have workers to carry their equipment for them as the soldier ants did.

Every year Pu Yi, with Woodhead in attendance, was a guest of honour at the parades to mark the Fall of the Bastille and American Independence Day. The Bastille Day parade was held in the French Park. Unlike Victoria Park, it was open to the Chinese, a fact which rankled with Woodhead who believed that the 'crafty French', as he called them, made political capital out of it. The saluting base, draped in blue, white and red, had the words *Liberté, Egalité, Fraternité* displayed on it in big gold letters. It was not Woodhead's favourite motto. Sitting in the stand among the chattering French, not a word of whose language he understood, Woodhead felt uneasy. The French never lost an opportunity of reminding the world that it was the British who had forced opium on China. If only they would leave the subject alone to die a natural death, he thought. But the French always found a fresh angle on the scandal of the opium trade. Recently one of their journalists had written an article on the plight of the Indians in Bengal province who had been forced by their British rulers to give up planting their normal crops in order to grow opium for the Chinese market.

Glancing about him, Woodhead viewed with distaste a row of French Marist Brothers. Their school was full of Siberian refugees. He dreaded to think what sort of citizens they would turn out to be. There, in the middle of the row, was Brother Superior and, beside him, the rascally Brother Faust, a Dubliner and a drinking companion of Inspector Kellaher. Behind them sat some fathers from the Jesuit College in Racecourse Road. If anything, Woodhead felt even more awkward in their presence. The Jesuits wore Chinese gowns and skull-caps, and spoke Chinese. He sometimes thought of them as a secret society. 'Goodness knows what their politics are. Pretty red, if you ask me,' he would say to his cronies in the Tientsin Club. 'Johnston is right,' he would go on to declare. 'The trouble with the French is that they are all Red Christians'.

Woodhead felt more comfortable among the Americans on Independence Day; in fact he felt distinctly superior to them. Was it not an article of his, headed 'Does That Star-spangled Banner Still Wave?', that had brought a whole brigade of American marines to help to defend Tientsin in 1927? The members of the Tientsin Club had a saying about Woodhead which he never denied: 'When Woodhead speaks, Washington trembles.'

In American eyes, Woodhead was the arch-colonist, and they idolized him for it. It was his style that fascinated them. They found him arrogant in the extreme, patronizing and unfailingly grandiloquent. The more vitriolic his anti-American tirades, the better they liked him. The title of Most Favoured Nation had been granted to Britain by an emperor of China, declared Woodhead, but it was being undermined by the American 'Open Door' policy. He accused the

Americans in China of being parasites and hypocrites. Warming to his charge, he described the American presence in Tientsin as a 'hermit crab that takes up its abode in the shell of another'. Tientsin, he said, was opened up by British arms. American businessmen and missionaries thrived there, yet they boasted of their righteousness in having no territorial concession. Worst of all, American pacifist missionaries were engaged in anti-British agitation.

The effect of all this was a flood of invitations to Woodhead to lecture in the United States. He repeated his anti-American charges in a series of public lectures in Chicago. Delivered in his haughty, imperial manner, they were received with enthusiasm.

If anyone, it was the British who were embarrassed by Woodhead's outbursts. Whitehall was appalled. The British consul-general in Tientsin protested. But the old China hand whose pen was his sword would not be silenced. His friends at the Tientsin Club believed that if he had not been so outspoken, Woodhead would have been knighted for his services to the British Empire.

The high point in Woodhead's year came on 11 November when the Armistice Day service and parade took place at the cenotaph in Victoria Park, to honour the dead of the Great War of 1914-18, Woodhead's war, in which he had striven so hard to interest his fellow-British settlers in Tientsin. The parade was modelled on the one held in Whitehall. This was the ceremony of Empire at its best, and Woodhead was proud to have Pu Yi with him. A company of the Argylls, a detachment of sailors from HMS *Hollyhock*, the Tientsin Volunteer Corps, members of the British Legion and the Boy Scouts were drawn up on three sides of the cenotaph. On the fourth side stood the consul-general, who represented the King. Behind him were the chairman and members of the British municipal council, and a group of foreign military attachés in a variety of uniforms. Now they would see how a parade should be put on, thought Woodhead.

With clockwork precision, the liturgy of service and military parade unfolded. The procession of clergy and choirboys, which had walked from All Saints' Church, arrived at the cenotaph at exactly ten minutes to eleven. The prayers, the hymns, the sounding of 'Last Post' from the ramparts of Gordon Hall, the two minutes' silence for those who had fallen in the Great War in Europe, reveille, and the pipers playing 'The Flowers of the Forest' the laying of the wreaths, all had been carefully rehearsed, and all went according to plan. Woodhead felt pride at the well-ordered ceremony. How different from the bustle of the Bastille Day parade! Solemnity, that was what the British were best at producing on State occasions. It probably never entered Woodhead's mind that the qualities of meticulous precision and solemnity, which he so admired, were new and alien to the English ceremonial tradition; the royal pageants such as coronations, State openings of Parliament, and parades, had always proceeded in a casual and spontaneous manner; that Queen Victoria herself was bored by precisely conducted ceremonies; and that it was only at the end of the nineteenth century and the begining of the twentieth, when the British Empire had begun to wane, that its rituals of State had become regimented and solemn.

Woodhead turned to Pu Yi. 'I shouldn't say so myself,' he said, 'but that went very well, don't you think?' Pu Yi's eyes were shut. The soldiers had been stationary for a long time. 'Very traditional,' he said, mechanically. Suddenly the colonel of the Argylls roared 'Quick March!' and the parade marched off down Meadows Road, led by the band playing 'It's a Long Way to Tipperary'. Pu Yi's face beamed. 'Thank you, thank you,' he said to Woodhead, clearly under the impression that the 'March of the Ants' had been specially requested for him.

Soon after Armistice Day in 1930 an announcement appeared in *The Peking and Tientsin Times* that stunned its readers. The editor-in-chief, H.G.W. Woodhead, CBE, had resigned. He was leaving for Shanghai to edit the journal *Oriental Affairs*, and to be the leading political commentator on the radio there. The commercial crusader's many admirers felt bereft, but the news of his departure brought a feeling of understandable relief to the staff at the British consulate. For years they had suffered the annoyance of seeing Woodhead treated as a kind of viceroy by foreigners of many nationalities as well as by leading Chinese businessmen. Some of his cavalier statements had become part of the concession's history. The British, in particular, remembered with awe Woodhead's frequent pronouncement that 'Britain should have conquered China rather than India'. If she had, Woodhead used to say, there would have been no limits to China's prosperity. China would have enjoyed an efficient police force, uniform taxation and, above all, a legal system second to none.

The Tientsin Club gave a farewell dinner in honour of Woodhead. He sat under Elgin's portrait at the top table, between Brigadier Burnell-Nugent, officer commanding British troops in Tientsin, and General Uenda, commander of the Japanese garrison. Viewing this scene from his place in the wings, the British consul-general thought it fitting that Woodhead should be surrounded by the senior officers of the profession he so admired. The consul noticed that Mr Okamoto, the Japanese consul, was not present. There was talk that the relations between the Japanese diplomatic corps and the Japanese high command were now more strained than ever before. He must find out more about that, he thought. It could be significant.

Before the toasts, Woodhead found time to ask the brigadier if he would keep an eye on Pu Yi after he had gone. 'You'll find the Emperor a likeable young man,' he said, 'but don't be put off by his odd behaviour at parades. Somehow, soldiers on the march always make him think of ants.'

The audience applauded as Woodhead rose to speak. It was being put about, he said with a twinkle in his eye, that his voice would no longer be heard on Tientsin affairs. He hated to disappoint his listeners, but he felt sure that he would find the time to write the occasional special article for his former paper. 'Old journalists,' said Woodhead, 'like old soldiers, never die.' He waited for the laughter to subside. 'As I stand here today and call to mind Lord Elgin's famous words. . . .' The audience hushed. Woodhead had reached the kernel of his speech.

CHAPTER EIGHT

THE DRAGON SAILS HOME

Now that both Johnston and Woodhead had gone, Pu Yi led a miserable existence at the Chang Garden. He received fewer invitations than ever to attend social functions in the British concession, where he was no longer even an object of curiosity. His Prince of Wales suit hung, unused, on a coat-rack.

One day a letter arrived at the Chang Garden for the secretary to the cabinet. It was from the owner of the house. With great regret, the letter said, the Chang family had decided that they must ask His Imperial majesty to pay rent, henceforth, for their house. The letter could not have come at a worse time. Pu Yi was in financial straits, his debtors were closing in, and he had been forced into the desperate measure of pawning some of his jewels. A cabinet meeting was called, and it was decided that the court must move to smaller premises. With the help of the Japanese consulate, a house was found for Pu Yi near the Japanese barracks. It was named the Quiet Garden.

Many of Pu Yi's officials, including the large and expensive team of advisers, now deserted him for wealthier clients. The two eunuchs of the presence also left, and all that remained of Pu Yi's court were the grand guardian, one other minister, and a few page-boys. The Empress kept one lady in waiting.

175

One by one the warlords, who had promised to fight for Pu Yi's restoration, changed sides and declared their support for the Nationalist government in Nanking. The late Marshal Chang Tso-lin's son, the 'Young Marshal' as he was called, also went over to the Nationalists, together with many Ching Loyalists living in southern Manchuria.

The impoverished Pu Yi's only visitors at the Quiet Garden were Major Mino and a staff officer from the Japanese garrison who gave Pu Yi lengthy briefings on the dangerous activities of the Anti-Ching Movement in the Native City of Tientsin. Pu Yi's eyes seldom opened. The Quiet Garden was a boring prison.

Then, in the autumn of 1931, everything changed. Captain Nakamura, a Japanese intelligence officer engaged in undercover work in southern Manchuria, was arrested and shot for spying by Nationalist soldiers in Mukden. On 18 September, a bomb exploded on the Japanese-owned South Manchuria Railway line outside Mukden station. Reacting with surprising speed, Japanese troops seized the city of Mukden. Within days a Japanese army corps was launched on a full-scale invasion of southern Manchuria. The whole plot had been organized by Colonel Doihara. He even gave it its name, 'the Mukden Incident'. A master of the vague euphemism, Doihara was particularly fond of the phrase 'The political situation demands', and he would use it to justify the most brutal action.

There was an outcry from the Chinese Nationalists. Many of them believed that Pu Yi was implicated in the Japanese plot. Threats were made against Pu Yi's life, and the Japanese guard at the Quiet Garden was doubled. Despite these measures, two grenades, relics from the Great War in Europe, were discovered in a basket of fruit that had been delivered as a present to the Emperor. The Quiet Garden was no longer boring.

Soon after the bombs in the fruit-basket scare Doihara arrived at the Quiet Garden to see Pu Yi. It was the first time that Pu Yi had met Doihara and he was struck by the permanent smile on Doihara's chubby face. On behalf of the Kwantung Army, Doihara was pleased to offer Pu Yi the position of head of the new state of Manchuria. There would be a salary of 600,000 dollars a year and, of course, the expenses of Pu Yi's household staff would also be met. Pu Yi asked if he would be restored as Emperor. The smiling Doihara assured him that the Japanese army would restore him to the throne as soon as the 'political situation was more settled'. He urged Pu Yi and the grand guardian to make up their minds quickly, for Tientsin was becoming highly dangerous for the Emperor.

No sooner had Doihara left, than Brigadier Burnell-Nugent was ushered in. Pu Yi shrank in his chair. The Brigadier was the officer who sat on a horse at the British parade-ground and bellowed orders at everyone. He gave Pu Yi the impression that he knew all about Doihara's plan. He brought the good wishes of the British in Tientsin, he said, and he also pledged his personal support for the Emperor in the exciting adventures that lay ahead of him. He envied the Emperor being surrounded by all those wonderful, wild Manchurian ponies. As he said this, the brigadier leaned forward and smiled. With his long nose and chin, and his protruding teeth, he looked alarmingly like a horse himself.

On the following day the Japanese consul called. Mr Okamoto assured Pu Yi that it was perfectly safe for him to remain at the Quiet Garden, which lay so close to the Japanese barracks. He advised Pu Yi not to leave the country, and made it clear that the Japanese government did not like the plan of the Black Dragon Society to make Pu Yi head of the Manchurian state.

Two days later Pu Yi received an emissary from the Nationalist government in Nanking. If Pu Yi promised not to go to Manchuria or Japan, said the emissary, the Nationalists would be prepared to revive the Articles of Favourable Treatment and pay Pu Yi a handsome annual salary.

The former grand guardian, Chen Pao-shen, who was now eighty-four years old, travelled to Tientsin and made a last pathetic plea to Pu Yi not to leave the country. He had heard from some Ching Loyalists living in Manchuria, he said, that the Japanese Kwantung Army itself was split over the plan to invite Pu Yi there.

Bewildered by all these pleas, offers and counter-offers, Pu Yi and his grand guardian did not know what to do. Doihara returned. He had evidence, he said, that the Anti-Ching Movement in the Native City of Tientsin was about to mount an attack on the Quiet Garden. The time had come for Pu Yi to escape.

Escape! Pu Yi's eyes opened wide. If only Johnston was there, he thought. Johnston *was* there! By an astonishing coincidence (if coincidence it was), Johnston had arrived in Tientsin from England at the very moment when Doihara was putting the finishing touches to his plot to take Pu Yi to Manchuria. Johnston spent the next two days with Pu Yi. The idea that his fledgling was about to leave for the land of his ancestors, the Great Ching Emperors, thrilled Johnston, and he could speak of little else. Would Johnston be coming on the great escape, too? Pu Yi asked him. There was an awkward silence. Unfortunately he had pressing duties in England, said Johnston. Perhaps he might follow later. Would it be a good idea for him to wear the Prince of Wales suit for the escape? asked Pu Yi. No, Johnston thought it would be most unsuitable. He recommended the Manchu gown and skull-cap. One day, said Johnston, carried away with emotion, Pu Yi would return in triumph from Manchuria, and they would walk together in the old courtyards of the Forbidden City. But before that could happen, there was important work for Pu Yi to do in Manchuria. Johnston sensed that he was present at a turning-point in history. Pu Yi was no longer his fledgling, he thought. He had become a dragon, and the Dragon was about to fly home.

Johnston left Tientsin on the night of 9 November. On the following morning he was in Nanking. Hearing that Johnston was in the city, Mr T.V. Soong, minister of finance in the Nationalist government, called to see him. The minister said he had information that the Japanese secret police were about to take Pu Yi to Manchuria. He begged Johnston to intervene and persuade Pu Yi not to go. China, said the minister, had protested to the League of Nations about the Japanese invasion of Manchuria. It would be a grave threat to world peace if the former Ching Emperor were to go there and show

178

his support for the invasion. Johnston's answer was a curt refusal. The Emperor was a free agent, he said, he could come and go as he pleased, and he was not being coerced by the Japanese in any way.

That night, 10 November, Doihara staged his 'Tientsin Incident'. Forty Chinese in the pay of the Japanese secret service crossed from the Japanese concession into the Native City, where they fired revolvers at a Chinese police patrol. The police returned fire. A squadron of Japanese armoured cars then trundled into the Native City and joined in the battle, killing several people with bursts of machine-gun fire. The sound of the firing could be heard as far away as the British concession.

During the chaos of the battle, which was a planned diversion, Doihara arrived by car at the Quiet Garden, where he was met by Major Mino. They disguised Pu Yi in a Japanese officer's overcoat and cap, and, allowing him to bring only his jewel bag, they bundled him into their car and drove away at high speed. Ill and frightened the Empress stood barefoot in the doorway, watching the car disappear. Once again she had been abandoned by Pu Yi.

Doihara's car crossed into the British concession and drove along Victoria Road, past Gordon Hall and the cenotaph where, in a few hour's time, the British residents would remember the glorious dead of the 1914-18 war. The car turned left at the Astor House Hotel and soon reached the bund. A motor launch was waiting. Seven helmeted Japanese marines lined the deck, which was protected by sandbags. Doihara and Major Mino said goodbye to Pu Yi and went back to their car.

Pu Yi was taken down to a small cabin in the hold. It was pitch dark and he felt confused and frightened. He had a vague idea that there were others in the cabin, but he did not dare speak to the shadowy figures. This was not the escape he had imagined. If only Johnston had come, too, he thought. He tried to console himself by remembering Johnston's last words to him: 'Just think of the joy of your Manchurian subjects when they see their Emperor!' The launch cast off and moved away down-river. After about half an hour, when

179

the launch was outside the protection of the foreign concessions, it was challenged by a group of Nationalist soldiers on the north bank, who flashed lights and then fired their rifles at the launch as it sped on its way and disappeared into the darkness.

Dawn had broken by the time the launch rounded the last of the many bends in the Sea River and entered the estuary. Beyond Taku Bar, silhouetted against the pale winter sky, the steamer *Awaji Maru* was waiting to carry Pu Yi to Manchuria. The Dragon was on his way home.

PART THREE

THE SALT PALACE

CHAPTER NINE

THE DRAGON LIMPS ASHORE

Early on the morning of 12 November 1931 the *Awaji Maru*, after a stormy passage up the Gulf of Liaotung, arrived at the small Manchurian port of Yingtow. During the night, Pu Yi, who had been seasick for most of the journey, was flung across his cabin, injuring a leg. But, as soon as the steamer docked, he made a brave effort, got up, and put on the Japanese army greatcoat over his Manchu gown. Feeling frail, he went up on deck, expecting to be greeted by cheering crowds of his Manchurian subjects.

All was strangely silent. Pu Yi went to the ship's rail and looked over it. Apart from one or two dock workers, the quayside was deserted. An empty train stood in a siding alongside the steamer. Below the gangway, a reception committee of six Japanese men were waiting. Not a single Manchurian subject was there to greet the Dragon as he limped ashore. Amakasu of the Japanese secret police raised his grey felt hat in greeting. Pu Yi remembered seeing him once before at the Quiet Garden. On behalf of Colonel Itagaki of the Kwantung Army staff, said Amakasu, he welcomed His Excellency to his homeland. The colonel regretted that he was detained at a meeting.

Pu Yi was ushered into the train. An armed Japanese soldier stood guard in the corridor. Amakasu pulled down the blinds. 'Security precaution,' he said, looking sheepish. With a jerk, the train moved off. Amakasu sat opposite Pu Yi. Every now and then he peered at Pu Yi over the top of his small, steel-rimmed spectacles. After about an hour, the train stopped at Tangkangtzu, a resort noted for its warm springs. Pu Yi and Amakasu left the train and went by taxi to the Railway Hotel.

Tangkangtzu, in the district of Kwantung, was a popular holiday centre for the troops of the Kwantung Army whose headquarters were nearby. The foyer of the Railway Hotel was crowded with Japanese officers. Pu Yi was shown up to the first floor. 'You are going to meet some old friends,' Amakasu told him on their way up. 'The whole of the first floor has been reserved for you'.

At the top of the staircase, waiting to greet Pu Yi, were the grand guardian and members of Pu Yi's former cabinet. Some had deserted him when he moved from the Chang Garden, others he had not seen since his escape from the Forbidden City, seven years before. Suddenly Pu Yi stiffened. A tall, lean man in a black skull-cap was standing behind the grand guardian. 'The Mantis!' Pu Yi whispered to himself.

Cheng Hsiao-hsu, the tall, lean man, was seventy-one years old. His shiny, bald head, hooded eyelids, and sharply drawn features gave him a strangely metallic look. He had a habit of holding up his hands in front of him like a praying mantis, and from the moment when Pu Yi first saw him in the Forbidden City, Cheng had become the Mantis. A strict Confucian, the Mantis was a close friend of Johnston, and had helped him to arrange Pu Yi's escape from the Northern Mansion to the Japanese legation. When Pu Yi moved to Tientsin, the Mantis was ousted by his rival, the grand guardian, and retired from the court, although he continued to serve Pu Yi on special missions. After the Mukden Incident he had gone to see the leading members of the Black Dragon Society in Tokyo to sound them out on the question of Pu Yi's move to Manchuria.

Amakasu bowed to Pu Yi and said, 'Your Excellency, for reasons of security, as I have already explained to your ministers, you must all remain on the first floor of the hotel. No one may go downstairs, and you may not have any visitors.' Amakasu bowed and departed.

Pu Yi did not seem to realize the full implications of Amakasu's remarks, namely, that Pu Yi and his court were under house arrest. 'Why does he call me Your Excellency?' Pu Yi asked the grand guardian petulantly. 'Am I not the Emperor?'

The grand guardian agreed that it was disgraceful that Pu Yi should not be addressed as Imperial Majesty. There were other distressing matters, he told Pu Yi. When the grand guardian had asked an officer of the Japanese secret service how long the court would have to remain at the Railway Hotel, he was told that Colonel Itagaki was at a meeting and would give his answer later. It was clear, said the grand guardian, that the staff of the Kwantung Army had not made up their minds what to do with Pu Yi and the ministers who now formed his cabinet.

A week later Pu Yi and his cabinet were taken by train to Port Arthur on the southernmost tip of the Liaotung peninsula. They were given rooms on the first floor of the Yamato Hotel. The same security arrangements applied. Once again they were forbidden to go downstairs. No visitors were allowed near the hotel. Pu Yi held a cabinet meeting in his suite. His ministers cried out in protest against the continued imprisonment of their Emperor. Taking his cue, Pu Yi warmed to his role of a sorely wronged monarch. 'The Japanese are treating me like a king in a pack of cards,' he stormed. The grand guardian agreed and said it was all Colonel Itagaki's fault. The Mantis advised caution. He suggested that Pu Yi should send the colonel a present. It would at least help the colonel to remember the existence of the court on the first floor of the Yamato Hotel, he said. Unfortunately Pu Yi had no signed photographs of himself, as his luggage had not yet arrived. With a sigh of reluctance, he dipped into his jewel bag and handed over a small brooch.

On the following day Amakasu brought two Japanese officers to see Pu Yi. They were university lecturers, attached to the Kwantung Army school of education, he explained.

185

Both the officers were experts on the battles of the Russo-Japanese war of 1904. Colonel Itagaki had kindly arranged for them to take His Excellency on a conducted tour of the old Russian forts which commanded the harbour.

For the next month, on two afternoons a week Pu Yi limped after the experts as they took him from fort to gun emplacement along the entire length of the old Russian fortifications. He was spared no detail. Sometimes the two experts had a slight difference of opinion which held up the tour. At one gun emplacement they disagreed as to the calibre of a giant Russian gun, and their politely phrased but acid comments to each other went on endlessly. Pu Yi, who had begun to wish that he had never complained about having nothing to do at the Yamato Hotel, was thankful when the last fort had been inspected, but there was to be no quick reprieve for him. 'Tomorrow', said one of the experts, 'we shall begin our naval tour of Port Arthur.'

Pu Yi was shown every exhibit in the naval museum. He was taken to a command post overlooking the harbour, where in 1904 the grand fleet of Tsar Nicholas II had lain at anchor. The experts informed Pu Yi of the exact disposition of every ship in the Russian fleet on the day before the fatal battle.

At last the six weeks' tour reached its climax. From the command post the experts showed Pu Yi how two squadrons of Japanese destroyers had sailed into the harbour at dead of night and, in a surprise attack, had sunk most of the Russian battleships. Surprise was the most important principle of war, the two experts chorused as they proudly surveyed the scene where Japan's victory over Russia had changed the course of the history of the Far East.

After Pu Yi's escape from Tientsin the Empress remained in her room at the Quiet Garden, with only the squawking cranes to keep her company. The Black Dragon Society decided that it would be dangerous to allow her to remain in Tientsin, where she might fall in with some faction opposed to their schemes in Manchuria. Acting on the instructions of Doihara, Major Mino called on the Empress and tried to persuade her to go to Port Arthur and join her husband. But the hysterical Empress felt sure that there was a plot against her life and refused to move.

Major Mino then sent for the Empress's only friend, Yoshiko. It so happened that Yoshiko had a house in Port Arthur which had been left to her by her father, the Mad Prince Su. Unknown to Yoshiko, the Japanese secret service had already requisitioned it.

When Yoshiko entered the Empress's room she was horrified at what she saw. The beautiful young woman of a few months ago was haggard and unkempt; and her room was a jumble of dusty furniture. Gradually Yoshiko calmed the wretched Empress, and even got her to take a little food. When she heard that Yoshiko had a house in Port Arthur and had been brought up there as a child, the Empress felt reassured and agreed to go and stay there as Yoshiko's guest.

The Empress and Yoshiko arrived at the Su house in Port Arthur to find it ringed with armed soldiers. Amakasu met them at the gate and informed them that His Excellency, Pu Yi, was in residence. The Empress was allowed a brief meeting with her husband, during which they uttered hardly a word. Amakasu led the Empress to her room and told her that she must remain in it unless sent for. Opium would be provided, he added with a sneer. After two or three days, Yoshiko, her only visitor, left for Shanghai. The small window of the Empress's room looked on to a high barbed-wire fence, beyond which were rows of oil drums. All she had to sustain her in her silent room were her opium and her dreams.

A week before the Empress's arrival at Port Arthur Pu Yi had been transferred from the Yamato Hotel to the Su House. At the same time, the grand guardian and the Mantis were allowed to leave the hotel, provided they observed the midnight curfew. During the next few weeks these two elder statesmen visited the Su House daily to call on Pu Yi, but neither of them made the least attempt to see the Empress or even enquire after her.

Meanwhile the other six officials were still confined to the first floor of their hotel. These hapless men, who had always

187

been so astute in looking to their own welfare, must have cursed their ill judgement in flocking to serve Pu Yi's cause in Manchuria too soon, much too soon, for their comfort.

The front balcony of the Su House gave Pu Yi a good view of the harbour. Every day he could see the huge transport ships unloading drums of oil and cases of munitions at the dockside while, on the horizon, another fleet of ships waited their turn to enter the port. Day and night a succession of trains steamed out of the docks, laden with supplies, northwards bound for Mukden and the battle zone.

By January 1932 the Nationalist government of China had made its official protest against the invasion of Manchuria to the League of Nations Assembly, and large sections of world opinion had expressed alarm at Japan's aggression. The Japanese government itself was divided over its army's invasion of Manchuria, and it took all the forceful advocacy of the Kwantung Army chief, and the influence of the Black Dragon Society, to win the day for the militants. In the United States there were strong protests from some senators, who accused their government of complicity in the invasion of Manchuria by allowing oil and iron ore to be exported to Japan. Without those supplies, claimed the senators, the invasion could not have proceeded. There was concern, too, among foreigners in the treaty ports of China. Suppressing the bandits around Mukden was one thing, people said, but a full-scale invasion of the whole province was quite another. Brushing aside these feeble protests, Woodhead came to Japan's defence. He was in his element again. Both on Shanghai radio and in special articles for *The Peking and Tientsin Times* he reminded the world that 'It is Japan's duty to keep the peace in the Far East. We should be grateful that Japan, alone of the allies, has staved off the final surrender of foreign rights in China.' Japan's policing action in Manchuria was no more than an extension of her 'Positive China Policy', said Woodhead, quoting Doihara's phrase with approval. Woodhead had long taken an interest in Doihara. There was an adventurous quality in the Japanese colonel that put Woodhead in mind of one of his heroes of the Great War, Lawrence of Arabia. The editor began to refer to

Doihara as the 'Lawrence of the East'. The name caught on, and in the smoking-room of the Tientsin Club the members were agreed that no number of *The Peking and Tientsin Times* was complete without a special article by Woodhead under the headline: 'Lawrence of the East in Mystery Journey' or 'The Lawrence of the East Does It Again'.

But Woodhead's euphoria did not last very long. Towards the end of January 1932 he was given an example of Japan's 'Positive China Policy' close to his own doorstep in Shanghai, and it was to shake his confidence in the 'Keepers of the Peace'. After a brawl between Japanese and Chinese in a Shanghai street, during which one Japanese and two Chinese were killed, the local Japanese commander, Admiral Shiozawa, sent for reinforcements. An aircraft-carrier and four destroyers arrived in the river. Not content with an apology from the Chinese mayor, Admiral Shiozawa ordered his marines to occupy Chapei, a densely populated district in which over 1½ million Chinese lived. The other foreign powers in the international settlement had agreed to this action; it was not the first time that Chapei, considered a danger spot, had been occupied by foreign troops during an emergency. But they were not prepared for what followed. The Chinese in Chapei resisted the Japanese troops, and fighting broke out. Admiral Shiozawa then gave orders that Chapei was to be bombed. For hour after hour relays of planes from the Japanese aircraft-carrier dropped their bombs on the crowded Chinese district until it was engulfed by flames. Many thousands were killed.

Woodhead watched the bombing from the comparative safety of a British command post, but he saw enough to be sickened by the carnage. After this, his first sight of a battle, he was a changed man. The voice that had spoken out so strongly in defence of Japan's policing of China now faltered, never to recover its strength.

Colonel Itagaki of the Kwantung Army staff at last sent word that he was ready to see Pu Yi. The date fixed for their meeting was 23 February, more than three months after Pu Yi's arrival in Manchuria. The gist of the Kwantung Army's plans for Pu Yi had already been leaked to the grand guardian and the Mantis by Amakasu. Pu Yi was to be chief executive of a new republic of Manchukuo. The name Manchukuo, which means simply Country of the Manchus, came as something of a shock to Pu Yi's elderly ministers, for the Chinese had always used the name North-East for that huge region which they regarded as a province of the Empire.

The meeting with Colonel Itagaki took place at the Su House. It was bound to be a formality, but the two senior ministers prepared a number of mild objections to the Japanese proposals as a face-saving gesture. Colonel Itagaki, who was short and dapper, had knife-edge creases in his trousers. He was another Adolphe Menjou, thought Pu Yi as he watched the way the colonel rubbed his hands together, just like a hotel manager welcoming an important guest. The colonel had the disconcerting habit of pacing up and down the room at meetings, as if he were inspecting his troops.

Having given Pu Yi a message of greetings from General Honjo, commander-in-chief of the Kwantung Army, and having also thanked Pu Yi for his kind present of a brooch, Colonel Itagaki outlined the proposals for the new republic. Then, with his hands behind his back, he paced up and down while the grand guardian made his objections: Was not the title chief executive somewhat demeaning for an emperor? Did not the word republic contain something repugnant? . . . Wisely, the Mantis kept silent.

The colonel dismissed these objections with contempt. He halted, paused for a few seconds, and then said, 'The capital of the Republic of Manchukuo will be at Changchun. There will be one political party in the republic. It will be named the Concordia Association.' With that, the colonel said he would like the court's decision by the next day, bowed to Pu Yi, and strode out of the room, followed by the scurrying Mantis.

That night Pu Yi and his cabinet gave a banquet at the Su House for Colonel Itagaki, the man who had kept Pu Yi waiting so long before deigning to meet him. The subject of the Republic was not mentioned. During the conversation, which could hardly be described as lively, the colonel addressed most of his remarks to the Mantis. Noticing this, the grand guardian feared the worst. For weeks he and the

190

Mantis had been vying with each other to win favour with the Japanese, and it now looked as if the Mantis had won. If that were so, thought the grand guardian with a sigh, he may as well retire from the court and go back to running his antique business with its branches in Tientsin, Peking and Mukden.

On the following day Pu Yi gave his formal assent to the proposals for the Republic of Manchukuo. Needless to say, no one gave a thought to any wishes the Empress might have in the matter. Another banquet was held. This time it was given by Colonel Itagaki in Pu Yi's honour. A toast was drunk to the Republic. Afterwards the Mantis saw the colonel to his car. When the Mantis returned, he approached Pu Yi with his hands held up in front of him and a beady look in his eye. He has just been appointed prime minister of Manchukuo, he said, and he looked forward to many years in Pu Yi's service.

CHAPTER TEN

THE PRINCIPLE OF BENEVOLENT RULE

On 6 March the train carrying Pu Yi to his new capital, 500 miles away in central Manchuria, steamed out of Port Arthur. From the window of his coach, Pu Yi had a last glimpse of the dreary Russian forts he had come to know so well. With Pu Yi in his coach were Amakasu and the Mantis. In the next coach were the Empress and an attendant nurse. In a third coach were the members of the cabinet, still complaining about the indignity of their detention in the Yamato Hotel. It was a slow journey. The train's engine seldom reached a speed of twenty miles an hour. On some stretches of the line there was only a single track. There were frequent stops to allow trains carrying soldiers and munitions to pass. Whenever the train entered a security zone where troops were concentrated, the guards at the door of each compartment would come in and pull down the window-blinds, and Amakasu would smile and nod with approval. Neither Pu Yi nor any of his cabinet was in the least inconvenienced when the blinds came down. Bred as they had been in the enclosures of palaces and urban mansions, they found even the distant views of the Manchurian landscape with its forests and snow-capped mountains an intimidating sight, and they would gladly have remained on the first floor of the Yamato Hotel for the rest of their lives rather than set foot in that wild country where bandits and tigers roamed.

After travelling for three hours they left the district of Kwantung and the Liaotung peninsula behind them and entered the 1,000-mile-long plain of Manchuria, which stretches from the Great Wall of China in the south to the River Amur and the arctic wastelands of Siberia in the north. The South Manchurian Railway line runs up the centre of that long narrow plain, through the towns of Mukden, Changchun and Harbin to join the Trans-Siberian line. On the west the plain is bordered by the high plateaux of Jehol, the Gobi Desert and Mongolia. On the east lies a belt of forest, above which tower the Long White Mountains. Changchun, which means Eternal Spring, was once an important staging-post for nomads on their long trek from the valley of the Volga to northern Korea. In 1932 it was a sprawling place comprising three settlements: a walled Chinese town of narrow lanes and many shops which sold furs, grain and spirits; an old Russian town with long houses which gave it the character of a Siberian settlement; and a Japanese town laid out in broad avenues, parks and Eurasian-style houses and office buildings. The most recent of the three settlements, the Japanese town, had a depressing, unlived-in-atmosphere.

Despite all the inducements offered to them by their government to settle in Manchuria, few Japanese had been prepared to leave their homeland for that vast, ungovernable country, bigger in extent than France and Germany combined. Since the Japanese invasion of Manchuria in 1931 the numbers of bandits there had actually increased, for thousands of disbanded Chinese troops had joined the gangs of professional bandits. The Secret Society of the Red Spear, deadly enemies of the Japanese, virtually controlled the forests and mountains in the east. Between the months of July and October, when the raw opium was brought in from the fields, the outlaws would come down to the plain to raid the towns and villages. Summer was also the time when the *gaoliang* in the fields stood over ten feet high, providing perfect cover for the raiders. Like most successful guerrillas, the Red Spear outlaws had the support of many villagers, who

194

provided them with a warning system against the approach of any Japanese troops. So powerful were the outlaws that in 1932 no night train ran on the South Manchurian line. Small wonder that the Japanese were reluctant to settle in their new colony.

On 8 March all the schoolchildren in the Japanese district of Changchun were given a holiday, and every available citizen was encouraged to be at the railway station to welcome the former Emperor who was about to become their head of state. With a feeble shriek from its whistle and grinding of brakes, the train from Port Arthur drew into Changchun station at the end of its two-day journey. It stopped with a sudden jolt, giving its occupants one last moment of acute discomfort. Pu Yi was thrown across his seat, but he quickly recovered. 'Listen!' he said. A brass band was playing. The platform was lined with children waving little Japanese red sun flags. 'Look!' said the Mantis, pointing to a small group of children who were waving the new, five-barred flag of Manchukuo.

Pu Yi stepped on to the platform, to be greeted by the Japanese mayor and a reception committee. The mayor then led him to the guard of honour, formed by a unit of the Kwantung Army. Beside them was a company of newly recruited Manchukuo troops in green uniforms. At the exit a large crowd cheered, and Pu Yi waved to them. The Mantis pointed out a small group of Manchu Loyalists in traditional long gowns who were waving their dragon flags; the delighted Pu Yi gave them a special wave, Pu Yi felt a glow of happiness. Everyone seemed so friendly, and there was not a single wild Manchurian pony in sight. This was the welcome that Johnston had promised him, he thought, and the one he had dreamed of on his way from Tientsin. Now all the bitter disappointment of his miserable arrival at Yingkow and the long weeks of waiting at Port Arthur seemed to have vanished with the wind.

A line of black cars waited to take Pu Yi, his family and his courtiers to his residence. Pu Yi sat in the first car with the mayor and waved to the crowd as the motorcade set off, led by two military policemen on motor cycles. The streets were empty as they drove through the western suburbs of the

Japanese district. 'Everyone must be at the station,' said Pu Yi. The mayor smiled. They passed some concrete blocks of flats, and one or two people put their heads out of the windows. Just beyond the flats the car stopped in front of an iron gate set in a high wall. 'This is your residence and office,' said the mayor. 'It is the biggest building in Changchun, and used to be the head office of the salt revenue administration.' The gate was opened by armed sentries, and the fleet of cars drove into a large compound that contained about four acres of derelict land. In the centre was the office, a grey brick building that reminded Pu Yi of Gordon Hall in Tientsin. At the back were a number of concrete bungalows with dark fly-screens covering the windows. 'Those are your residential quarters,' said the mayor. Pu Yi pointed to some sheds with red-painted corrugated-iron roofs, and looked inquiringly at the mayor. 'Ah!' said the mayor. 'Those are the old sheds where the reserve salt was once stored.' The bleak, rectangular compound with its air of a disused factory was surrounded by a fourteen-foot-high castellated brick wall. In each angle of the wall stood a round tower with loopholes for guns which could command all the approaches.

Pu Yi fell silent. 'There are recreational facilities,' said the mayor as he led Pu Yi towards his bungalow. Between the office building and Pu Yi's residence was a concrete tennis-court with a tattered net. Beside it was an empty swimming-pool. 'They were put in by an American.' the mayor said. He was not to know, of course, that the American he spoke of had once met Pu Yi. Twenty-three years before in the Hall of Supreme Harmony in the Forbidden City, Mr Esson Gale, then a young interpreter, had been in the American delegation which was received in audience by the child Emperor, and Mr Gale had noticed that the three-year-old Pu Yi's arms and legs were stretched out so stiffly under his padded robes that he looked like a mechanical toy. Since that dawn audience Mr Gale had been transferred to the salt administration. In 1922 he was appointed chief inspector at the administration's head office in Changchun. During their time there, he and his wife had installed those essentials of life, the tennis-court and swimming-pool which the mayor was now pleased to call 'recreational facilities'.

The next day, 9 March, was Inauguration Day for the chief executive of Manchukuo. From nine o'clock in the morning a continual succession of cars arrived in the compound, bringing Japanese military and civic dignitaries as well as some old Chinese officials. Among the latter was the grand guardian, who had come up from Mukden for the occasion. The ceremony was held in a large reception-room on the first floor of the office building. The room had been specially decorated and smelt of fresh paint. Pu Yi wore the evening-dress suit made by Whiteway & Laidlaw. He sat on a large cane chair. On one side of him stood General Honjo and Colonel Itagaki; on the other side were the Mantis and Mr Uchida, director of the South Manchurian Railway. Before the proceedings began, General Honjo announced that, in order to celebrate the birth of the new state, the Japanese government had decided to change the name of Changchun to Hsingking, which means new capital. His statement was greeted by a ripple of applause.

Two elderly subjects of Manchukuo presented Pu Yi with the seal of the chief executive. The Mantis then read out a proclamation on Pu Yi's behalf: 'Our new country,' he said, 'is founded on the principle of Wang Tao, the kingly way of benevolent rule. If we follow that principle, Manchukuo will become a paradise for the people.'

The ceremony over, everyone trooped outside, where photographs were taken of Pu Yi surrounded by the leading dignitaries. The new, five-barred, flag of Manchukuo was raised on the flag-pole. The officers saluted, and the civilians raised their hats.

In the afternoon Amakasu showed Pu Yi around the office building. Much to Amakasu's amusement, Pu Yi called it the salt office. The long corridors were full of musty, unused rooms which depressed Pu Yi. On the second floor they climbed up a staircase, which gave on to the flat roof. It was the only place in the compound from which one could see over the perimeter wall. On the east side of the compound were the blocks of flats and other buildings of the Japanese town. On the other three sides *gaoliang* fields stretched as far

197

as one could see. Between the wall of the compound and the *gaoliang* fields on the south side was a small park with yellow trees and a pond. It looked very inviting, Pu Yi thought.

A banquet was planned for Inauguration night, but before it began, Pu Yi decided to take Beautiful Countenance for a walk in the park. They had just reached the pond, where to their delight they saw some ducks bobbing about, when they heard loud shouts. A police patrol came running up, followed by Amakasu. 'Come back at once!' he shouted. 'This is strictly forbidden.'

On their way back to the salt office Amakasu explained that the alarm had been raised when it was reported that Pu Yi was missing from the compound, and that the police had been searching for him. 'Your Excellency and your family must never leave the compound without a military escort,' said Amakasu.

That night at the banquet Pu Yi was subdued. While toast after toast was drunk, he kept thinking of the unused rooms in the salt office and of the enchanting pond in the forbidden park.

One day the Mantis sidled into the chief executive's office and placed a pile of documents before Pu Yi for his signature. They were the terms of a treaty between Japan and Manchukuo, the Mantis explained. He had agreed to everything with General Honjo. Perhaps he might run through some of the principal terms in order to put Pu Yi in the picture. The Mantis recited them: Japan was to have control over the defence and security of Manchukuo; Manchukuo would supply all the food and equipment needed by the Japanese armed forces: Japan would continue to control the railways.

Pu Yi signed the documents. All that remained was for the Kwantung Army commander to come to Hsingking for a formal ceremony, said the Mantis. The Concordia Association would then ratify the treaty and Japan would give its official recognition to the Republic of Manchukuo. Other nations would surely follow Japan's lead. The Mantis had good reason to feel pleased. He had handled his first affair of state, and it seemed to be going without a hitch.

Before the treaty ceremony General Honjo retired, and his place as commander of the Kwantung Army and governor of the Kwantung province was taken by General Muto. A white-haired, fatherly figure of sixty-five, General Muto had commanded the Japanese forces in the ill-fated allied expedition to Siberia in 1918 when the general had distinguished himself by his speedy withdrawal of the Japanese troops in the face of the Bolsheviks.

General Muto duly came to Hsingking for the treaty ceremony. Afterwards toasts were drunk in champagne. Feeling in an expansive mood, the general took Pu Yi on one side. 'As man to man,' said the general, slapping Pu Yi on the back and nearly sending him flying, 'republics may do for other countries, but you and I know that the Chinese and the Japanese prefer to be governed by an emperor. Mind you,' said the general, wagging his finger at Pu Yi and roaring with laughter, 'I'm not promising anything, you understand?'

Thrilled at what he heard, Pu Yi could hardly sleep that night. One day soon he would wear the dragon robes again, and the beady-eyed Mantis who gave those stiff little bows would have to kowtow when he came into the office. It was a pleasing thought.

The Mantis entered Pu Yi's office, bowed more stiffly than usual, and said, 'Your Excellency's old friend has arrived from Tientsin. May I show him in?'

H.G.W. Woodhead strode in and gave Pu Yi's limp hand a hearty shake. The Mantis went out, leaving Woodhead with Pu Yi and an interpreter from the office of information.

Woodhead, who was on a fact-finding mission in Manchuria, was delighted to be the first journalist to interview the chief executive. 'Thank you for sparing me some of your time. I know how busy you must be,' Woodhead said with a smile. Pu Yi remained silent. Woodhead, a little disconcerted, tried again. 'It's good to see you looking so well,' he said, less breezily. To his astonishment, Pu Yi turned to his interpreter and exchanged a few rapid words with him in Chinese. 'His Excellency thanks you for your kind reference to his health,' said the interpreter in his carefully phrased English.

Woodhead was baffled. His conversations with Pu Yi had always been in English. Woodhead himself had hardly any Chinese, and when forced to speak it he would eke out the few words he had in pidgin English. Could Pu Yi have forgotten his English so soon? he wondered. Recovering his composure, he explained to the interpreter that he would like to put one or two questions to the chief executive. The interpreter translated his words to Pu Yi, who smiled and nodded.

'Why did His Excellency leave Tientsin for Manchuria?' asked Woodhead.

There was a flurry of Chinese and the interpreter replied, 'Firstly, His Excellency felt that the welfare of the Chinese people was being neglected by the Nationalists. Secondly, Manchukuo, the homeland of his tribal ancestors with its forests and mountains, has always had an irresistible appeal for His Excellency.'

'Is there any truth in the report that His Excellency was forced to come here by the Japanese, and that they have placed him under restraint since he landed in Manchuria?'

The interpreter spoke to Pu Yi, who smiled broadly. 'At no time,' said the interpreter, 'has His Excellency been under the restraint of the Japanese.'

Pu Yi rose from his chair to signal the end of the interview. As he did so, he turned to his interpreter and said, 'Wang Tao'.

'His Excellency says that no one need fear being put under restraint in a country such as Manchukuo, where the principle of benevolent rule is carried out,' the interpreter said to Woodhead.

At the door, Pu Yi offered Woodhead his hand and then said a last few words in rapid Chinese. 'His Excellency', said the interpreter, 'wishes you to convey his greetings to the British people in Tientsin, especially to the society dedicated to St Andrew.'

When, later, Woodhead wrote a detailed report of his visit to Pu Yi, he made no mention at all of the 'lovely girl who resembled a piece of delicate porcelain'.

Woodhead had just left Pu Yi's office and was walking down the corridor when he was stopped by a Japanese officer who introduced himself as Colonel Yoshioka. Saying that he was honoured to meet the famous editor of *The Peking and Tientsin Times*, the colonel explained that he was in charge of the office of information. He felt sure that Woodhead would be interested in some literature about Manchukuo. With that, he handed Woodhead a huge pile of pamphlets and brochures. Weighed down by the bundle, Woodhead staggered to his car which was waiting to take him back to the Railway Hotel.

Colonel Yoshioka was of medium build with a remarkably slim waist, over which his belt was always tightly buckled. He had high cheek-bones and a sallow complexion. Ever eager to communicate, he spoke in an incessant whine, and his voice would rise to a high pitch when he became excited. Pu Yi called him the Wasp. The Wasp had been on Colonel Doihara's staff in Mukden, and he had accompanied Doihara on some of his visits to Tientsin, where he had once met Pu Yi. When Pu Chieh, the younger brother of Pu Yi, was a pupil at the Japanese army cadet school, the Wasp had been one of his instructors, and it was partly through the recommendation of Pu Chieh that the Wasp had obtained his present post. Shortly after the Wasp's arrival, Amakasu was transferred to a secret service unit in Hsingking. Thanks to Doihara's influence, the Wasp had become a skilled propagandist. But, unlike the Lawrence of the East, who spoke in the concise slogans of an advertiser's copy writer, the Wasp tended to be verbose. He had, however, succeeded in adapting for his purposes a succinct Chinese phrase, of which the Lawrence of the East would have approved: Wang Tao, the principle of benevolent rule. The Wasp drafted all Pu Yi's speeches and he coached Pu Yi in the art of handling interviewers. So far, judging from the Woodhead interview, the Wasp was satisfied with his pupil's progress. A much sterner test, however, awaited Pu Yi.

Peter Fleming, a special correspondent of *The Times* of London, had arrived in Manchuria, via Siberia. The title of Fleming's book on his travels in Asia tells one a lot about the man. He called it *One's Company*. It was typical of Fleming, devoid as he was of conventional wisdom, and an intrepid wanderer by nature, that he should manage to persuade a Japanese officer to allow him to accompany an anti-bandit expedition to the densely forested foothills of the Long White Mountains. Fleming later compared the troops' efforts on that expedition with those of an elephant trying to seek out and destroy a swarm of mosquitoes.

Fleming had not been in Manchuria long, before he offended the many special correspondents there by referring to them as 'members of an overrated profession who never went off the beaten track, but sat about the lounges of railway hotels, waiting to be given the official line in propaganda'.

The Wasp knew what he was up against in this idiosyncratic journalist who had recently described the Japanese town in Hsingking as 'having an atmosphere thick with humbug, as well as possessing that symmetrical, sanitary, and entirely characterless appearance imposed by Japanese influence on all the railway towns in the Manchurian plain'. As for the Wasp's propaganda, Fleming treated it with contempt. And the Wasp was unhappy when Amakasu reported that the Wasp's 400-page treatise, 'Manchukuo before and after the Mukden Incident', which had been sent to Fleming, had been found dumped on a spitoon in the foyer of the Railway Hotel. Fleming later confessed that, having read 'several kilometres' of the treatise, he had given up in exhaustion, for it was full of indigestible statistics, and, worst of all in Fleming's view, totally humourless.

When the dreaded Fleming was ushered into the chief executive's office, he found Pu Yi wearing dark glasses, a frock coat, white waistcoat and white spats to match. Once again Pu Yi answered all the questions through his interpreter. Unlike Woodhead, Fleming was prepared for the universal formula: Wang Tao. And he knew that his questions must contain specific charges, if they were not to be easily deflected.

'Was it not true', Fleming asked, 'that the government of Manchukuo was making profitable business out of its monopoly in opium?'

The interpreter shuddered. He managed to arrive at Wang

Tao, but his circuitous journey did not sound convincing.

'Had not the use of bombers on anti-bandit operations resulted in the destruction of much innocent life and property?'

The interpreter gasped and made another despairing and futile attempt to reach Wang Tao.

Having won his moral victory, Fleming decided that it was time to be generous. He offered an easier question: 'Which has been the happiest time in His Excellency's Life – the old days in the Forbidden City, his exile in the Japanese concession in Tientsin, or the present in Manchukuo?'

Pu Yi and the interpreter both smiled with relief as they discussed the charming question. The interpreter began to translate: 'His Excellency says that so long as you feel benevolent towards everyone, so long as you practise the principle of Wang Tao, happiness is surely only a question of . . . ' he droned on.

Fleming found Pu Yi a rather touching figure. He was, Fleming later wrote, better looking than one would suppose from his photographs, which gave him a tortoise-like appearance. When Pu Yi learned about that remark, he was puzzled. He was very fond of tortoises, and would not in the least mind looking like one of them.

CHAPTER ELEVEN

MOON TO THE MIKADO'S SUN

Pu Yi sat at a large desk in his office. He was wearing his black frock coat, white waistcoat, and, a new touch, a grey cravat with a pearl tie-pin. The Mantis stood at one side of the desk with the disconsolate air of an underemployed master of ceremonies, while the Wasp fussed about the desk, arranging bundles of paper on it, to make it look like the desk of the managing director of a thriving company. The Wasp was highly nervous today. The League of Nations commission of inquiry was coming to interview Pu Yi. As if that was not enough, Colonel Itagaki was coming with them. Word had reached Itagaki that Fleming had scored something of a victory at his interview with Pu Yi. The Wasp, who was producer, director and scriptwriter for the performance which was about to begin, knew that his career depended on it. He gave a last word of instruction to the interpreter, placed an easy chair beside the desk, cast an eye over the six chairs that had been arranged in a semicircle in front of Pu Yi, and satisfied that the stage had been set, went off to await Itagaki.

The buglers sounded a fanfare, and the guard presented arms as the commission's fleet of cars swept through the gate into the compound. Itagaki led Lord Lytton, the British chairman of the commission, and his members into the chief executive's office and introduced them to Pu Yi.

205

When the interview began, Pu Yi moved from behind his desk and sat in the easy chair exactly as planned. Lord Lytton and his colleagues from America, France, Italy and Germany took their places in front of Pu Yi. Itagaki sat behind them. At the very back of the room the Mantis sat motionless on a stool, looking like a dry old stick. Lord Lytton, who was dressed in a black coat and striped trousers, conducted the proceedings as if he were a genial old high court judge and Pu Yi was a shy young barrister appearing in court for the first time. Smiling to put Pu Yi at his ease, and speaking in his most soothing voice, Lord Lytton asked the friendliest of questions, couched in the simplest language. Pu Yi, who was unable to take his eyes off his lordship's striped trousers, lost track of some of the questions, but it hardly mattered, for his interpreter was master of the situation.

Lord Lytton came to his last question: 'I wonder if you could say something on how the state of Manchukuo came to be founded?' he asked.

Pu Yi listened to his interpreter, smiled, and replied, 'Wang Tao'. The interpreter translated: 'The Manchurian masses have long yearned for the principle of benevolent rule . . .'

At the end of the interview Pu Yi took Lord Lytton to a side-table and proudly pointed out to him the signed photograph of King George V. His lordship was touched by this personal gesture.

Outside in the corridor the Wasp anxiously awaited his fate. When he saw Itagaki emerge from the office, gently rubbing his hands together, and behind him the Mantis raising his hands as if in a prayer, he knew that all was well.

A few weeks later, the Lytton commission presented its report to the League of Nations. The report treated Japan with remarkable leniency. It sympathized with Japan's concern that law and order should prevail in that region, so close to her border with Russia. Although the commission found that Japan had violated China's sovereignty and had established the new state of Manchukuo for her own purposes, it did not recommend Japan's withdrawal. On the contrary, it recommended that the government of Manchukuo, with Pu Yi at its head, should continue in being, with, perhaps, the help of some foreign advisers. The truth is that the League could do little to halt Japan's aggressive designs in the Far East even if it had wanted to. The League of Nations had been sponsored by President Wilson of the United States, but his government had promptly disowned it, and without American support the League was powerless.

Towards the end of 1932 the new state of Manchukuo suffered a setback in its fortunes. Beyond its western borders lay the province of Jehol. The Chinese governor of Jehol had come out for Manchukuo when it was founded, but he now changed his mind and declared that Jehol was once more back in the fold of China. This desertion was more than the Japanese government could tolerate. Japan had a new foreign minister, Mr Uchida, who when he was a director of the South Manchurian Railway had attended Pu Yi's inauguration. Uchida had many close friends in the Kwantung Army, and he was a strong believer in the Positive China Policy. He ordered General Muto of the Kwantung Army to recover Jehol. Waves of Japanese bombers flew over the province, pounding Chinese troops and civilians alike, to prepare the way for Muto's divisions. Chinese resistance crumbled, and the Japanese advanced rapidly to occupy Jehol city, the capital. That night Pu Yi gave a banquet at the salt office to celebrate General Muto's victory.

Outside the city of Jehol stand the ruins of the Summer Palace of the Ching emperors, unlived in since the Hsien Feng Emperor, husband of the Venerable Buddha, died there, a fugitive from Peking. On the mountainside above are a number of temples. Towering over them all is the Potala. A copy of the Potala Palace of the lamas of Tibet, the Jehol Potala was built in the eighteenth century by the famous Chien Lung Emperor, ancestor of the Empress Beautiful Countenance, Pu Yi's wife. In the spring, the lower slopes of the mountains and the fields in the valleys below are covered with mauve-coloured poppies. Beyond those purple valleys and the mountains that enclose them lie the steppe lands of the Interior and the legendary Western Isle of the Empress's dreams.

The invasion of Jehol brought a strong condemnation of Japan by the League of Nations. At Geneva, delegate after delegate denounced Japan's action. The indignant Uchida ordered his delegation to march out of the assembly in protest, and on 27 March 1933 he announced that Japan had quit the League.

General Muto now had a free rein. His troops marched southwards, crossed the Great Wall into China, and soon threatened Peking. Chiang Kai-shek's Nationalist government in Nanking panicked and sought an armistice on Japan's terms. By the Tangku Agreement, China agreed to withdraw all her troops from an area of about 5,000 square miles between the Great Wall and Peking, leaving the Japanese army in control of northern China.

The flag of the rising sun fluttered over the camps of General Muto's victorious troops in northern China, but the general soon found that he had to face a more elusive and deadly enemy than Chiang Kai-shek's Nationalist army. The White Wolf was active again, and every day the general received reports of his men being ambushed by guerrillas. These attacks occurred most frequently on the Japanese army's weak and extended flank in the province of Shensi, west of Peking, where the terrain was ideally suited to guerrilla warfare, as Yuan Shih-kai's Northern Army had so often found to their cost.

In Shensi province the Great Wall runs along the southern edge of the great desert plateau which the Mongols call the Ordos. In several places the wall's long spine is broken, and blocks of stone lie half-buried in the sand. Below the wall, on the Chinese side, was the small hill town of Pao An. There the White Wolf had his lair. The enemy of landlords, government officials and tax-collectors, the White Wolf was regarded as a hero by the local peasants. His daredevil escapades were famous. Once, he and a few of his followers were invited to a banquet by one of the war-lord Feng Yu-hsiang's generals. The general's plot was to poison the White Wolf, but during the banquet the White Wolf and his men disarmed their hosts and, seizing twenty guns, made off into the hills. It was exploits such as these which led the peasants to attribute magical qualities to the White Wolf. No one was his equal as a swordsman, and he was even said to be invulnerable to bullets.

The White Wolf had links with the Red Army, which was fighting Chiang Kai-shek in the south, and he was said to be a Red himself. None of that mattered to the peasants; to them, he was the White Wolf who killed officials and made their hill town and its surrounding terraces impregnable against tax-collectors and soldiers.

By the spring of 1932 the White Wolf and his peasant guerrillas controlled no fewer than eleven counties in the north-west of China. Chiang Kai-shek sent an army against him, but the White Wolf slipped across the broken wall into the desert region of the Interior, where no army dared pursue him. The Japanese had then invaded northern China, and Chiang Kai-shek withdrew, leaving General Muto to deal with the White Wolf as best he could.

Earlier in the year, from their base in the far south of China, Mao Tse-tung and his comrades in the Red Army had declared war on Japan for her invasion of Manchuria. Few people in the world had heard about Mao Tse-tung, let alone his declaration; and even those who did learn about it, will not have taken much notice. In time, however, even the Western historians were to recognize that Mao's declaration of war on the Japanese was the first signal that the Second World War had begun.

Harried by the Nationalist forces, which were intent on exterminating the Reds in the south, Mao Tse-tung and his Red Army began their long march to the north-west. In the autumn of 1935 the advance guard of Mao's depleted army reached Yenan in Shensi province, within the White Wolf's territory. The Reds sent a senior party official with their advance guard to Yenan, to make arrangements for the arrival of the main army.

The Communist official, whose name was Chang Ching-fu, became known to the local guerrillas as the Inspector. Shocked by the anarchistic behaviour of the White Wolf and his men, which he termed 'Robin Hoodism', the Inspector began to collect evidence to prove that the White Wolf had deviated from the party line. The White Wolf and a hundred of his men were arrested.

When the Red Army arrived at Yenan in October, and

Mao learned of the White Wolf's arrest, he immediately released him and his men. It was a wise move, for it prevented trouble among the local peasants and, at the same time, it freed for active service against the Japanese a brilliant commander who led his men from the front, unlike the generals of orthodox armies.

In March 1936 the White Wolf was mortally wounded during an attack on a Japanese-held fort on a bank of the Yellow River. He was carried back to Pao An, where he died. Shortly afterwards, peasants reported having seen him riding along the top of the Great Wall. Like the Yellow Lotus of the marshlands, the White Wolf never dies.

In July 1933, while his troops in China kept an uneasy watch for the White Wolf and his guerrillas, the white-haired little General Muto died peacefully in his sleep. Pu Yi missed him. Muto had always taken a paternal interest in Pu Yi. For his part, Pu Yi enjoyed Muto's company, especially at banquets, when, after a few glasses of champagne, Muto would put on one of his swashbuckling performances and then roar with laughter at the gloomy Mantis and the anxious Wasp.

Muto's funeral was held at Port Arthur, the Kwantung Army's main base. The ceremonies were typical of that unhappy blend of Eastern and Western customs that Fleming found so vulgar. A Shinto religious service was followed by a Western-style military parade at which Muto's coffin was borne on a gun-carriage drawn by Japanese marines, while a band played Chopin's funeral march. On the coffin were Muto's cap and a sword, and his many decorations including the stars for his retreat from Siberia and his conquest of Jehol. No award had yet been made for the campaign in northern China.

General Hishikari, Muto's successor as commander-in-chief, had the hatchet-like face of a hardened campaigner. He too, like Muto, was a believer in imperial rule. The Emperor of Japan was the supreme Mikado, of course, but there was room for a satellite emperor, thought Hishikari. At their very first meeting, Hishikari told Pu Yi that there was little doubt that the Japanese government would shortly recognize Pu Yi

210

as Emperor of Manchukuo. Pu Yi hopped about his office with delight at this news, while the Mantis looked on benevolently.

There was an air of excitement in the salt office as the word spread that the chief executive was to become an emperor. Acting on his own initiative, the Wasp travelled to Tokyo, where he sought to further Pu Yi's cause by calling on members of the Black Dragon Society. He also visited some relatives of the Japanese Emperor, and was given a few presents to take back to Pu Yi. The staff of the Kwantung Army were furious when they heard about the Wasp's mission, and Colonel Itagaki administered a reprimand that checked the Wasp's enthusiasm for several weeks.

At last the Japanese government issued a communiqué stating that a ceremony would be held soon in Hsingking, at which Japan would officially recognize Pu Yi as Emperor of Manchukuo. The news that he was to be an emperor again was published in the Peking newspapers and shortly afterwards a horde of his relations, most of whom he had never met, descended on the salt office. They were Pu Yi's three sisters, who were Prince Chun's daughters by various concubines, their husbands, and three young male children, Pu Yi's nephews. Their journey to Hsingking was arranged by the Kwantung Army staff who saw propaganda value in this demonstration of family affection and loyalty to the new regime in Manchukuo.

One of Pu Yi's newly arrived brothers-in-law, Cheng, was the grandson of the Mantis. He and his wife had just spent two years in London, where they had stayed in Johnston's house. Mr Cheng, as he liked to be called, was inclined to put on airs because of his travels abroad. He also made the fatal mistake of boasting of his connection with the Mantis, not knowing that his grandfather was out of favour with both Pu Yi and the Wasp. Not surprisingly, Pu Yi formed an instant dislike for Mr Cheng.

Any expectations that this family brood may have had of a life of grandeur at Pu Yi's court quickly died when the iron gates of the compound clanged shut behind them and they found themselves confined within the tall grey walls. All the bungalows being occupied, they were accommodated in a derelict salt shed that had been hastily converted. There was no plumbing in the shed and they were forced to share the outdoor lavatory. By night they suffered in their bitterly cold rooms, and by day they were pursued by the Wasp, who delighted in inflicting on them a large number of house rules and other petty restrictions. Within a week Mr Cheng's one thought was to find a way of returning to Peking, but as he was to discover, it was one thing to gain entry to the salt office, and quite another to gain permission to leave it.

Colonel Itagaki arrived at the salt office to discuss the arrangements for the enthronement. Pu Yi told him, with great excitement, that he had sent for the imperial dragon robes. They had been cared for by one of the high consorts, and would be brought from Peking by a veteran Manchu nobleman in time for the enthronement.

There was a frosty silence. 'It has already been decided,' said Itagaki, 'that Your Excellency will wear the uniform of generalissimo of the land, sea and air forces of Manchukuo.'

Pu Yi stamped his foot in anger. 'But I must wear the dragon robes,' he cried. 'They are the only dress an emperor can possibly wear on his throne.'

'I must remind Your Excellency,' said Itagaki, 'that you are to be enthroned as Emperor of Manchukuo. You are not being restored as the Emperor of China.' Itagaki turned to the Mantis.

'I fear the colonel is right,' said the Mantis. 'This is not to be a restoration. Perhaps one day when the Japanese army has conquered China, you may become the Great Ching Emperor again.'

Pu Yi gave the Mantis a sour look. He was becoming more and more displeased with him. Every night Pu Yi sat up until the early hours, playing mah-jong with the Mantis and two other members of the cabinet, and the Mantis always won. Sometimes, just when Pu Yi was on the brink of victory, the Mantis would stretch out his long fingers, snatch a lucky piece from the wall, and announce with a beady look in his eye that his hand was complete.

Pu Yi told Itagaki that he would have to consider the question of what he would wear at the enthronement, and left the office in a huff.

The next day the Mantis was able to inform Pu Yi that a compromise had been reached. Pu Yi could wear the dragon robes for the dawn sacrifice at the Altar of Heaven, but he must wear the uniform of generalissimo at the enthronement.

On the eve of his enthronement Pu Yi was in the bedroom of his bungalow behind the salt office when the Mantis and an old Manchu nobleman arrived with a cloth bag containing the imperial robes. The nobleman knelt and kowtowed to Pu Yi, whom he had not seen for many years. Pu Yi was pleased by this act of homage, and he enjoyed performing the gracious gesture of helping the nobleman to his feet.

The faded yellow robes were taken out of the bag, and the two men helped Pu Yi to try them on. Pu Yi turned to face a long looking-glass while the nobleman adjusted the collar of the mantle. As he looked at himself in the mirror, Pu Yi said to the nobleman behind him, 'I was a child when I last wore the imperial robes. Mine were much smaller than these. Can you tell me who was the last emperor to wear these old robes?'

'Your Imperial Majesty,' replied the nobleman, 'the high consort who kept them told me that they were the robes of your predecessor, the Kuang Hsu Emperor.'

There was a long silence. The Mantis and the nobleman looked at each other, then, bowing to Pu Yi's back, they slipped away and left him staring at himself in the looking-glass.

At dawn on 1 March 1934 Pu Yi stood before a wooden altar that had been erected in the forbidden park outside the walls of the compound. Behind the altar the first red streaks of sun could be seen through the naked branches of a willow tree that bordered the pond. The Mantis heaped incense on a piece of burning charcoal. Dressed in his heavy yellow robes, Pu Yi bowed to the altar and the sun behind it. He then made the brief Address to Heaven, bowed again in the direction of the sun, and, the ceremony over, he turned round to face the Mantis and the nobleman who were in attendance. The two men should have bowed to the Emperor, but they stood there, petrified. The figure in the yellow robes who now faced them was not the young Pu Yi of the evening before, but a man with the sad and ageing eyes of one who had lived too long alone.

213

The Wasp flitted about the chief executive's office, putting the finishing touches to the scenery for the enthronement ceremony. A red carpet had been laid, stretching from the door to a high-backed chair at the end of the room. Behind the chair, which served as a throne, the wall was covered in silk curtains of a bright blue colour. Two large vases filled with yellow chrysanthemums stood one on either side of the throne. There was no place for the Empress, who was said to be indisposed. The Mantis and the other members of Pu Yi's court came in and lined up in front of the throne. A fanfare was sounded by the buglers at the door, and Prince Chichibu, the brother of the Emperor of Japan, entered, escorted by General Hishikari and Colonel Itagaki. All three wore British-style full-dress uniforms. The Wasp, bowing obsequiously, ushered them to their places beside the throne. A second fanfare was sounded, and all present turned to watch Pu Yi's entrance. Ten page-boys, recruited from the Hsingking orphanage, walked in file, leading the imperial procession. Next came Pu Chieh, Pu Yi's brother, in the uniform of a Japanese army cadet. He was followed by his three young nephews. Last of all came Pu Yi. Even the Wasp, who had seen Pu Yi's uniform on a coat-hanger earlier that morning, had to gasp. Pu Yi wore a grey double-breasted Napoleonic coat which reached to his knees. Gilt epaulettes hung from each shoulder. His dark blue trousers were much too long for him. Attached to the white belt around his waist was a curved sword. On his right arm he carried a large gilt helmet. Dark red feathers hung down from its crown, and there was a chin-strap in the form of a chain. The whole headpiece looked as if it had been designed for a centurion in a Hollywood film about ancient Rome. This was the uniform of the generalissimo of the land, sea and air forces of Manchukuo.

Itagaki had stressed that the ceremony must be carried out with military precision and, in order to impress his chief, the Wasp had gone to a lot of trouble to teach Pu Yi the goose step. Now, kicking out his legs before him, Pu Yi marched stiffly down the red carpet.

When Pu Yi was seated on the throne, the Mantis and the rest of the cabinet bowed three times. Pu Yi had asked for the kowtow to be restored, but his request had been rejected by Itagaki. Instead, the colonel had ordained that the single bow formerly given to the chief executive should be increased to three bows.

General Hishikari stepped forward and presented his credentials as the Japanese ambassador to the imperial court of Manchukuo. This, as far as the Japanese were concerned, was the crux of the entire proceedings.

Afterwards, photographs were taken outside the entrance of the salt office, which was now named the Imperial Palace, although Pu Yi irritated the Wasp by insisting on calling it the Salt Palace. Toasts were drunk to celebrate the beginning of the new dynasty. No one was in a happier mood than the Wasp. Itagaki was pleased with the way the ceremony had gone. He not only forgave the Wasp for his indiscretions, but he promoted him to the post of 'attaché to the imperial household'.

In the afternoon Pu Yi was taken on his first imperial motorcade to be shown to his subjects. Wearing his general-issimo's uniform, he sat beside General Hishikari in an open car, surrounded by Japanese army motor cycles. When the imperial car passed the railway station, a crowd of schoolchildren waved the flags of Japan and Manchukuo, crying 'Long live the Emperor!' at the figure in dark glasses, hidden under the Roman centurion's helmet.

A few days after Pu Yi's enthronement, his father, Prince Chun, arrived from Peking to pay his son a visit. Pu Yi's elevation to Emperor seems to have gone to his head, for he treated the simple family reunion as if it were a formal military exercise. Rather than go to the railway station to meet his father, he sent an officer with a guard of honour. Dressed in his generalissimo's uniform, he waited for the old prince at the main gate of the compound.

Having heard that Prince Chun was coming, the Empress went to the gate to join Pu Yi. It was the first time she had been seen in public since her arrival from Port Arthur. When the prince stepped out of his car, Pu Yi gave him a stiff salute, but, to Pu Yi's surprise, the Empress knelt on the ground in the old Chinese way of venerating the elderly. The prince, who was very fond of the Empress, was moved to tears at seeing her

215

again. He lifted her up gently and, giving her his arm, led her into the palace, followed by the goose-stepping generalissimo.

That night Pu Yi gave a private dinner party for his father. The Empress appeared again and sat next to Prince Chun. Noticing that his father was paying her a lot of attention, Pu Yi began to feel peeved. He brightened up a little, however, when his brother, Pu Cheih, raised his glass and called out 'Long live His Majesty the Emperor!' Everyone joined in the toast, and Pu Yi lowered his eyes modestly.

As Pu Chieh sat down again, he made a joke that Pu Yi could not quite catch but that made his sisters giggle. Pu Yi frowned. Memories returned to him of that day in the Forbidden City when he had caught Pu Chieh wearing the imperial yellow in the lining of his gown. There was something dangerous about Pu Chieh, he thought. He probably wanted to become Emperor himself. He would have to be watched.

It was time for Prince Chun to leave for home. Seizing this opportunity, Mr Cheng, who made no mention of his own wife or the rest of the family, implored the prince to take him with him. The embarrassed prince referred his request to the Wasp, who replied sharply that it was out of the question for Mr Cheng to leave.

After Prince Chun returned to Peking the Empress withdrew to the solitude of her room. The people of Manchukuo knew her only from her photograph taken on her wedding day when she was a beautiful young girl of sixteen. It was hung beside Pu Yi's photograph in schools, army barracks and other public places. The Japanese attached great importance to the image of their own Mikado, whose photographs were venerated as icons. Unlike the Mikado, Pu Yi was not regarded as sacred, but schoolchildren and soldiers were instructed to bow to the picture of Pu Yi and his Empress whenever they passed them.

In the year following his enthronement Pu Yi was allowed out of his palace three times to be shown in person to his subjects. On two of these occasions he went on an imperial progress by motorcade. The third involved a visit to the headquarters of the Concordia Association. Pu Yi received a standing ovation from the party members when he appeared. Seated on a gilt chair in front of the portraits of himself and his Empress, he read out the speech written by the Wasp, who had introduced a new keynote. Pu Yi was honoured, he said, to be the moon to the Mikado's sun. Together their alliance would shine over Asia. The speech over, there was a second ovation, and Pu Yi left the stage to return to his grey palace in the suburbs.

Pu Yi was never accompanied by his beautiful Empress on these State visits, and it was only natural that rumours should spread about the secret life that went on behind the walls of the palace compound. The Empress, it was said, languished in a basement dungeon while Pu Yi lived a depraved life above stairs. Whatever the truth of these rumours, there is no doubt that from the time of his enthronement Pu Yi returned to his old vice of flogging the page-boys for the slightest offence. He rarely left his bed before midday and took no exercise except to go ant watching among the nettles in the grounds of the compound.

Inevitably, one day a page-boy escaped from the palace and told of his trials there. Japanese newspaper reporters asked the attaché to the imperial household for a statement. It was the Wasp's duty to protect Pu Yi's reputation, and he went to work with zest. He held a press conference at which he lectured his audience on the vigorous, outdoor life led by the Emperor. Pu Yi, he said, possessed the ancient tribal instincts of the Manchu race which, of course, included a knowledge and love of horses. Pu Yi always rose early in the morning, and after the simplest of breakfasts he could be seen galloping on horseback over the hills, far beyond the palace. An expert in the traditional Tartar sport of equestrian archery, Pu Yi would race through the grounds of the compound loosing off quiverfuls of arrows at his targets. So fearsome an archer and a horseman was he, that it was hardly necessary for the palace to be guarded by its sentries any longer. As usual, the Wasp had excelled himself.

At about nine o'clock one morning in the winter of 1934 a Japanese cavalry officer and two troopers clattered into the palace compound on horseback. One of the troopers led a riderless horse, a magnificent chesnut mare. When the Wasp arrived on the scene, the cavalry officer explained that the mare was a present from His Imperial Majesty, Hirohito, Emperor of Japan, who, having heard of Pu Yi's prowess on horseback, was delighted to send him this thoroughbred from his own stables.

All aquiver, the Wasp entered Pu Yi's bedroom, wakened him and, in his high-pitched whine, passed on the terrible news of the Mikado's gift. At the word horse, Pu Yi buried himself in his bedclothes, not to emerge all day.

At the end of 1934 General Hishikari, in consultation with the Mantis, decided that the time had come for Pu Yi to pay a State visit to the Emperor of Japan. Thus, Pu Yi would repay the courtesy of Prince Chichubu's attendance at his enthrone-ment, and cement the alliance between Japan and Manchukuo. The Mikado and the Japanese government gave their consent to the proposed visit, and a date was fixed for early April 1935.

Undeterred by the consequences of his previous labours on Pu Yi's behalf, the Wasp began a new propaganda campaign to acquaint the citizens of Tokyo with Pu Yi's many fine qualities. The cornerstone of his campaign was a lengthy tome entitled *A Respectful Record of His Majesty's Virtues*, which must have impressed many a Japanese matron.

Pu Yi, the *Respectful Record* said, was a distinguished poet and calligraphist. As a painter he had few equals, even among professional artists. He had an extensive knowledge of English literature, and his English writing style was Shakespearian in its richness. But, the Wasp reminded his readers, Pu Yi was not only an artist, he was a man of action. And the *Respectful Record* gave its readers a picture of Pu Yi, the lone horseman, armed with a bow and a quiverful of arrows, riding along the mountain ranges of Manchukuo, ready to do battle against any invader.

On 2 April Pu Yi boarded the Japanese battleship *Hie Maru* in Dairen harbour. Although Manchukuo possessed no warships, Pu Yi wore the new dark blue uniform of the supreme commander of the Manchukuo Navy. There had been no invitation for the Empress, who remained behind in her concrete bungalow.

Before the battleship set sail, Pu Yi, the poet Emperor, sat in his beautifully decorated cabin composing a poem with the help of the Wasp, as a tribute to his Japanese allies:

> The sea as flat as a mirror,
> I make a long voyage.
> The two countries hold hands
> To consolidate the East.

The sea did not remain flat for long, and soon after the *Hie Maru* set sail Pu Yi was violently seasick. He remained in that condition for the entire four days of his journey, while the Wasp hovered anxiously about him.

On the morning of 6 April the *Hie Maru* entered Yokahama harbour. A fly-past by a hundred Japanese naval aircraft had been arranged in Pu Yi's honour, and everyone was on deck to see the spectacle, but the supreme commander of the Manchukuo Navy remained below, stretched out on his bunk, as the planes roared overhead.

Prince Chichibu was waiting to greet Pu Yi and escort him to Tokyo in a special train. When Pu Yi finally emerged from his cabin, he was wearing a German-style army uniform with peak cap and jackboots of the kind worn by Adolf Hitler. On his breast were six stars and a number of campaign medals. Hidden behind large dark glasses, his face was barely visible as he hobbled down the gangway, relieved to be on land again.

At Tokyo station Emperor Hirohito, the Mikado, welcomed Pu Yi and invited him to say a few words to the assembled crowd. The Wasp handed Pu Yi his speech: 'I am honoured', said Pu Yi, 'to be the moon to the Mikado's sun. Together our alliance will shine over Asia.'

A group of journalists followed Pu Yi everywhere during his three weeks' visit, and the Wasp was kept busy fending off awkward questions and supplying titbits of information about the poet and man of action.

The Wasp was delighted by the number of photographs of

Pu Yi that appeared in the papers daily. Pu Yi was pictured gallantly helping the Mikado's aged mother up a slope in her garden; attending a religious shrine as a pilgrim; and receiving the papal legate to Japan. The Vatican had recently announced its *de jure* recognition of the Empire of Manchukuo, and the papal legate had called on Pu Yi to present the Pope's greetings to him.

The climax of Pu Yi's visit was drawing near. He and the Mikado were to review ten thousand troops of the imperial bodyguard, together with many squadrons of cavalry and tanks, at a grand military parade. The day before the parade an elderly general, who was aide-de-camp to the Mikado, arrived at Pu Yi's hotel to discuss the details for the parade. When the Wasp saw that the general was in riding-breeches and boots, he had a terrible foreboding. The general explained that the Mikado would be mounted on his favourite charger at the parade, and that another superb charger would be provided for the famous horseman, Pu Yi, whom everyone was looking foward to seeing as he rode along the ranks of the parade. To the general's amazement, Pu Yi fled from the room, crying out that he would rather die than be put on a horse. The Wasp explained to the general, as best he could, that Pu Yi was still suffering from the effects of his sea trip, and would not be fit to ride for at least a month.

The flags of Japan and Manchukuo flew from two flag-poles in the centre of the vast parade-ground, around which were formed the imperial bodyguard, the cavalry and the tanks. There was an air of expectancy as troops and spectators alike awaited the Mikado and the lone horseman of the mountain ranges. Buglers sounded a fanfare, and into the arena trotted a pair of chubby grey ponies pulling a carriage, in which sat the Mikado and, beside him, a slight figure in dark glasses, under an ancient Roman helmet.

The Wasp spent all his energy that day and for the remaining days of Pu Yi's visit doing his best to avoid the attentions of the gentlemen of the press.

CHAPTER TWELVE

THE DUNGEON

On a beautiful day in 1935 a black motor car drove up to the gates of the Salt Palace. When the sentries had inspected the papers of its single passenger, a distinguished looking foreign gentleman, the car was waved on to the office building, where the Wasp was waiting.

'Sir Reginald Johnston?' said the Wasp with a bow.

'Yes. You are . . .?'

The Wasp clicked his heels. 'Colonel Yoshioka, attaché to the imperial household. His Majesty received your letter. He is at his residence but will be here soon. Will you please wait in his office.' The Wasp led the way down the corridor.

Two page-boys stood at the office door; they bowed as Johnston entered the dark room. Although it was after eleven o'clock in the morning, only one curtain had been drawn, allowing a single shaft of sunlight into the room. The air smelt of stale cigarette-smoke, and Johnston wondered whether the windows had ever been opened. He walked over to a side-table. A signed photograph of King George V stood beside one of Benito Mussolini. Beside them was the imperial ant album. It was open at a page illustrating a queen ant being followed by her retinue of kings, soldiers and workers. Johnston sighed. He felt weary at the thought of all those years he had spent trying to encourage Pu Yi to lead a healthy, outdoor life.

'Ah! You are looking at my album.'

Johnston turned round. Pu Yi was wearing his Prince of Wales suit with a carnation. In his hand he held an ebony holder with a lighted cigarette. Johnston bowed. Pu Yi asked him to sit on the sofa. They were both unusually self-conscious, like two friends who have not met for a long time and have become uncertain of their relationship.

'Did you know that the Italian army has marched into Ethiopia?' Pu Yi asked.

'Yes, I just heard the news,' said Johnston.

'If the Italians had a regiment of white ants, they could carve their way through Ethiopia in a few days. The Italians are our allies, you know. The King of Italy was one of the first to recognize Manchukuo. And now the German chancellor, Herr Hitler, has recognized us too.'

'Yes, I've been following your country's fortunes with great interest, Your Imperial Majesty,' Johnston said, stiffly.

The Mantis came in, carrying a pile of documents. Having greeted his old friend Johnston, the Mantis explained that Pu Yi had some urgent letters to attend to, and he suggested that Johnston might like to stroll in the grounds until lunch-time.

Walking by the concrete tennis-court with its tattered net, Johnston thought of the old days in the Forbidden City when he had watched his young fledgling growing up. He recalled the poem which Pu Yi had given him:

> O that we were a pair of herons,
> That we could fly home together.

Now they were exiled from that old home, and he regretted ever having left it.

Johnston had not been happy since his days as Pu Yi's tutor. In 1931, the year of Pu Yi's escape to Manchuria, Johnston retired from the colonial service and was awarded a knighthood. He hoped to be appointed governor of Hong Kong, or failing that, vice-chancellor of Hong Kong University, but, with the deadly timing that comes naturally to many academics, a scholar of the university now revealed that the book attacking the Christian missions in China, published in 1911 under the pseudonym of Liu Shao-yang, was in fact the work of Johnston. The fatal discovery ruined Johnston's chances of any suitable employment in China.

In 1931 Johnston became head of the Chinese department at the School of Oriental Studies in London. His pupils noticed that, whatever the subject-matter of his seminar, be it the *Analects of Confucius* or the *Three Hundred Tang Poems*, after a few minutes Johnston would stray from his topic and begin to reminisce about his days in the Forbidden City. His eyes would light up as he talked about the magnificent ceremonial in the Hall of Supreme Harmony or the sight of the imperial yellow palanquin borne by a team of bearers on its way to the Palace of Mind Nurture. Sometimes, however, he would fall silent, and his eyes would cloud over. Was he, perhaps, inadvertently recalling the days when he was forced to read a passage from *Alice in Wonderland* to his bemused pupils in the imperial class-room while the eunuchs of the presence grinned in the background?

In 1934 Johnston published *Twilight in the Forbidden City*, a memoir of his days as imperial tutor. He dedicated it to Pu Yi 'in the earnest hope that, after the passing of the twilight and the long night, the dawn of a new and happier day for himself, and also for his people on both sides of the Great Wall, is now breaking'. For years Johnston had been looking forward to his reunion with Pu Yi, and he had often pictured to himself the mellow atmosphere of a real palace in the hills, where loyal retainers served at table, and the company included a fine body of Manchu noblemen. Now, sitting at lunch in the gloomy salt office dining-room, served by insipid page-boys, with the silent Mantis on one side of him and the whining Wasp on the other, while at the head of the table Pu Yi's tortoise-like face was largely hidden behind his dark glasses, Johnston had an unpleasant sensation that the scene about him was unreal, that it was part of some wonderland, inhabited by strange creatures.

After lunch Johnston said goodbye to Pu Yi at the doorway of the office building. He asked Pu Yi to give his respects to Prince Chun and Pu Chieh. He did not mention the Empress.

As he was waiting for the driver to turn the car's starting handle, he waved to Pu Yi who was standing in the doorway. Johnston thought of their last farewell at the bund in Tientsin, and the nostalgic words on the fan came back again: 'O that we were a pair of herons,' The car moved off, and Johnston looked back over his shoulder. Pu Yi was still waving. Someone was standing behind Pu Yi. Johnston caught only a fleeting glimpse of him, but he could have sworn that it was the grinning face of a eunuch of the presence.

Johnston retired from his teaching post in 1937 and went back to his native Scotland. He never married, but lived alone on a small island, Eilean Righ, which means the Island of the King, on Loch Craignish in Argyllshire. During the few months that remained to him, he spent most of his time in his study, surrounded by his collection of Chinese books and a few treasured mementoes: a black mandarin's button of the highest grade, a sable robe, a fan on which a Chinese poem was written, and a white jade ring.

Johnston died in Edinburgh on 6 March 1938. In his will he ordered the destruction of all his private papers, letters and diaries.

In the winter of 1936 Pu Chieh completed his studies at the Japanese army cadet school and returned to Hsingking. He was made a lieutenant in the imperial guard and took up residence in one of the concrete bungalows close to Pu Yi's. Knowing of Pu Yi's passionate interest in the Prince of Wales, Pu Chieh gave his brother a Japanese illustrated magazine entitled *Year of the Emperor*. Pu Yi devoured it. There were pictures of the funeral of King George V, the Prince of Wales as Edward VIII, the new King Emperor taking the salute at various parades, Edward VIII on a Mediterranean cruise and, sadly, Edward VIII in a dark suit on the day of his abdication. On the last page was a picture of Edward VIII's brother, who had taken his place on the throne as George VI. Pu Yi frowned. He looked across the room at his own brother in his splendid guards' uniform. Everyone at the Salt Palace had been making a fuss of Pu Chieh since his return from Japan. The Mantis let slip a remark, which his enemy the

Wasp reported to Pu Yi. It was good, the Mantis had said, to have a fully qualified officer in the household for a change. The remark would have cost him his head during the old regime in the Forbidden City, but more civilized forms of punishment now prevailed. The Mantis resigned as prime minister, his bank account was frozen, and he lived under house arrest in Hsingking. He died there three years later.

The Kwantung Army staff appointed as prime minister Chang Ching-hui, a pro-Japanese member of Pu Yi's cabinet, whose vague and indecisive manner gave him the appearance of an oriental Peebles. He always kept a fan up his sleeve, and Pu Yi swore that the fan's black handle contained a knife. By now, Pu Yi had begun to suspect that there was a plot to force him to abdicate.

Pu Yi's suspicions were strengthened in the following year when Pu Chieh went off to Japan in search of a bride. He was fortunate to be accepted by Hiro, daughter of the Marquis Saga and a second cousin of the Mikado himself. The wedding took place on 3 April in the officer's club near Hsingking railway station, Pu Yi having decided, ungraciously, that the palace was not a suitable venue. This was just as well for Pu Chieh, for it was unlikely that Hiro, who found the officers' club depressing enough, would have had the heart to go through with the ceremony once she had seen the shabby compound and the grim little bungalow surrounded by disused salt sheds which was to be her future home.

Immediately after the wedding Pu Chieh took his bride back to Tokyo, where he was due to attend a course at the military staff college. While Pu Chieh was away, the state council of Manchukuo, acting on orders from the Kwantung Army staff, drew up rules for the imperial succession. In the event of the Emperor dying childless, said the rules, Pu Chieh would succeed him, and he in turn would be followed by his son. The rules seemed sensible enough, but Pu Yi saw them as further proof that everyone was conspiring against him.

Pu Chieh and Hiro returned to Hsingking in October 1937. The sight of the grey bungalow in a wasteland of nettles and corrugated-iron sheds made Hiro shudder. Greater horrors awaited her inside her four-roomed home. Her furniture and wedding presents had been thrown in a heap on the floor of one of the rooms. There was no telephone, and none of the comforts to which she was accustomed. Worst of all for a Japanese of her sensitivity, no one had thought of putting even a vase of flowers in the house to welcome her.

Reluctantly, Pu Yi gave a family lunch party at the Salt Palace as an official welcome for his brother. The Empress attended. It was the first time she had been in Pu Yi's company since the visit of Prince Chun. Although she looked emaciated, and her shoulders stooped, she was still hauntingly beautiful, and Hiro, who had not met the Empress before, found her full of charm.

After the first course, a roasted turkey was carried in on a large dish and placed near Pu Yi for him to carve in the traditional Western manner. There was a lull in the conversation as everyone watched Pu Yi. Suddenly the Empress lunged across the table, attacked the turkey with her long finger-nails, tore off a piece with her hands, and chewed it like a ravenous animal. The whole company sat paralysed with fear as she growled and snatched at more and more of the turkey. Then, giving a wild cry, she wrenched at one of its legs. It was obvious to Hiro that the wretched woman was crazed with hunger.

Pu Yi rose from the table and began to tiptoe out of the room, retreating from the awful spectacle. The others followed him. Hiro was the last to leave. She looked back to see the beautiful Empress, her head-dress wreathed in flowers and jewels, lying on the ground, moaning as she gnawed at a bone.

At the lunch party, Hiro had noticed that one of the page-boys was treated differently from the others. He stood behind Pu Yi's chair, smiling, while the other boys, who looked glum, did all the work. In the weeks to come, by piecing together snatches of conversation and by talking to her husband, the innocent Hiro learned to her embarrassment that Pu Yi's favourite page-boy was known at court as the male concubine, and that Pu Yi had kept a male concubine for his pleasure ever since the days at the Chang Garden in Tientsin, and possibly before that in the Forbidden City. Hiro came to the conclusion, as she noted in her diary, that it was the existence of this boy concubine in the household that had broken the Empress Beautiful Countenance's heart and first led her to take opium.

Every day the male concubine, followed by a page-boy carrying a tray of food, went to a small bungalow which lay between Hiro's bungalow and Pu Yi's. Sometimes a pretty little girl would be seen leaving the bungalow, followed by two fat men who, Pu Chieh told Hiro, were probably eunuchs. No one but the page-boys and the eunuchs were ever allowed to approach the mystery bungalow. At last the day came when Pu Yi could no longer conceal from his brother who the little girl was. He told Pu Chieh that some nine months earlier he had married the daughter of a Manchu family, and made her his secondary consort. Her name was Yu-ling, or Jade Years, and she was sixteen years old.

Grudgingly, Pu Yi took Pu Chieh and Hiro to the mystery bungalow one day and introduced them to Jade Years. The first thing Hiro noticed about the shy young girl was that she was wearing the beautiful string of pearls which Hiro had brought from Japan as a present for the Empress. As Hiro and Pu Chieh were leaving, two eunuchs of the presence, who were standing in the doorway, bowed to them. They gave Pu Chieh the uncanny feeling that he was back in the Forbidden City again.

Pu Yi had begun to import eunuchs from Peking soon after he had taken up residence in the salt office, when he was still chief executive. The eunuchs were not on the official staff of the household but led a shadowy existence in the labyrinth of rooms in the basement of the office building, which was known as the Dungeon. To begin with, there were only two eunuchs of the presence, but their number had increased to eight. There was no chief eunuch in charge of them, but Pu Chieh noticed that the eunuchs all deferred to the male concubine when he was about.

One day a eunuch of the presence, keen to ingratiate himself with Pu Yi, reported to his master that he had discovered that Hiro was keeping a diary. Alarmed, Pu Yi gave orders that she was to be watched. He felt sure that she must be spying on him. The Wasp, who could hardly be expected to accuse the second cousin of the Mikado of spying, did his best to calm Pu Yi, but it was no good. Pu Yi now relied increasingly on his eunuchs, and they obliged by feeding his fears.

The next report Pu Yi received from his eunuchs was even more alarming than the first. Hiro, who had been looking more and more bulky, was almost certainly bearing a child, a fact that Pu Chieh was happy to corroborate. A child! An heir to his throne! Pu Yi clutched at his throat like a despairing monarch in a play. Now he was in dire peril indeed!

By an unfortunate coincidence, Hiro, who had grown tired of the food that was cooked in the Dungeon, chose this moment to suggest to Pu Yi that he might like to try some Japanese food for a change, and that she would be glad to prepare it. Japanese food! Prepared by Hiro! Threatened with poison, the doomed monarch tottered around his throne as if he were being pursued by a harpy, while the matronly Hiro watched, astonished by his performance.

Hiro duly gave birth to her baby. It was a girl. For the first time in many weeks Pu Yi was seen to smile. He sent a message of congratulation to Pu Chieh and even deigned to call at their bungalow to see Hiro and her baby, perhaps to make sure that it really was a girl. At first Hiro was terrified of Pu Yi, who behaved so monstrously towards his wife. But he appeared so pathetic that she began to take pity on the captive Emperor of the Salt Palace, a role which Pu Yi played to perfection.

A large number of presents for Hiro's baby arrived from her family in Japan, including a jack-in-the-box from the Mikado. When Pu Yi saw the jack-in-the-box he was beside himself with wonder. Day after day he called at Hiro's bungalow and he would sit on the floor for hours playing with the miraculous toy while the baby looked at him and gurgled.

When Pu Yi was not playing with Hiro's daughter's toys, he found a sadistic pleasure in his old pastime of flogging the page-boys. The seldom visited palace, with its high walls and rambling basement, was the perfect setting for him to indulge his old vice. Pu Yi, with the help of his male concubine, drew up a list of household rules and punishments for the eunuchs and page-boys. Each of them had to report at once any breach of the rules, however slight, on the part of his fellows. Pu Yi would sit in judgement on the offender and pronounce sentence. If Pu Yi pointed to the ground, the wretched boy would be dragged down to the Dungeon to be flogged. If the offence was serious, torture might be used, and afterwards the victim would be left in solitary confinement. Sometimes Pu Yi and his male concubine would watch the sentence being carried out.

The severest punishment was awarded to anyone who attempted to escape from the compound. The orphan boys who tried to escape were easily caught as they wandered about in the surrounding countryside or in the suburbs, but the more resourceful eunuchs might make their way south of the Great Wall to Peking and safety; or so they hoped. Pu Yi would stop at nothing to seek them out, as his letter to a Manchu nobleman in Peking shows:

> One Kuo Te-shun, a eunuch in attendance upon Our Person, escaped from the Palace on August 3rd. You are requested to look for him in Peking. . . . You are reminded that the last such fugitive, Liu, has still not been traced. It is essential that the man Kuo should be found. When this is done, first return his Palace badge by messenger, and then have Kuo himself escorted back to Hsingking.

It was only a matter of time before the Dungeon became a place of death. A small page-boy named Sun Po-yuan, newly recruited from the orphanage, tried to escape one day and he was given a beating and a month's solitary confinement in an unlit cellar in the Dungeon. The boy, Sun, made a second attempt to flee, but was caught trying to climb the compound wall. This time he was given such a savage beating that he died soon afterwards. The boy's death frightened Pu Yi, who prayed in front of a statue of Buddha that the boy's soul would cross safely into the next world.

In all her time at the palace Hiro never managed to discover the Empress's rooms. Hiro worried about her. There were frightening rumours that the Empress was kept in the Dungeon. Ominously, Pu Yi himself put about the allegation that the Empress had committed adultery with an unknown person, possibly a servant, and deserved the severest punishment. No shred of evidence was ever produced to support the accusation, and Hiro did not believe a word of it. She did, however, believe Pu Yi when he told her one day that he kept Jade Years as he might keep a bird in a cage, and that he had married her only in order to punish the Empress.

Death came again to the palace. Jade Years, who was then twenty-one, was taken ill with fever. Pu Yi said it was nothing serious, but when the Wasp saw her he insisted on sending for a Japanese doctor. The doctor diagnosed meningitis. By the following morning the young girl was dead.

Jade Year's place was taken by a Chinese girl aged twelve. Hiro watched the little thing, who wore her hair in plaits, making her way to the secondary consort's bungalow, escorted by two huge eunuchs. Within three days, to Hiro's relief, the girl escaped. She was never found.

The Wasp, acting on his own initiative, soon found a successor to the runaway child. Yu-chin, or Jade Lute, was the daughter of a waiter in a Hsingking restaurant. She was fifteen years old. Pu Yi found her a welcome change from flogging the page-boys. He devised a special ritual for her. He made her write out a list of rules and punishments, stipulating what would happen if she were disobedient. She was made to sign it. Whenever the eunuchs reported her for breaking a rule, Pu Yi, sitting in judgement, would produce the document, force her to read it, and then, personally, flog her. Flogging Jade Lute proved an absorbing sport for Pu Yi, and the male concubine must have felt neglected and perhaps uneasy about his position of supremacy at court.

The captive Emperor of the Salt Palace had never given up hope that one day he might return to the Forbidden City as the Great Ching Emperor. His hopes had been raised and dashed many times, but in the summer of 1937 (three months before the wedding of Pu Chieh and Hiro) it seemed that they must surely be fulfilled at last. On 7 July a shot was fired at a patrol of Japanese soldiers who were on duty at Marco Polo Bridge (Lukouchiao) outside Peking. In the confusion that followed, the Japanese exchanged fire with the Chinese Nationalist troops. The Japanese brought up a squadron of tanks, and a pitched battle took place. The Chinese retreated, and shortly afterwards the Japanese occupied Peking.

Pu Yi hopped about his office with delight when he heard the news. 'Peking is ours again!' he cried. The Wasp smilingly agreed.

'Marco Polo Bridge Incident!' ran the headline in *The Peking and Tientsin Times* report of the battle. Doihara himself could not have worded it better. The fracas at the bridge bore his hallmark, and it was to have momentous consequences, for that first shot fired on Marco Polo Bridge was the signal for the Japanese invasion of the whole of China.

The Lawrence of the East had struck again! Woodhead's old friends in the Tientsin Club found it bracing to read of the swift and decisive capture of Peking by the Japanese. But as the days passed, and the Japanese poured reinforcements into Tientsin, which they used as a bridgehead, the whole affair came too close for comfort, bringing as it did many minor irritations. It was impossible to hire a rickshaw, for instance, because they had all been commandeered by the Japanese to carry the equipment of the thousands of troops who disembarked at the bund. And there must have been some British residents who had uneasy premonitions as they watched the columns of unsmiling Japanese soldiers marching along Victoria Road towards the Japanese barracks.

Shanghai fell to the invaders, and then Nanking and Hankow, as the Japanese advanced into central China, forcing Chiang Kai-shek and his Nationalists to take refuge in distant Chunking. Every day Pu Yi expected a message to arrive from the Kwantung Army staff, inviting him to return to his throne in Peking. But the Japanese had other plans. A leading Nationalist, Wang Ching-wei, had recently deserted to the Japanese and, with their support, he set up a government in Peking. Pu Yi was not wanted south of the Great Wall, and his Japanese allies did not even bother to tell him so.

The British concession in Tientsin was now a small island in Japanese-occupied China. Trade flourished, and there was an air of prosperity in the concession. It seemed that Woodhead's constant support for Japan's Positive China Policy was amply justified.

The social life of the concession went on much as before. 1937 brought King George VI's coronation, and an open-air service was held in Victoria Park, with firework displays and other celebrations in the evening. In one corner of the park a model English country village was erected, with a fun-fair and a maypole. Outside the park railings a Chinese crowd watched in awe as British soldiers, dressed as country yokels, rollicked about the stalls.

In November the St Andrew's Society held a grander ball than usual. All mention of Pu Yi, their guest of honour of seven years before, had disappeared from the social columns of the papers long since, and it is hardly likely that any of the dancers at this coronation year ball would have given a thought to the quaint figure in dark glasses who had watched them hurtling about the floor of the Astor House Hotel, performing their Highland flings. There is a possibility, however, that one person in that ballroom did remember the Emperor across the Great Wall. When the shouting and the wail of the pipes died down, Herr Schneider looked up to heaven, sighed, and then led his trio in the lament for Bonnie Prince Charlie:

> Will ye no come back again?
> Will ye no come back again?
> Better loved ye canna be,
> Will ye no come back again?

CHAPTER THIRTEEN

THE GENERALISSIMO

Slowly, imperceptibly at first, like the ebbing tide in its muddy creeks, the atmosphere of confidence in the British concession began to die away. The year 1937 was also the year of Guernica, and German bombers devastated the Basque city as the Japanese had devastated Chapei. Japan was a member of Hitler's Anti-Comintern Pact, and she took strength from Germany's belligerent attitude.

Early in 1938 the commander of the Japanese garrison presented a series of brusquely worded complaints to the British municipal council. There had been a bomb outrage in the British concession in which a Japanese businessman had been killed. The Japanese were convinced that a number of anti-Japanese terrorists had found refuge in the British concession, and they demanded the right to enter the concession to seek them out. For a time the British resisted this infringement of their sovereignty, but at last they gave way and a secret agreement was reached. From time to time the Japanese police would send the British authorities, in advance, a list of suspected terrorists thought to be living in the British concession whom the Japanese wished to interrogate. Then, in the company of a British inspector, the Japanese would visit the suspects, usually late at night. Sometimes a suspect would escape on the eve of his interrogation. The numbers of these last-minute escapes increased, and Major Mino of the Japanese secret service was called in. He realized at once that someone at British police headquarters, who had access to the list, was tipping off the suspects. Mino also had a shrewd idea who that someone might be.

One night Inspector Kellaher was walking along Gordon Road when a car, which was following him, drew level. Two men fired on Kellaher from the car, which then sped away, leaving the dying inspector to be tended by a passing coolie. 'Inspector Kellaher slain by bandit gang,' said the headline in *The Peking and Tientsin Times* the following day.

A second Great War in Europe loomed nearer and the Japanese, who were about to join the Axis powers, demonstrated their contempt for the British in Tientsin by erecting barricades at the British concession's exits. Anyone, woman or man, who wished to come and go from the concession was stripped and searched by Japanese soldiers. The small island of the concession was now a beleaguered outpost, and many of its residents realized for the first time that the existence of the British concession was threatened by the very people who were supposed to guard it, the keepers of the peace. The irony was too terrible to contemplate.

There was a time when Woodhead's strong and decisive voice would have rallied the worried British residents, but Woodhead himself now doubted that Japan was 'playing the game'. He paid a visit to Tokyo and was granted an interview with Prince Konoye, the premier. The two men were photographed afterwards, shaking hands and smiling. The charming and cultivated Japanese premier did not look at all like the rugged generals who had led the Japanese government in recent years, and some people may have felt a little reassured by the picture, but, behind Prince Konoye, it was the Kwantung Army staff who dictated Japan's policy in China. After a few months Prince Konoye was replaced as premier by the militant General Tojo.

War broke out in Europe, and Britain withdrew her forces from China. A small group of residents watched sadly as HMS *Hollyhock* sailed away from the Tientsin bund for good.

On the next day the last British regiment, the East Surreys, marched down Victoria Road to the railway station, leaving the commercial crusaders to their fate.

German Panzer divisions tore through the fields of France. Ahead of them, Stuka dive-bombers screamed down on the fleeing allied columns. On the beach at Dunkirk thousands of British troops flung themselves to the ground as Messerschmitt fighter planes strafed them. The German infantry goose-stepped, six abreast, through the Arc de Triomphe in Paris. At Notre-Dame a German corporal played a Bach fugue on the organ high up in the loft while Hitler stood alone in the aisle, savouring his triumph in the national shrine of France. A ray of sun shone through a stained-glass window on to his head. The sight of Hitler caused a ripple of applause to break out in the audience. Pu Yi joined in the clapping. He was sitting in the front row of the cinema at the Japanese army barracks in Hsingking. Beside him was General Yamashita of the Kwantung Army. They were watching the German film documentary *Victory in the West*. At the end of the film Pu Yi led a further round of applause.

Pu Yi was fascinated by Hitler's technique. The way he stood in his open car, wearing a high peak cap and long trench coat, and raising his arm in salute; and the way he bent down to receive a simple bunch of flowers from a pretty little girl.

Nearly every day Pu Yi wore his Hitler-style army uniform with jackboots, and once or twice the Wasp was startled when he went into Pu Yi's bungalow to see him standing in front of the looking-glass, with a lock of hair pulled down over his forehead, looking surprisingly like Hitler.

Pu Chieh returned home one day and found Pu Yi in the baby's nursery, wearing a small false moustache, with his hair pulled down. 'I was making the baby laugh, pretending I was Hitler,' said Pu Yi on seeing his brother's look of astonishment. But the baby was playing quietly in another corner, and Pu Chieh wondered what his brother was up to.

In the autumn of 1940 Japan joined the Axis and, with

Germany and Italy, signed the New Order Pact. Pu Yi attended a celebration at the officers' mess in Hsingking to celebrate the occasion. When a group of brown-shirted Hitler Youth leaders, who had been serving as training advisers to the Kwantung Army, stopped at Hsingking on their way home via Siberia, Pu Yi gave a reception for them at the Salt Palace.

Now that his country was virtually at war, Pu Yi had no intention of letting his fully qualified, staff officer brother forget that he, Pu Yi, was generalissimo. A rifle-range was built in the grounds of the compound, which echoed with the deafening noise of the imperial guard at firing practice. A small office was turned into a map-room, and when Pu Yi was not playing in Hiro's nursery or chastising his staff he would pore over military maps with the Wasp or attend parades of his soldiers in the compound.

'Surprise is the most important principle of warfare,' the Kwantung Army lecturers had told Pu Yi at Port Arthur. The words came back to him when he heard the news of Japan's devastating attack on the American fleet in Pearl Harbour on 7 December 1941. How simple it all was! Pu Yi thought. The ships lying side by side, making a perfect target for the Japanese aircraft flying out of the early morning sun.

There was more exciting news to come. General Yamashita's Kwantung Army divisions invaded Malaya and, in the most brilliantly executed operation, swiftly overran the country. This was in many ways a victory for Manchukuo, for Yamashita's men had been trained there. With the Wasp's help, Pu Yi composed a long and glowing message of congratulations to his friend, the victorious Yamashita. At the Concordia Association's headquarters Pu Yi read out a proclamation, pledging all Manchukuo's resources to Japan in her war effort.

Pu Yi was enjoying the war. Almost every day brought news of another victory for the Axis powers. In the west, Hitler launched his armies into the heart of Russia. Japan had a non-aggression pact with Russia; nevertheless, the people of Manchukuo drew comfort from the fact that the great Russian

236

bear which prowled along their northern frontiers was fighting on a distant front.

There were more Japanese surprise attacks. On 10 December 1941 Japanese aircraft sent the British battleships *Prince of Wales* and *Repulse* to the bottom of the South China Sea, and on 25 December Hong Kong itself fell to the Japanese.

Then came the greatest victory of them all. Early in 1942 General Yamashita captured Singapore after only token resistance by the much larger British force. From his map-room at the Salt Palace Generalissimo Pu Yi sent a tribute to Yamashita and the men of the Kwantung Army in Singapore.

Meanwhile the Japanese army extended its hold over China and mopped up the remaining British territories there. In one such minor operation Pu Yi took a personal interest. On the day of their surprise attack on Pearl Harbour, Japanese troops marched in to occupy the British concession in Tientsin. The foreign residents were rounded up, and most of them were sent to a detention camp at Weihsien in Shantung province. The Union Jack was hauled down, and the flag of the rising sun now fluttered from the ramparts of Gordon Hall. In the hall's entrance lobby, where Pu Yi had so often been received by Peebles of the municipal council, hung four portraits of English monarchs: King George V and Queen Mary on one side of the lobby, and on the other side King George VI and Queen Elizabeth. When the commander of the Japanese troops entered the lobby and saw the imperial portraits, he stood nonplussed, like someone who had wandered into a temple hung with icons. Recovering himself, he barked out an order. His troops sprang to attention, and the commander saluted each of the monarchs in turn with a flourish of his sword. When these proper courtesies had been paid to the king emperors of England and their consorts, the Japanese commander went into the hall to confront Peebles, the chairman, and to receive from his reluctant hands the last symbol of British rule in Tientsin, the keys of the safe of Gordon Hall.

At the very hour when the Japanese marched into the British concession in Tientsin, Woodhead, who lived near the bund in Shanghai, was wakened by the sound of explosions. Japanese aircraft were attacking British and American ships moored in the river. Afterwards Woodhead described the scene: 'Smoke billowed from a number of ships. I was just in time to see HMS *Petrel* going down with her flag flying in the best traditions of the British Navy.'

Later that morning Woodhead picked up the news of the Japanese attack on Pearl Harbour on his radio. From his window he could see steel-helmeted Japanese soldiers patrolling the street. He knew then that it would only be a matter of hours before the Japanese arrested him. For some months past, ever since Prince Konoye had been replaced as premier of Japan by General Tojo, Woodhead's radio broadcasts and newspaper articles had been increasingly hostile to the Japanese. The British consul had warned Woodhead more than once that it was not safe for him to remain in Shanghai, but the commercial crusader, ever independent, would not think of leaving. It would not be playing the game to desert his public now, he said.

When the Japanese police came for Woodhead, Inspector Kawai noticed a bronze statue of a Japanese soldier on the mantelpiece in Woodhead's sitting-room. He asked Woodhead about it. Woodhead told him that it was a gift from the then premier of Japan, General Hayashi, adding as an afterthought that the statue had come with a message from the Emperor of Japan himself.

Woodhead was taken to a detention centre for enemy aliens, named Bridge House. He was stripped of his possessions and thrown into a small, unlit cage which he shared with about twelve others. With great fortitude he endured the squalor and cruel treatment, which varied from subtle forms of torture and interrogation to beatings. When he could bear no more, he would sit on the floor of the cage reciting to himself again and again Kipling's lines: If you can force your heart and nerve and sinew/ To serve your turn long after they are gone. . . .

Compared with the other wretches in his cage, some of whom were not to leave it alive, Woodhead, the enemy propagandist, was easily the most serious offender in

Japanese eyes. His friends despaired of seeing him again. In June 1942 *The Times* of London anticipated the next and inevitable Japanese step. Under the headline 'British orientalist on espionage charge' it reported: 'Mr H.G.W. Woodhead, a well known British authority on the Far East, has been tried by a Japanese court martial on charges of espionage and of conducting subversive propaganda against Japan.' But there was to be no trial for Woodhead. One morning, three months after his arrest and detention, he was informed that he was to be freed that day, and would be deported from Shanghai in a Japanese steamer. He was given no reason for his unexpected release.

Lice-ridden, half-starved, with his right arm and leg paralysed, Woodhead was lifted out of his cage. Had someone in high authority come to his help? Blurred ideas crossed his confused mind. Had he not been so dazed and ill, he might have seen what it was that had spared his life. When his gaolers helped him along the corridor to the door of Bridge House, Inspector Kawai clicked his heels, shook Woodhead by his good hand, and reverently handed back to him the bronze statue of the Japanese soldier.

In the salt office compound the only piece of ground that was not covered with rubble and weeds was the small garden which Hiro had made outside her grey bungalow. Another small garden was laid out in 1940. It surrounded a shrine that had been built on to a wing of the office building. The shrine was in honour of the great Sun Goddess of the Shinto religion. The Sun Goddess had founded the Japanese Empire over 2,500 years ago, and the Mikado was her descendant. If the people of Manchukuo were to share the same faith in the Sun Goddess as did the people of Japan, then, naturally, their two nations would be as one. So argued the Kwantung Army staff, and they set about instructing Pu Yi in the Shinto religion. The Wasp, assisted by a Shinto mystic, gave Pu Yi daily lessons, and retreats were held when the three would contemplate the mysteries of the Sun Goddess. It was during one of these retreats that Pu Yi was inspired to build the shrine.

In June 1940 Pu Yi paid a visit to Tokyo. At a private meeting with the Mikado Pu Yi humbly declared his conversion to the Shinto faith. Pu Yi then went on a pilgrimage to the holy shrine of Ise, where he was presented with copies of three sacred relics of Shintoism: two objects of bronze and jade, and a sword. Pu Yi brought these relics back to the Salt Palace, and at a special ceremony of dedication they were placed in a tabernacle of the shrine.

Shortly after that solemn ceremony Pu Yi issued an imperial proclamation, which had been drafted by the Wasp. It was read out in all the schools of Manchukuo, and at an assembly of the Concordia Association. Their Emperor, said the proclamation, had come to realize that the prosperity which Manchukuo enjoyed was due to the Sun Goddess and to the protection of her descendant, the Mikado. In order that his people should be one in virtue and mind with the people of the 'parent country' Japan, the proclamation went on, the Emperor hereby dedicated the nation to the great Sun Goddess.

The new shrine at the Salt Palace became an object of interest to Japanese residents in Manchukuo, and great men came to visit it. General Tojo, the new premier of Japan, paid it a special visit in 1942, and he was followed by the victor of the campaigns in Malaya and Singapore, General Yamashita. Both the generals inspected Pu Yi's map-room and praised him for the interest he was taking in the war. The Wasp, too, received a commendation for his wall-chart, on which the flags of the warring nations were pinned.

But the mood of celebration at the Salt Palace did not continue for long. In the autumn of 1942 things began to go badly for the Axis. At Stalingrad, the Russians held out against wave after wave of desperate German attacks which went on through the winter. Then in February 1943 the Russians broke out to encircle and destroy von Paulus's German army. General Yamashita, who had a strategist's eye, saw Stalingrad as the turning-point of the war.

After Stalingrad, the Russian bear went on the rampage. Smolensk fell, followed by Kiev as the Germans retreated, and the swastika was replaced by the hammer and sickle in town after town. The Axis powers were defeated in North Africa, Italy was invaded, and in the summer of 1943 Mussolini resigned. Manchukuo lost her first ally when Italy formally surrendered in the autumn, and there was gloom in the map-room at the Salt Palace when the Wasp removed the last Italian flag from the wall-chart.

By 1944 the Americans had regained their full strength in the Pacific theatre. They invaded the Japanese-occupied Philippines, and in October they inflicted a crushing defeat on the Japanese grand fleet in the Philippine Sea.

Pu Yi was no longer enjoying the war. He gave up wearing his Hitler-style uniform and seldom went into the map-room, where the stars and stripes of America hemmed in the dwindling flags of the rising sun. The shadow of the old enemy, the Russian bear, fell across Manchukuo again, as the Kwantung Army staff had always feared. On 5 April 1945 Russia renounced her neutrality pact with Japan. General Yamashita was brought back to assume command in Manchukuo, but the position of his forces was hopeless. The best divisions of the Kwantung Army were far away in South-East Asia; the frontier with Russia was long and difficult to defend. Pu Yi met Yamashita again about this time and found him a changed man, sad and resigned.

Pu Yi tried not to think about the war, but the Wasp insisted on giving him the sordid details about the end of Mussolini and of Hitler. These terrified Pu Yi and gave him nightmares. On 28 April Mussolini was shot and his body, together with that of his mistress, was later hung upside-down outside a garage in a suburb of Milan. Two days later Hitler shot himself in his underground bunker in Berlin before the Russian hordes could reach him.

Japan battled on, alone. In Manchukuo everyone dreaded the coming of the bear. Okinawa fell to the Americans on 21 June, but still the Japanese fought on. Then came the American surprise. On 6 August the atomic bomb was dropped on Hiroshima. By the next day confused reports reached Hsingking and the Salt Palace that something terrible had happened to Japan which had never happened in the world before. On 8 August the Russian bear struck. Four Red

241

armies crossed the border into Manchukuo, three from Siberia and one from Outer Mongolia. On 9 August the new commander-in-chief of the Kwantung Army called to see Pu Yi. The capital would have to be moved from Hsingking to Tunghua in southern Manchuria not far from the Korean border, he said. While he was talking, the air-raid sirens sounded, and within a few minutes a stick of Russian bombs landed close to the compound as Pu Yi and the general ran down the steps to the basement.

That night there was another air-raid, and the entire court, Pu Yi, Jade Lute, Pu Chieh, Hiro and her child, Pu Yi's sisters and nephews, the Wasp and the cabinet ministers rushed to the basement, where they found eunuchs and page-boys crouching, panic-stricken. Only the Empress was missing from the party cowering underground.

Early in the morning after the air-raid Pu Yi held a council of war in his office. Pu Chieh, the Wasp and a Japanese staff officer attended as well as the cabinet. Pu Yi wore his grey Napoleonic coat. He looked the perfect figure of a defeated warrior emperor, grave and dignified. Before the meeting began, Pu Yi ordered tea to be brought for everyone, but the Wasp reported that the kitchen was closed and that all the servants had fled, together with the male concubine, eunuchs and page-boys. Worse than that, said the Wasp, the gates of the compound were wide open and there was no sign of the imperial guard. The Warrior Emperor now wore the stricken look of one who had been deserted by his army. While his ministers talked excitedly about what they should do, Pu Yi remained silent, with his head bowed. Then the Wasp announced the view of the Kwantung Army staff: the Emperor must escape. Pu Yi raised his head. Escape! Of course, he thought, he would escape, and in a last noble gesture, he would wear his grey Napoleonic coat. As for the mere details such as where he might escape to, and who should escape with him, they could be left with the Wasp to decide.

Hsingking was in a state of total confusion. Crowds of people besieged the railway station, and they had to be held back by

242

armed troops. The few available trains were filled with senior Japanese officers and administrators fleeing to Korea. On 14 August a sullen crowd watched as the grey-clad figure of the Emperor, protected by a platoon of Japanese soldiers, climbed on board a special train. He was followed by his bedraggled looking courtiers. The last person to board the train was the Empress, who wore a black veil over her face.

After they had been travelling for about eight hours, they reached Tunghua in eastern Manchukuo, about a hundred miles from the Korean border. The original plan had been for the court to stay there, but the Wasp explained to Pu Yi that air raids were expected and the court would be safer at a mining town in the mountains where the deep shafts would provide them with shelter. Slowly the train began to climb into the foothills of the Long White Mountains. In their compartment the Chinese ministers looked more and more anxiously at the walls of sheer rock-face which began to appear above the dark fir trees. On the craggy peaks above those walls of rock were the hideouts of the Red Spear guerrillas, an enemy who would show them far less mercy than the Russians.

Another four hours on from Tunghua the train stopped at the small mining town of Talitzu. The imperial party left the train and went to their temporary home, an old miners' hostel built of logs. They were now high up in the mountains. Three hundred years before, in this wild region, the Manchu clans had gathered to invade China. They had poured down on to the great Manchurian plain, through the pass in the Great Wall at Shanhaikwan, and gone on to seize the Forbidden City and found the Ching dynasty. Now the last emperor of that dynasty and his small group of ministers sat huddled around a stove in the hostel, fearful of even showing their faces outside.

The next day, 15 August, Pu Yi and Pu Chieh heard on the radio that Japan had surrendered. The Mikado came on the air to tell his people in solemn words that the war was over. Pu Yi called a meeting in the hostel canteen. Conducted as if it were a scene in a play, with a strict regard for imperial protocol, the meeting decided unanimously that Pu Yi should abdicate. An edict was drawn up, and for the third time in his life Pu Yi was stripped of his role as Emperor.

Pu Yi shook hands with each of his cabinet ministers and thanked them for their loyal service. As soon as they left the canteen, the ministers, who had already packed their belongings, hurried to the two motor cars that were waiting to take them to the station. They knew that a train, possibly the last, was due to leave for Hsingking soon, and their one object in life was to escape from the menacing guerrillas. On the following day, when they were back in Hsingking, Pu Yi's former cabinet began to make overtures to Chiang Kai-shek, saying that they would be pleased to serve any future Republican administration which might be set up in Manchuria.

The Wasp now proved himself a man of action. They must make their way to Japan immediately, he told Pu Yi. He had made all the arrangements. A plane was waiting in Tunghua. It would fly Pu Yi, Pu Chieh and the Wasp to Korea, where they would change planes for Japan. The plane was a small one and there would be room for only seven others besides themselves. Pu Yi must decide who would fill the vacant places. Pu Yi chose his three nephews, a doctor, a servant, and two of the brothers-in-law. There was no place in the escape party for Mr Cheng, the only male to be left behind.

The women and Mr Cheng stood outside the door of the hostel to see Pu Yi and the rest of the men depart. As their luggage was being loaded in a car, Mr Cheng fell on his knees and begged for one last chance, but he was brushed aside. Jade Lute kept crying out 'What are we to do? The guerrillas will kill us.' Embarrassed by the scene she was creating, Pu Yi said to her, 'You can always catch a train to Mukden and find your way to Japan from there.' At this, Jade Lute became hysterical. Hiro, who was carrying her child in her arms, was weeping. Pu Chieh muttered some advice to her about making her way across the mountains to Korea. But she knew as well as everyone else that the Japanese troops had withdrawn from the area, and that at any moment the guerrillas might descend on them.

One figure watched this frantic scene of departure in

244

silence: the Empress. She was to be abandoned once more.

Glad to be down from the mountains and the threat of the guerillas, Pu Yi and his party arrived at Tunghua, where they boarded their plane. Instead of flying to Korea, however, where bad weather was reported, the plane took them to Mukden. There they waited in the airport lounge for the connecting plane for Japan. Pu Yi sat in an armchair with his shoulders hunched and took no notice of the dismal surroundings. He did not even bother to look up when the Wasp announced that their plane had arrived. A large transport plane touched down and, with a roar from its engines, taxied towards the lounge. The Wasp and Pu Chieh went outside to make arrangements for their seats. To his horror, the Wasp saw that the plane had Russian markings. Just then a group of soldiers, armed with sub-machine-guns, left the plane, ran across to the airport buildings and disarmed the Japanese guard. The soldiers ordered the Wasp and Pu Chieh back to the lounge. A Russian officer went in after them. There, slumped in an armchair, was the resigned figure of the defeated Napoleon. No one could say that Pu Yi was not properly dressed for his part.

Had Pu Yi been betrayed? It is difficult to account otherwise for the switch of route from Korea, and the remarkable timing of the arrival of the Russian plane at Mukden. One or more of Pu Yi's ministers, seeking to ingratiate themselves with the Russian authorities who had taken over Hsingking, could easily have given Pu Yi's escape plan away.

Pu Yi and the others in his party were put on the Russian plane and flown to Tungliao in Outer Mongolia, where their plane was refuelled. During the stop Pu Yi asked to see the Russian officer in charge, and, pointing at the Wasp, pleaded to be rescued from 'that terrible man' who was responsible for all his ills. The Russians obliged, and the bewildered Wasp, who had been Pu Yi's producer, director and close companion for thirteen years, was handcuffed and led off the plane, protesting. Leaving behind a cloud of dust, Pu Yi's plane took off for Siberia.

At Talitzu, in the Long White Mountains, the frightened

women in the hostel lived from day to day, not knowing when the enemy would come for them. At night they could see the camp-fires of the guerrillas, high above the town. There were rumours that the Russians, who had taken Tunghua, were closing in on Talitzu. The women saw little of Mr Cheng, who spent most of his time in the town. Jade Lute kept wailing for her mother. The Empress, whose supply of opium had run out, suffered agonies and would cry out at night, pleading for more. Hiro, as well as looking after her five-year-old daughter, took charge of the entire household. She no longer wore her kimono but disguised herself as a Chinese.

With the women Pu Yi had left behind all the imperial baggage, including several boxes of art treasures. Twenty years before, he and Johnston had removed them from the Forbidden City, and they had followed him on his travels ever since. Hiro soon had good reason to curse Pu Yi's treasures, for they were to imperil her life and cause her and her companions untold misery.

On 21 September, about a month after Pu Yi's flight, the first Russian troops reached Talitzu. They did not stay.long, but handed over the town to their allies, a regiment of Mao's Red Army whose forces had begun to occupy southern Manchuria. The women at the hostel were treated courteously by the Red Army men, and it seemed that there was a good chance that they might be released. Just then Mr Cheng paid a visit to the Red Army commander and revealed to him the identities of himself and all of the women. Taking the commander to the hostel, Mr Cheng showed him where the boxes of treasures were hidden and denounced the women for their part in stealing the national treasures of the Chinese people. Having had his revenge on Pu Yi's family, Mr Cheng disappeared, leaving his wife and the other women to their fate.

Hiro, her child, Pu Yi's three sisters, Jade Lute, and the Empress were sent under escort to the prison in Changchun (Hsingking had reverted to its former name). They were kept there in freezing conditions throughout the winter of 1945. Pu Yi's former cabinet ministers did not visit them once. In April 1946 Jade Lute was set free and went home to her mother, whom she had not seen since she entered the Salt Palace as Pu Yi's concubine at the age of fifteen. Some time later the three sisters were also released on probation.

Hiro and the Empress were not so fortunate. They were sent back to the Long White Mountains, a journey of 300 miles, in an open cart. A banner was fixed to the cart, bearing the words *Traitors of the Imperial Puppet's Family*. When the cart, drawn by ponies, stopped in a town, people would gather round it and point at the Empress, saying, 'That is the Puppet's wife.' Sometimes the Empress would yell at them, begging for opium, and the crowd, shocked by her ghastly cries, would fall silent.

At last, a month after leaving Changchun, the cart trundled into the hill town of Yenchi, its destination, and stopped outside the prison. People came running up to see Hiro, her child and the Empress being carried from their cart. Hiro and her child were put in a cell with some French nuns, two of whom were in chains. The Empress was given a concrete cell of her own. Word spread in the town and its neighbouring villages that the last Empress of the Ching dynasty was in their local gaol, and the queue of men and women formed at a small iron grating to watch the spectacle of Beautiful Countenance writhing in agony on the floor of her cell. Now and again she would moan and plead for a bath and some clean clothes. Then, all of a sudden, seized by her craving for opium, she would scream and petrify her audience.

Early in June Hiro and her daughter were released. Although her gaolers would have been glad to get rid of the Empress as well, she was too weak to travel. Hiro made her way across the border into China and eventually reached Peking, which was then in the hands of the Nationalists. She called on Prince Chun at the Northern Mansion. The old man's first thoughts were of Beautiful Countenance, and he was deeply distressed to hear of the dreadful conditions in which she was living. 'How beautiful she looked on her wedding day!' he said again and again. 'How beautiful she looked. . . .'

Did he but know it, Beautiful Countenance had been released from her misery. In the middle of June some peasants, taking pity on her, carried her to a farmhouse high up in the mountains. She was washed, given a change of clothing and a *kang* on which to rest. It is pleasant to think that, in the few lucid moments that remained to her, she was dimly aware that she was being cared for. Beautiful Countenance died in her simple room before the end of June. She was forty years old.

CHAPTER FOURTEEN

THE MODEL CITIZEN

Night was falling as Pu Yi's plane circled above the Trans-Siberian railway town of Chita and came in to land at a military airstrip. Pu Yi, his brother and his nephews were ushered into a staff car. After driving for about an hour through a forest of dark firs they came to the edge of a lake and stopped outside a large hotel which also served as a sanatorium for Russian officers on sick-leave. The general commanding the Russian garrison in Chita was in the entrance hall to welcome Pu Yi. He was shown to a comfortable room where his luggage was already waiting. An excellent dinner was served in a private dining-room for Pu Yi and his party. No monarch could have been better treated, and it all seemed too good to be true.

On the journey from Outer Mongolia to Siberia Pu Yi had not dared to look out of the plane window at the vast desert plateau, but spent his time wondering anxiously what his Russian captors were going to do with him. He kept thinking of Johnston's terrible tale of the execution of the Tsar and his family by the Bolsheviks. And he remembered Johnston saying that the Red Christian, General Feng Yu-hsiang, was sure to behave even worse than had the Bolsheviks if Pu Yi did not escape from the Forbidden City. When Pu Yi was told that his plane was to land at Chita, he felt even more anxious.

Chita had been the base of the ogre Semenov, the hated enemy of the Bolsheviks, and they were bound to have found out all about the money Pu Yi had given Semenov, and about the anti-Bolshevik convention that Pu Yi had signed. Now, delighted as Pu Yi was with the attention that was being shown to him, his fears disappeared, and he glowed with well-being. Judging from this spacious hotel, with its central-heating system, Siberia was a very desirable place, he thought. And that intriguing uniform of the Russian general's with the leather belt worn over the casual smock! Pu Yi could see himself in it, a glass of vodka in his hand.

Each morning Pu Yi was visited by two charming nurses, who saw that he was provided with any medicines he might need. Pu Chieh and his nephews acted as his personal servants and made a great fuss over him. After lunch a Russian orderly would take Pu Yi for a walk along the lake shore. This was followed by English-style afternoon tea in the lounge, where Pu Yi was serenaded by gramophone records of the Red Army choir, accompanied by the twang of balalaikas. Vodka and caviare were served on the terrace before dinner.

Never had Pu Yi been so comfortable as he was in this haven. After a few weeks he decided to apply for asylum in Siberia. In all, he made three written applications to remain in Siberia, but he received no reply from the Russian authorities. Perhaps the time had come to offer them a present, he thought. He had brought with him a large quantity of jewels, the best of which were hidden in the false bottom of a suitcase; and he wondered whether he might offer a few of them to the general in return for his help. But Pu Chieh advised his brother that the Russians might not take kindly to being bribed.

One afternoon the staff car drove up to the entrance of the hotel just as Pu Yi was returning from his walk. He was astonished to see all the members of his cabinet emerge from the car. They looked very sheepish when they saw Pu Yi. After fleeing from the hostel at Talitzu they had gone into hiding in Changchun, where they tried to make contact with Chiang Kai-shek's Nationalists, but they had been captured by the Russians. Pu Yi had as little to do with them as possible, and spurned all their approaches. He was the aloof Emperor. In another age he would have ordered their deaths by a thousand cuts.

In the autumn of 1946 the Russian general informed Pu Yi that he was going to be called as a witness for the prosecution at the international tribunal in Tokyo, where several leading Japanese, including General Tojo, the premier, were to be tried for war crimes. Pu Yi was moved to Khabarovsk on the River Amur in Eastern Siberia, where the Russian prosecution team was assembled.

Witness for the prosecution! Pu Yi was full of enthusiasm for his new role. He surprised the Russians with his eagerness to accuse the Japanese of every offence he could think of.

When the trial opened in Tokyo, Pu Yi was the chief witness against the Japanese leaders. The court-room was packed; never had Pu Yi seen so impressive a theatre. He would have liked to wear a Siberian smock with a leather belt over it, but the Russians supplied him with a blue suit, white shirt and red tie. Pu Yi spent eight days in the witness-box giving his testimony. It was a *tour de force*. His voice rang out across the court-room as he denounced the villainous Japanese who had kidnapped him, carried him away from China, and used him to suppress the unfortunate people of Manchuria. And he revealed with a sob of anguish how he, an ardent Buddhist who spent much of the day sitting cross-legged in meditation, was forced to worship the Shinto Sun Goddess.

It was when he came under cross-examination that Pu Yi showed his highest skills as a prosecution witness. When an aggressive American lawyer for the defence attacked Pu Yi and suggested that he was partly to blame for what went on at the Salt Palace, he hung his head in silent outrage at the grave accusations. And when his speech to the Emperor of Japan was repeated to him — 'I am honoured to be the moon to the Mikado's sun' — Pu Yi looked at the tribunal with the puzzled air of an injured innocent, as if to say, how could they believe such things of me? Feeling increasingly protective of the frail, long-suffering Pu Yi, the judges began to speak sharply to the defence lawyers.

There were, however, two moments when Pu Yi's

composure was shaken. The first was when the aggressive defence lawyer challenged Pu Yi's account of how he came to leave Tientsin. The lawyer quoted from Sir Reginald Johnston's book *Twilight in the Forbidden City*, in which Johnston said: 'Pu Yi left Tientsin and went to Manchuria of his own free will.' There was a silence in court for a few moments. Then Pu Yi shouted in a hoarse voice, 'Lies! Lies! Lies! That book of Johnston's is full of lies. He wrote it to make money for himself.' Pu Yi went limp. He had broken his last link with his former master.

The lawyer then said to Pu Yi, 'You put all the blame on the Japanese, but sooner or later the Chinese government will capture you and make you pay for your crimes.' Pu Yi turned pale and clutched at the sides of the witness-box. The judges immediately ordered a recess to give him time to recover.

The international tribunal sentenced many of the Japanese prisoners to death. Among them were General Tojo and Colonel Doihara. Pu Yi went back to his Siberian haven. As he sipped his vodka by the lakeside in the evenings the only thing that spoiled his peace was an occasional glimpse of his cabinet as they went mincing by, bowing obsequiously to him in the distance.

On several mornings a week a Chinese-speaking official from the bureau of current affairs held classes in the hotel library for Pu Yi and the other Chinese residents. The man from the bureau would read extracts from Russian news bulletins, interspersed with maxims culled from the works of Marx and Lenin. Pu Yi found these classes dull, and his eyes would remain shut most of the time, but an occasional titbit of information would catch his attention. One day an item from the radio report brought back a ghost from the past. The Red Christian, General Feng Yu-hsiang, whom Johnston had so detested, had died on board a Russian steamer cruising in the Black Sea. The Red Christian had been watching a film, *The Three Musketeers*, when the ship's cinema caught fire, and he was suffocated.

The man from the bureau announced with great pleasure one morning that India had been granted independence; this meant, he said, that the British Empire had come to an end, just as Marx had predicted. Pu Yi remembered how Johnston, an ardent believer in Empire, used to dream of the day when the British and Chinese Empires would rule the world in harmony. A strange mood came over Pu Yi. After the class he went up to his room, took from a leather folder a signed photograph of Johnston, held it over a waste-paper basket, and set it alight. The face of his old tutor curled, blackened and then flaked into ashes.

Pu Yi found the news from China more and more disturbing as the Red Army of Mao Tse-tung, allied with the peasant militia, began to drive the Nationalists out of the north. The prospect of being returned to Red China loomed closer. Pu Yi asked the man from the bureau for his help, but he was told that nothing could be done to hurry the department of immigration which was considering his case.

In October 1949, when Pu Yi had been in his Siberian haven for five years, Mao Tse-tung entered Peking and proclaimed the People's Republic. Pu Yi was alarmed at this news, but his cabinet, ever ready to shift their allegiance, asked the man from the bureau for permission to send Mao a telegram expressing their humble and respectful congratulations. Terrified of being sent back to China, Pu Yi sent a last, desperate appeal to the Russian general, begging to be allowed to remain in Siberia, but his plea was in vain. In August 1950 he was informed that he was to be handed over to the Chinese Communists.

At the border between Siberia and Manchuria Pu Yi and his fellow-prisoners were met by a genial, middle-aged man in a grey uniform buttoned at the neck. He introduced himself as a 'cadre'. Pu Yi noticed that the green-uniformed Chinese soldiers and the blue-uniformed railway workers were quick to do this man's bidding. A cadre, as Pu Yi was soon to learn, was the jargon for a State official in the People's Republic of China. The word conveys the impression of a skeleton élite awaiting the day when it might swell into a vast army of civil servants again with some, if not all, of the privileges enjoyed by the old imperial bureaucracy. Already in 1950, the year of Pu Yi's return from Siberia, citizens of the newly founded Republic had begun to level charges of nepotism against senior cadres. A few years later, when Chairman Mao Tse-tung ordered that all, irrespective of status or occupation, should do manual work in the countryside, the official *Red Flag* magazine had to appeal to cadres to stop favouring their own families by granting them exemptions from going to the countryside.

The cadre offered cigarettes to the new arrivals and lit one himself. He would like to welcome them back to their motherland, he said, exhaling a cloud of blue smoke. They had nothing to fear, he added, but should regard themselves as students who were about to learn a new way of life. Some soldiers, wearing the red star of the People's Liberation Army in their caps, carried the luggage of the 'students' across the platform, where a Chinese train was waiting to take them to Mukden.

Breakfast was served by the soldiers as the train clattered along on its way southwards, and Pu Yi, who had been dreading what the Reds might do to him, began to feel more relaxed. The train stopped at Changchun where, twenty years before, Pu Yi and his Empress had alighted to cheers from the schoolchildren and the sound of a brass band. Now the station was deserted, except for a few Chinese soldiers. Less than a mile away, hidden behind the grey concrete blocks of flats, was the Salt Palace. Curious to learn what had become of the place, Pu Yi asked one of the soldiers, but neither he nor his comrades had ever heard of the compound with its iron gates, watch-towers and office building.

At Mukden, Pu Yi and his fellow-students were taken to a rest centre. The canteen table was laden with fruit, cakes and cigarettes. A haze of smoke filled the room, where the students talked and joked with the cadre until it was time for them to catch another train for the short journey of forty miles to the mining town of Fushun.

The detention centre for Manchukuo war criminals at Fushun was a former barracks. The governor, a short, chubby, soft-spoken man, wore the grey uniform of a cadre. Addressing the new arrivals, he stressed that they were there as students rather than prisoners. Pu Yi noticed that his favourite word was 'remould'. There was a new China, said the governor, and in order to become worthy citizens, each must work hard to remould his character.

The new arrivals were asked to declare in detail the contents of their luggage, and were then allotted rooms. Pu Yi shared a large room with his brother and one of his nephews. Before Pu Yi had been at the detention centre for a week, the governor and his wardens discovered that he was incapable of looking after himself, and that Pu Chïeh and the others did everything for him. The governor tried putting Pu Yi on his own for a week, but it was a disaster. Although Pu Yi was nearly forty-five years old, he could not dress himself. His limbs seemed to lack any co-ordination, and the simplest things like doing up a button, or tying his shoelaces, were beyond him. He would appear for meals in the canteen with only one shoe on, and wearing his jacket inside-out. In the afternoon, as part of their physical exercise, the inmates were asked to weed the garden, but Pu Yi was forbidden to go anywhere near it, for he would pull up all the flowers and plants in mistake for weeds. This was in fact a clever ploy of Pu Yi's; he had survived for many years in Manchuria without his feet once touching the ground, and he did not intend to begin doing anything so earthy now.

Athough the governor was disappointed in Pu Yi's lack of physical effort, he was impressed by his progress in political studies. The students were divided into groups, and each group was given a textbook to read and discuss. They were also asked to write individual essays in which they set out their reflections on what they had learned. Pu Yi's group was given a book called *On New Democracy*. At first Pu Yi found it difficult to do more than just quote from the textbook. Then, one day, he hit on a clever idea. Recalling how he used to compare the Mikado of Japan with the sun, he wrote a series of essays in praise of Mao Tse-tung in which he produced sentences such as 'He is like the sun which shines on all mankind', and 'As long as I live, I shall follow this mighty sun.' Remembering the governor's favourite word, Pu Yi always took care to end his essays with the climax: 'I firmly resolve to remould my character and become a new man.' Whenever visiting cadres and inspectors came to the detention centre, the governor would proudly show them Pu Yi's essays.

There was one little matter concerning Pu Yi's character, however, that spoiled the governor's pleasure at his student's undoubted progress. The governor decided that it was time to bring it out into the open. One day Pu Yi received a hint from a member of his study group that it would be better for him if he owned up to hiding in his luggage something he had failed to declare. Realizing that the governor knew his guilty secret, Pu Yi decided to make a full confession. He carried his suitcase into the governor's office. Hanging his head in shame, he confessed that he had failed to declare some of his possessions. This breach of the regulations had weighed so heavily on his conscience, he said, that he could bear the strain no longer. Opening the suitcase, Pu Yi turned it upside-down over the table and pressed a secret catch. A cascade of jewels – diamonds, pearls and ornaments of jade, sapphire and gold – poured on to the table. There were 468 pieces in all. The embarrassed governor, who had never seen anything remotely like this mountain of treasure before, mumbled something about Pu Yi's having finally remoulded his character. He would make a list. . . . There was no need for a receipt, Pu Yi said, magnanimously. The jewels belonged to the Chinese people, and he was glad to return them. With the noble air of a proverty-stricken student without a pearl to his name, Pu Yi walked back to his room with his empty suitcase.

After this episode Pu Yi's advance as the most zealous student and champion of the new democracy was unchallenged. In July 1956 the governor informed Pu Yi that he was to be the principal witness for the prosecution at the forthcoming trial of a number of Japanese. All the accused had been administrators in Manchukuo when Pu Yi was Emperor there. They were all charged with committing war crimes.

Witness for the prosecution! Pu Yi was delighted to perform that role again. Once more his voice rang out in court as he denounced with scorn the Japanese prisoners who cringed in the dock. This time Pu Yi was not troubled by any hostile defence lawyers. All forty-five of the accused pleaded guilty to the charges against them, and they were sentenced to long terms of imprisonment.

Pu Yi returned to the detention centre as a hero, and the governor shook him warmly by the hand. As he listened to his words of congratulation, Pu Yi gazed with envy at the governor's grey uniform with its two breast pockets, in one of which a fountain-pen was clipped, two side pockets, and its smart collar, buttoned at the neck. It was a uniform at once business-like and yet pleasingly casual, thought Pu Yi, and he found himself hoping that one day he, too, might be qualified to wear the sober dress of a cadre.

In 1955, when Pu Yi had been in the detention centre for five years, he was given the privilege of receiving letters and visits. A number of letters came from his many relations in Peking. None of them seemed to have come to any harm since the Communist revolution; on the contrary, some had been appointed to positions of responsibility. The most influential post of all was held by Pu Yi's uncle, Tsai Tao, who, when he was a young prince, had been sent on a military mission to Germany in 1910. Now Tsai Tao was a member of the National Congress.

One pathetic letter for Pu Yi came not from Peking, but from Changchun. Jade Lute, his former concubine, who had gone back to live with her mother, wrote to tell Pu Yi that she was now working in a wool mill. Pu Yi answered her letter and asked her to visit him. Trains were scarce, and it was a long and difficult journey for her to make for the sake of an hour's meeting, but Jade Lute managed it. Pu Yi was surprised to see that his little schoolgirl had become a sturdy woman with the strong hands of a factory worker. Jade Lute found Pu Yi completely unchanged. In the following year Jade Lute got a job in Changchun municipal library. She went on exchanging letters with Pu Yi for a few months. Their letters, which were confined to the subjects of Pu Yi's health and the new democracy, became fewer and fewer and then ceased altogether as Jade Lute disappeared from Pu Yi's life.

There came the day the governor announced that, as part of their education, all the inmates at the centre would be taken on visits to various towns in Manchuria, so that they could see the works of socialist reconstruction which were being carried out. One of these visits took Pu Yi back to Changchun. An army lorry met Pu Yi's group at the station. The warder in charge explained that they were going to visit a new factory where army vehicles were being manufactured. The lorry drove into the western suburbs and soon came to a pair of large iron gates. 'This is the Number One Motor Works,' said the warder as the gates were opened and they drove into the compound. A row of newly made lorries stood in front of the old office building. Pu Yi and his companions walked round to the side of it, past the concrete tennis-court and the empty swimming-pool. Loud hammering noises came from the bungalows which had been turned into workshops.

'The manager is expecting us,' said the warder as he led the party back to the office building. They walked down the corridor and entered a large office. The factory manager was sitting in a cane chair. He welcomed his visitors and then motioned them to sit on the row of chairs drawn up before him. Cigarettes were passed round, and the manager began to address the group on the importance of socialist reconstruction. Pu Yi gazed about him at the old walls. At the far end of the room, exactly where he had last seen it, was the stool on which that dry old stick, the Mantis, used to sit. He half expected to see the Wasp come in and buzz about, arranging the papers on the manager's desk. The manager was coming to the end of his speech. 'We have done our best to make use of the derelict buildings here. You would be surprised at the amount of rubbish we had to clear away when we came in. The strangest things had been left about. Do you know that in this room there was a long red carpet on the floor, stretching right up to my desk? We couldn't think what to do with it, and in the end we gave it to the library.'

Pu Yi's uncle, Tsai Tao, came to visit him at the detention centre. The governor made a fuss over this distinguished member of Congress. The news had reached Foshun that Chairman Mao himself was behind Tsai Tao's visit. One day, outside the newly built Hall of the People in Tien An Men Square in Peking, Premier Chou En-lai had introduced Tsai Tao to Chairman Mao, who shook Tsai Tao by the hand and said, 'I hear that Pu Yi's studies are going well. Why don't you go and visit him?'

258

Tsai Tao gave Pu Yi news of the family, including the details of Prince Chun's peaceful death at the Northern Mansion. No Chinese family, said Tsai Tao, could have received so many favours from the government of the People's Republic as the former imperial family of Prince Chun. He looked foward to the day when Pu Yi's remoulding was complete and he returned to Peking.

Although Jade Lute had not detected any change in Pu Yi, the governor was pleased with his progress. At New Year the inmates always held a party in the canteen, during which plays were performed. For the New Year party in 1957 Pu Chieh wrote a short play called *The Defeat of the Aggressors*, based on newspaper reports of Britain's invasion of Egypt to regain control of the Suez Canal. Pu Yi was given the part of a left-wing Labour MP. His biggest scene took place in the House of Commons, where he clashed with the foreign secretary, Selwyn Lloyd. The audience were gripped by Pu Yi's entrance. Wearing his blue suit, white shirt and red tie, he strode into the House of Commons, and with a menacing look at the Conservatives, took his seat. Even the governor, playing the part of the speaker, quailed at the sight of him. The foreign secretary began his speech, justifying the invasion of Egypt. This was Pu Yi's cue to intervene in a short statement of about six lines. Pu Yi leapt to his feet, and then completely forgot his lines. He glared at the foreign secretary, pointed at him, and shouted at the top of his voice 'Out! Out! Out!' in heroic opposition. The audience were spellbound, and so were the other players in this dramatic improvisation. Everyone joined in the thunderous applause as they chorused 'Out! Out! Out!' in support of the defiant member in the red tie.

In 1959 the People's Republic celebrated its tenth anniversary. To mark the occasion, Chairman Mao proposed that a number of war criminals who were sufficiently remoulded should be granted special pardons. Congress unanimously endorsed his proposal, and there was joy in the detention centre at Fushun when the students heard the news. The students were to be released in batches, priority being given to those who had made the most progress in their studies. On 4 December everyone gathered in the canteen to hear the names of the lucky ones who were to be released first. There was a hush as the governor came in. He began to read from his list: 'Pu Yi. . . .' a burst of applause greeted Pu Yi's name. Pu Chieh, too, was named in the first batch. As he shook hands with Pu Yi the governor, who was visibly moved, looked like a headmaster saying farewell to his favourite pupil.

The train carrying Pu Yi from Mukden passed through the gateway in the Great Wall at Shanhaikwan, leaving Manchuria behind, Pu Yi was fifty-four years old. Save for five years in Siberia, he had spent the last twenty-eight years of his life in the land of his Manchu ancestors. He had been chief executive, emperor, witness for the prosecution, and star pupil among war criminals. He could congratulate himself on the fact that not once had he mounted a Manchurian pony, nor had his feet touched Manchurian soil.

Shrouded in a white cloud of steam, the train from Manchuria came panting and hissing into Peking station. Pu Yi's uncle, Tsai Tao, Hiro and her daughter, now aged twenty-one, and many other members of the family were there to greet the remoulded heros. A cheer went up as Pu Yi and Pu Chieh stepped on to the platform. Pu Yi was taken to his new home, a house once owned by his late father, Prince Chun. The State had requisitioned it in 1949, but made it available now for Pu Yi. He was to share it with Hiro and Pu Chieh, who would look after him.

The day after Pu Yi's return to Peking the entire family was given the rare privilege of being received by Premier Chou En-lai. 'You know all about emperors,' the premier said to Pu Yi. 'You have been Emperor of China and Emperor of Manchukuo. But remember, the Emperor now is the Chinese people.' Pu Yi smiled in agreement.

That evening a party was held at Pu Yi's house. The many guests, who included several former courtiers, filled the reception-room to overflowing, making it look like a gathering of the Manchu clans. 'How good it is to be back in Peking!' Pu Chieh kept saying, and Hiro, the wife he had abandoned, unprotected, in the mountain town of Talitzu, echoed his sentiment. Yes, it was good to be back. It was good to be alive, too, she might have added.

At the climax of the evening, Tsai Tao, a member of the People's Congress, stood in front of a portrait of Chairman Mao and called for a toast to be drunk in honour of Pu Yi, now safely back from the wilds of his ancestral homeland.

Pu Yi's grandfather, the secret police officer, and first Prince Chun, would have been proud of his descendants who had recovered from all their setbacks and were showing such admirable resilience in remaking their lives under the new regime. The family motto he had coined, and which used to hang in the Northern Mansion, would not have seemed out of place in Pu Yi's home that night:

> Wealth and Fortune breed more Fortune,
> Royal Favours bring more Favours.

It would have spoiled the party, of course, if anyone had been tactless enough to mention the tragic Empress who had not returned with Pu Yi. Judging from their behaviour towards her during her lifetime, few if any of the celebrating clansmen would have spared even a passing thought for Beautiful Countenance, who lay buried in an unmarked place in the Long White Mountains.

After the celebrations there was work to be done for the State. Pu Yi's first official post was assistant at the Peking Botanical Gardens. This was to give rise to the legend that he was employed as a gardener in his former palace, but Pu Yi's work hardly involved manual labour; he spent his time in a large greenhouse, studying the cultivation of seeds. The appointment was not a success, and Pu Yi felt more at home when he was transferred to the department of historical archives. At the same time, as part of his official duties, he began to work on the story of his life.

A team of writers assisted Pu Yi to produce his autobiography, which was given the title *From Emperor to Citizen*. Apart from a number of political editors, the team included Pu Chieh, author of some short plays, Lao Shih, a master of the written word, and the novelist Wen Da, author of the highly acclaimed *The Girl Who Loves to Throw Her Pigtails*

To and Fro. Johnston, whose *Twilight in the Forbidden City* had caused Pu Yi so much embarrassment in the witness-box at the war crimes trial in Tokyo, is one of the villains in Pu Yi's book. Johnston, that 'testy Scot whose clothes smelt of moth-balls', was always avid for honours, according to Pu Yi. The vainest of creatures. Johnston loved to have his photograph taken, dressed as a mandarin in his sable robe, and wearing his black button of the highest grade; and he distributed copies of the picture all over the world. In a poignant sentence which might well be in Pu Yi's own words, the book says that by the time Pu Yi left the Forbidden City at the age of nineteen, 'Johnston had become the major part of my soul,' The 'testy Scot' lured Pu Yi away from his love of ancient Chinese music and introduced him to British brass bands, the book claims. Johnston constantly sang the praises of 'the great British Empire on which the sun never sets', and he persuaded Pu Yi that he, Johnston, was the most learned member of the empire. Obsessed by his admiration for imperial rule, Johnston, says the book, convinced Pu Yi that the Chinese people longed for the restoration of the Ching dynasty. What the people really longed for, of course, was a Communist republic under the protection of the Red Army, but at the very mention of the word Red, the 'testy Scot' would panic and set about preparing to escape.

Leaving out no details in their efforts to vilify Johnston, Pu Yi and his ghost writers descended to the pettiest of sneers. Pu Yi claims that one day he copied out some verses by a celebrated Ming poet and pretended that they were his own work. Johnston, who prided himself on his Chinese scholarship, was completely taken in, seeing the verses as evidence of his pupil's poetic gifts – so Pu Yi says. Nowhere in the book, which so cruelly ridicules his old tutor, is there any mention of the 'pair of herons' who might fly home together one day. In the last contemptuous dismissal of the 'testy Scot', Pu Yi refers to Johnston's lonely end in Scotland: 'He even flew the flag of Manchukuo from an island he had bought, to show his loyalty to the Emperor.'

Throughout the autobiography, the few references to the Empress Beautiful Countenance are hostile and vindictive, save for one revealing sentence near the end when news of her death in the Long White Mountains reached Pu Yi in Siberia. 'If', he wrote, 'her fate was not determined at her birth, her end was inevitable from the moment she married me.'

From Emperor to Citizen pleased the authorities and, as a reward for all his good work, Pu Yi was provided with a new wife, Li Shu-hsien, a buxom nurse aged forty. He was also given a voter's card, entitling him to full citizenship of the Republic. The department of historical archives promoted Pu Yi to the position of cadre, and from now on he always wore the flat cap and grey uniform that he found so business-like, especially when a fountain-pen was clipped to his breast pocket. He added one exotic touch, however, that made him stand out among his fellow-cadres — a pair of dark glasses.

The next step in his advance up the State ladder came when he was elected to the People's Political Committee, a body concerned with 'the reconstruction of the motherland'. The governor of the Fushun detention centre for war criminals must have been proud of his star pupil, who had become every inch the model civil servant.

EPILOGUE

THE FAIRY ISLE

'You must be our guide now,' the official from the ministry of state security said to Pu Yi with a smile.

They were standing inside the Meridian Gate at the heart of the Forbidden City. The curator and the rest of the party of twelve, all wearing grey uniforms, clapped their hands in agreement. Some of them cried out '*Hao, hao* ... Good, good!' and gathered around Pu Yi, peering at him with morbid curiosity.

Pu Yi struggled with his face-mask and at last he managed to remove it. His mouth smiled at his audience, but behind his dark glasses his eyes were cold and expressionless. He knew these former generals and senior civil servants well. He had spent ten years in their company at the Fushun detention centre for war criminals. Although, like him, they professed a new-found faith in the Communist Party, he was in no doubt that if the Empire were to be restored that very day, they would fall on their knees and kowtow to him. After their release from prison, he had hoped not to see his fellow-traitors again, for they knew too much about him for his comfort, but the Peking municipal authority had arranged for Pu Yi and his comrades to visit a number of places of interest as part of their political re-education. A few weeks before, they had been sent to a commune in the Interior, north-west of Peking. It was a drought-stricken region where dust covered everything, and the sullen peasants made no secret of their contempt for their urban visitors. When a band of rebels ('vagabond elements', the official called them) was reported in the vicinity of their hostel, the men in grey panicked. Besieging the official in charge, they begged him to cut short their tour in the countryside and allow them to return to Peking.

Today's visit to the Forbidden City had been organized at the special request of Pu Yi's comrades, who were much taken with the idea of being shown round the Imperial Palace by the former Emperor himself. The municipal authority had given its sanction, and Pu Yi could hardly refuse. This was to be his last performance in public.

Pu Yi had been in a daze from the moment he passed through the Gate of Heavenly Peace into the Forbidden City. He lagged a little behind the others as they walked through the long forecourts of the outer palaces. Now and again something caught his eye and made him stop. Near the Presidential Palace, the former board of punishments, he noticed a clump of tall shrubs that had not been pruned for many years. Was Yuan Shih-kai's armoured car still hidden there? he wondered.

Now, having been put in charge of the party, Pu Yi led the way from the Meridan Gate, across a bridge, through the Gate of Supreme Harmony, and into the Great Within. Before them stood the Hall of Supreme Harmony, surrounded by terraces of white marble; beyond the hall, a sea of yellow-tiled roofs stretched as far as the distant Gate of Spiritual Valour. After the dust-storm that had raged in Tien An Men Square and pursued them into the outer courts, the silence in this sanctuary was uncanny. As Pu Yi walked among the inner palaces he was amazed at the stillness. These courtyards, terraces and gardens, which used to be full of the bustle of officials, sedan-chair bearers, eunuchs, concubines, page-boys and guards, were as deserted as an empty stage. He led the group into hall after hall. Stripped of their ornaments, the great audience halls with their musty air seemed depressingly alike. The merest whisper brought an echo. He said something about each place they entered, but in this other

266

world, which his companions could not possibly understand, he could only bring himself to give a few bare facts.

In the Palace of Mind Nurture, Pu Yi stood in the empty schoolroom where, like Alice, he had plunged down and down a deep well to find himself in that strange land where the footmen were frogs dressed in livery, the Duchess ordered a beating for the child who sneezed, the soldiers acted as executioners, witnesses were threatened, and the Queen of Hearts ordered the direst punishment for the slightest offence. This underworld had so fired Pu Yi's imagination that he peopled it with hierarchies and armies of different coloured ants. Of all this, Pu Yi could say nothing to the men in grey.

He took them into the eunuch's theatre where the Venerable Buddha had spent so many hours. The puppet theatre was still in its place. A faded damask curtain concealed the miniature stage. Pu Yi remembered watching with fascination as the curtain was drawn back to reveal the violent and cunning humpbacked Punch. After each performance the puppet master would emerge from behind the curtain with a smirk on his face to receive the applause of the audience. Once Pu Yi watched from behind the stage as the puppets were manipulated. He had then given the unsuspecting puppet master a cake filled with iron filings. Such a pity his nurse had interfered and revealed what it was in the cake! Pu Yi smiled as he recalled the look of panic in the puppet master's eyes. Even after all these years he relished the image of the abject puppet master and his kowtows.

Seeing Pu Yi smile, his comrades looked at him in-quiringly, but the only words he uttered were 'This was the theatre.' How could he explain his hatred for the puppet master and his kind? And how could he speak of his craving to avenge the humpbacked Punch who had been used as a villain and then had been thrown, so contemptuously, into a box at the end of a play?

They walked through the courtyard of the Palace of Tranquil Old Age, once the residence of the Venerable Buddha. In the centre of the yard Pu Yi hesitated by a well, covered by an old iron lid. He looked as if he was about to say something, but he changed his mind and walked on. A path, overgrown with weeds, led from the courtyard to the shore of the West Lake. Here they were exposed once more to the strong wind and swirling dust. Pu Yi replaced his face-mask. Only a little way out from the shore was the Fairy Isle with its pavilion, half hidden by a willow tree.

'What a beautiful place! Was this your retreat?' one of his comrades asked Pu Yi.

He did not answer. Here, least of all, could he speak a word. Standing with his back to the group, he gazed at the island. Hidden in its miniature palace was the Empty Room, that place of death where, so many years ago, he had left his childhood behind. A violent gust of wind blew across the Fairy Isle, whipping up the lake water and making a moaning sound that rose to a scream as it forced down the branches of the willow tree. A limp figure with hunched shoulders, Pu Yi turned to face his companions. Not one of them could tell that behind those dark glasses and the mask was the tear-stained face of an old man.

For another seven years Pu Yi lived placidly at home, nursed by his young wife, and doing and saying all the things expected of a cadre who followed the correct party line. In that unchanging scene he was not given any other roles to play. He died on 17 October 1967.

He was quickly forgotten. In books, including his own, he is always shown in the company of the eminent, and more often than not surrounded and propped up by officials. Even in the printed word, fate has decreed that he should be overshadowed by that unholy matriarch, the Venerable Buddha. As for his former subjects, China's millions, they regarded the last Emperor, if they thought of him at all, as an unwanted puppet that had played its part in an old play and had been consigned to the litter of history.

A different place was given to Beautiful Countenance, his tragic Empress. Within a few years of her death a legend grew up about her: she had come to life again, and the peasants claimed to have seen her frail yet fearless figure in the Long White Mountains, where she was in league with those other immortals, the White Wolf and the Yellow Lotus. The wandering story-tellers included Beautiful Countenance in their repertoire, and not only in Manchuria, but in her beloved Interior, tales about her were recited with affection. They tell of a beautiful and noble woman whose special mission is to come to the rescue of those who are imprisoned and cruelly treated. These tales of immortal outlaws are taken seriously by the government officials who need no reminding that, among the peasant masses, legend easily becomes reality. In the spring of 1985, at a time when China was boasting of her 'modernization programme', the authorities in Peking were forced to issue a statement denouncing the spirit of 'Robin Hoodism' that still prevails in the country regions surrounding the capital.

Unlike the Puppet Emperor, Beautiful Countenance lives on. One dies only when one is forgotten.

GLOSSARY

ANCESTRAL TABLETS   Also known as spiritual tablets, they consisted of plain, oblong pieces of hard wood on which were written the name and age and other particulars of the dead ancestor. As a mark of filial piety, at certain times of the year gifts of fruit, cakes, pieces of silk and incense were offered before the ancestral tablets which stood in many houses. In the Imperial Palace at Peking the tablets of deceased emperors were hung in the Temple of Ancestors.

CONCUBINES   The first Emperor of China, the tyrant Chin, kept a harem of beautiful women as concubines. (They paid a terrible price for that honour: they were buried alive in his tomb at his death.) The practice of keeping concubines for the Emperor's pleasure was continued in future dynasties. It was not an imperial prerogative, however. Most wealthy officials possessed a few concubines as well as a wife. But the Emperor's harem was much the largest. During the Manchu dynasty (1644-1911) only Manchu girls were chosen as imperial concubines.

CONFUCIANS see TAOISTS AND CONFUCIANS

THE DRAGON THRONE   Stood in the Hall of Supreme Harmony at the centre of the Forbidden City. On this throne was carved the symbol of the dragon, sacred emblem of the Emperor, Son of Heaven, who was also called 'The Dragon'.

THE FORBIDDEN CITY   Built by Yung Lo, the third Ming emperor (1403-24), the citadel of the Forbidden City or 'Great Within' lies at the centre of the Imperial City in Peking. In this citadel, where only the

271

privileged few might enter, were situated the great audience halls and inner palaces.

GAOLIANG   A type of maize. Extensively cultivated in the North China Plain and in the lowlands of Manchuria, it grows to a height of about ten feet in the summer months. Its coarse, yellow grains provide the staple diet as well as a bitter tasting wine for peasants and for coolies in the towns. The strong *gaoliang* stalks yield many by-products, such as thatching for roofs, matting, baskets and brooms.

IMPERIAL YELLOW   The colour yellow, symbolizing the sun, gold and magnificence, was exclusively reserved for the Emperor's usage. For instance, only the Emperor might own yellow porcelain.

KANG   A raised platform of bricks, used as a bed. It was heated by means of an oven in which wood or coal was burnt.

KOWTOW   The act of prostration and striking the head on the ground in homage or worship.

MANCHUS   Known to the Chinese as 'the Eastern Tartars', the Manchu tribes lived by hunting and animal husbandry in the region north of the Great Wall. Foreign atlases called this region Manchuria; the Chinese have always referred to it as the 'North-East'. By the sixteenth century Manchu tribes had begun to attack the Chinese garrisons stationed in Manchuria. Early in the seventeenth century, when the Ming dynasty in China was nearing its end, the Manchus united under their dynamic leader Nurhachi. In 1618 he defeated a large Chinese army at Mukden. A few years later his successor founded the 'Great Ching' dynasty of the Manchus there. They were now poised to invade China. Meanwhile sporadic peasant risings had been taking place in north-western China. In 1640 an outlaw, a skilled horseman-archer named Li 'The Harrier', led an army of peasants against Peking, the Ming capital, which he seized in April 1644. Whereupon the last Ming emperor hanged himself in his palace garden. 'The Harrier' was proclaimed Emperor, but within a month his reign was over. A treacherous Chinese general, who commanded a vital gateway in the Great Wall at Shanhaikwan, opened it to the Manchu cavalry. The Manchu hordes swept into China, and by May 1644 a 'Great Ching' emperor reigned in Peking. 'The Harrier' fled into central China, where he found refuge in a monastery. Other peasant leaders were to emerge, however, and, nourished by secret societies, peasant resistance to imperial officials continued to flare up during the 300 years of Manchu rule over China.

PIGTAIL   When the Manchus invaded China in 1644 they ordered Chinese men to adopt the Manchu style of head-dress. Instead of having long hair gathered in a top knot, the Chinese fashion, men were compelled to shave the front of their heads and wear a pigtail at the back. The only men exempted from this rule were Buddhist monks whose heads were shaven, and Taoist priests who continued to wear the top knot. The rebellious minded regarded the pigtail as a badge of humiliation. On the other hand, many Chinese of the mandarin class, eager to obtain official appointments, were only too willing to please their Manchu rulers by wearing the pigtail.

TAEL A weight of money equivalent to an ounce of silver. In 1908, the year of Pu Yi's accession to the imperial throne, the rate of exchange was, approximately, 6 taels per £1 sterling.

TAOISTS AND CONFUCIANS The Taoists were nature mystics. Their ideas, which were widespread in China from the sixth century BC onwards, still permeate Eastern thought. (Buddhism, for example, which reached China in the middle of the first century AD, came under the influence of the Taoists and travelled on as Zen Buddhism to Japan, where it flourishes.) Tao means a road or way. For the Taoists it symbolized the way of nature. 'Do nothing against nature,' they counselled. Only the contemplation of nature in all its moods could free one from fear and disappointment. 'He who can face the harsh realities of nature and not flinch from anything as too trivial or painful, will ride upon the clouds.' Fascinated observers of the elements, their insight into nature inspired Chinese art and formed the basis of magic, divination, medicine and science. (The Chinese art of siting houses so as to harmonize with the natural surroundings, *feng-shui*, led them to invent the magnetic compass.) It is not surprising that Taoist thought has been misunderstood by most Western scholars, trained as they are to think of a world of separate things – a world, for instance, in which time is divided into countable units. For the Taoist, past, present and future are one. He sees the universe as indivisible; it is also spontaneous and ever flowing like streaming clouds or the action of a galloping horse. 'Look around you!' says the Taoist sage. 'Attune yourself to the rhythm of the seasons. Until we know more about nature we shall not be able to organize society.'

Confucius (552-479 BC) also used the symbol of Tao or way, but for him and his followers it signified the right way of life within human society. Their ideal was a paternalistic government in which a virtuous prince set a good example to his people, and where the traditional rites and ceremonial were properly observed. In time Confucianism became the official doctrine of the bureaucratic society which existed under the emperors. Confucian scholastic knowledge was masculine and managing; it was opposed by the Taoists, who favoured a feminine and receptive wisdom, which they termed 'the valley spirit'. Far from insisting on respect for the male head of each family, as did the Confucians, the Taoists stood for a primitive, sharing community where woman was man's equal. 'When the Tao prevailed, the whole world was one community . . . men cherished the children of others as their own. But now the Tao is eclipsed, selfish scheming abounds, and men love only their own parents and children.' In the *Chuang Tzu* (The Book

273

of Master Chuang), the Taoist sage says: 'I have heard of letting the world go its own way, but not of governing the world successfully.' A Confucian asks: 'If the Empire is not to be governed, how are we to keep order?' The Taoist replies: 'Be careful not to interfere with the natural goodness in the heart of man.' Affronted by the Taoists, the Confucian sages called them 'irresponsible hermits'. But the less polite imperial officials had a harsher name for them: 'anarchists'. During the Ching dynasty of the Manchus, Taoism was the cult of masses of disaffected peasants, and the Taoists who had close links with the secret society of the White Lotus were seen as the deadly enemy of the State.

TARTARS The name given to the mounted nomadic tribes who roamed the steppe lands between the Caspian Sea in the west and the Great Wall of China in the east. From the eleventh and twelfth centuries AD their chief staging-posts were situated west of the Ordos Desert in the heartland of Asia, which the story-tellers of China spoke of as the 'Interior'. Fine equestrian archers, Tartar mercenaries formed the cavalry regiments of the Chinese imperial army right up to the end of the Empire in 1911.

YAMEN The office and residence of a local imperial official and his subordinates. It was also a court of law, prison, barracks, arsenal and granary (the peasants paid their taxes in grain). Surrounded by high walls, the *yamen* had the appearance of a fortress. A hated symbol of State power, it was the first place to be sacked and burned when the peasants rose up in rebellion.

CALENDAR OF EVENTS IN PU YI'S LIFETIME

1906   *7 FEBRUARY* birth of Pu Yi.
1908   *14 NOVEMBER* death of Kuang Hsu Emperor.
        15 NOVEMBER death of Empress Dowager, Tsu Hsi.
        2 DECEMBER Pu Yi enthroned as Hsuang Tung Emperor.
1911   Republican revolution led by Sun Yat-sen.
1912   *12 FEBRUARY* abdication of Pu Yi. *15 FEBRUARY* Yuan Shih-kai is provisional president of China.
1914   war breaks out in Europe.
1916   *13 APRIL* death of Yuan Shih-kai.
1917   *1 JULY* army revolt; Pu Yi restored as Emperor.
        8 JULY revolt put down; Pu Yi abdicates again.
        14 AUGUST China declares war on Germany.
        OCTOBER Russian revolution.
1918   Allied expedition against Bolsheviks in Siberia.
1922   *1 DECEMBER* wedding of Pu Yi and Beautiful Countenance (Wan Jung).
1924   *5 NOVEMBER* imperial family ordered to leave the Forbidden City. Pu Yi goes to his father's house.
        29 NOVEMBER Pu Yi 'escapes' to Japanese legation, Peking.
1925   *23 FEBRUARY* Pu Yi arrives in Tientsin.

1927   Chiang Kai-shek sets up Nationalist government in
        Nanking. Civil war between Nationalists and
        Communists.
1931   *SEPTEMBER* Japanese forces invade Manchuria.
        10 NOVEMBER Japanese secret service take Pu Yi to
        Manchuria.
1932   *JANUARY* Japanese bomb Chapei district, Shanghai.
        23 FEBRUARY Pu Yi appointed chief executive of
        Manchukuo (formerly Manchuria). *MAY* League of
        Nations commission of inquiry arrives in Manchukuo.
1934   *1 MARCH* Pu Yi enthroned as Emperor of
        Manchukuo.
1935   *APRIL* Pu Yi pays State visit to Japan. *OCTOBER* long
        march of the Red Army ends at Yenan.
1937   *7 JULY* Marco Polo Bridge Incident; Japanese invade
        China.
1939   Second World War breaks out in Europe.
1940   *SEPTEMBER* Japan joins the Axis powers of Germany
        and Italy.
1941   *7 DECEMBER* Japanese destroy US fleet at Pearl
        Harbour. *8 DECEMBER* Japanese declare war on
        United States and Great Britain. *25 DECEMBER*
        Japanese capture Hong Kong.
1942   *15 FEBRUARY* Singapore falls to Japanese. Pu Yi
        pledges support of Manchukuo for Japan.
1945   *6 AUGUST* atomic bomb dropped on Hiroshima.
        8 AUGUST Russia declares war on Japan, invades
        Manchuria. *15 AUGUST* Pu Yi flees to Korean
        border, abdicates (for third time). *17 AUGUST* Pu Yi
        attempts to escape to Japan but is seized by the
        Russians and flown to Siberia.
1946   *JUNE* Empress Beautiful Countenance dies in the
        Long White Mountains. *OCTOBER* Pu Yi gives
        evidence for prosecution at war crimes trial in Tokyo.
1949   *OCTOBER* Mao Tse-tung proclaims People's
        Republic of China.
1950   *31 JULY* Russians return Pu Yi to China. He is
        imprisoned in Fushun detention centre for war
        criminals.

1959   Pu Yi, a convert to communism, receives a special pardon. *4 DECEMBER* he returns to Peking.

1962   *1 MAY* Pu Yi takes a new citizen wife.

1967   *17 OCTOBER* Pu Yi dies.

SOURCES OF REFERENCE

In reconstructing the life of Pu Yi, the chief written sources I consulted were:

Bland, J.O.P. and Backhouse, E. *China under the Empress Dowager*. London, 1911.
——. *Annals and Memoirs of the Court of Peking*. London, 1914.
Chesneaux, Jean. *Peasant Revolts in China 1840 – 1949*. London, 1973.
Creel, H.G. *Chinese Thought from Confucius to Mao Tse-Tung*. Chicago, Ill., 1953.
Dmitriev-Mamonov, A. and Zdziarski (eds). *Guide to the Great Siberian Railway*. (David & Charles Reprints) Newton Abbot, 1971.
Fleming, Peter. *One's Company*. London, 1934.
Gale, Esson. *Salt for the Dragon*. Michigan, Ind., 1953.
Haldane, Charlotte. *The Last Great Empress of China*. London, 1965.
Hummel, A. J. W. (ed.). *Eminent Chinese of the Ching Period*. Washington, DC, 2 vols, 1943.
Johnston, Reginald F. *Twilight in the Forbidden City*. London, 1934.
McAleavy, Henry, *A Dream of Tartary*. London, 1963.
Pu Yi, Aisin-Gioro. *From Emperor to Citizen: The Autobiography of Aisin-Gioro Pu Yi*. Peking, 2 vols, 1964.
Riencourt, Amaury de. *The Soul of China*. London, 1959.
The Peking and Tientsin Times, 1925 – 40.
Trevor-Roper, Hugh. *A Hidden Life: The Enigma of Sir Edmund Backhouse*. London, 1976.
Varè, Daniele. *Laughing Diplomat*. London, 1968.
Woodhead, H.G.W. *A Journalist in China*. London, 1934.

INDEX

Note: There is no distinct entry for Pu Yi, the Hsuan Tung Emperor.

Palace of Tranquil Old Age, Forbidden City, 28, 36, 39, 45, 267

Palmerston, Viscount, 35

Pearl Concubine (Chen Tai Fei), 34, 36, 40, 58

Pearl Harbor, 236, 237

People's Republic of China, 16, 253, 259

'pigtailed general, the': see Chang Hsun

Prince of Wales, Edward, 93, 94, 96, 149, 152, 153, 158, 167, 175, 178, 222, 224

principle of benevolent rule (Wang Tao), 197, 200-2, 206

Pu Chieh, 26, 67, 68-70, 89, 99, 131, 201, 214-15, 223, 224-8, 231, 235, 241, 242, 244, 245, 250, 255, 259, 260, 261

Pu Lun, 28, 48, 138

Punch and Judy, 69, 267

Quiet Garden, Tientsin, 176, 178, 179, 183, 186

Ransom, Nona, 161

Red Army, Chinese, 209, 246, 253, 262

'Red Christian, the': see Feng Yu-hsiang

Red Spear, Secret Society of the, 194, 243

Reform Movement, 34, 59

Republic of China, 67, 70, 72, 79, 85, 98, 100, 105, 106

Ricci, Father (Matteo), SJ, 81

Saga, Hiro, 225-9, 236, 239, 242, 244-8, 260

St Andrew's Society, Tientsin, 156-8, 200, 232

Salt Palace, 215, 221, 224, 226, 228, 230, 236, 237, 240

Schneider, Herr, musician, 149-52, 159, 232

School of Oriental Studies, London, 223

Semenov ('the ogre of Chita'), 131, 140-1, 250

Seymour, Admiral, 36

Shigera, Japanese consul, 113, 130, 131

Shiozawa, Admiral, 189

Soong, T.V., 178

Stalingrad, 240

Su ('the Mad Prince'), 84, 161, 187

Summer Palace, 33-4, 40, 99, 105, 106

Sun Yat-sen, 63, 72, 101,

Sung Chiao-jen, 72,

Taft, President, 54

Taiping (Great Peace) rising, 33,

Taisho: see Emperor of Japan

Taku Bar, Sea River estuary, 117-18, 135, 180,

Tanaka, General, 143, 164

Tangku Agreement, 208

Taoism/Taoists, 134, 163-5, 273-4